Social Motivation, Justice, and the Moral Emotions

An Attributional Approach

Social Motivation, Justice, and the Moral Emotions

An Attributional Approach

Bernard Weiner
University of California–Los Angeles

LAWRENCE ERLBAUM ASSOCIATES, PUBLISHERS

2006   Mahwah, New Jersey   London

Lawrence Erlbaum Associates, Inc., Publishers
10 Industrial Avenue
Mahwah, New Jersey 07430
www.erlbaum.com

Cover design by Kathryn Houghtaling Lacey

Library of Congress Cataloging-in-Publication Data

Weiner, Bernard, 1935–
Social motivation, justice, and the moral emotions : an attributional approach /
   Bernard Weiner.
      p. cm.
   Includes bibliographical references and index.
ISBN 0-8058-5526-2 (cloth : alk. paper)
ISBN 0-8058-5527-0 (pbk. : alk. paper)
1. Motivation (Psychology)—Social aspects. 2. Social justice. 3. Emotions.
   4. Social justice. I. Title.
BF503.W45   2005
153.8—dc22   2005041459
                                                                      CIP

Books published by Lawrence Erlbaum Associates are printed on acid-free paper,
and their bindings are chosen for strength and durability.

Printed in the United States of America
10 9 8 7 6 5 4 3 2 1

Contents

Why is it we want so badly to memorialize ourselves? Even while we're still alive. We wish to assert our existence .... We put on display our framed photographs, our parchment diplomas, our silver-plated cups; we monogram our linen, we carve our names on trees, we scrawl them on washroom walls. It's all the same impulse. What do we hope from it? Applause, envy, respect? Or simply attention, of any kind we can get?

At the very least we want a witness. We can't stand the idea of our own voices falling silent finally, like a radio running down.

—Margaret Atwood
From *The Blind Assassin* (p. 95)

Preface

It was about 10 years ago that my book, *Judgments of Responsibility: Foundations for a Theory of Social Conduct* (Weiner, 1995) was published. In the subsequent decade, the theoretical and empirical work presented there has expanded in many directions. These extensions are reflected in the title of this book: *Social Motivation, Justice, and the Moral Emotions: An Attributional Approach.*

The book is organized as follows. A short prologue is followed by five chapters, each representing a main theoretical and/or empirical legacy, concluding with an epilogue. The first chapter considers the logical development and structure of a theory of social motivation and justice. I examine how the metaphors of the person is a judge and life is a courtroom, and the concepts of causal control and responsibility, allow the theory to address phenomena related to achievement evaluation, stigmatization, help giving, reactions to transgressors, and aggression. In so doing, I document the breadth and relational fertility of the conception. Inferences of responsibility and the emotions they generate are the key mediators within the theory. Chapter 2 examines: (a) the testing of the theory within the contexts of help giving and aggression; (b) cultural and individual differences, particularly political ideology; and (c) broad characteristics and special features of the theory as compared with other motivational conceptions. Thus, the theory presented in chapter 1 is placed under an empirical and conceptual microscope, and moderators are introduced and placed beside mediators. Emotions are the theme in chapter 3 with the discussion focusing on so-called moral emotions, which were restricted to anger and sympathy in chapters 1 and 2. There is an analysis of emotions not considered in my prior work, including admiration, envy, gratitude, jealousy, regret, Schadenfreude, and scorn. I also examine perceived arrogance and modesty and communications eliciting these personality inferences, for they relate to moral emotions. This also is a new direction, not previously considered from this theoretical perspective. In addition, in chapter 3 the creation and management of impressions are considered in the context of excuse giving, confession, and other social communications that alter causal beliefs and feelings of others. Chapter 4 contains a discussion of reward and punishment, two themes closely linked to social justice. This chapter continues to pursue the goal of documenting the breadth of the theory and its ability to address traditional topics of motivation from a different vantage point. Included within this chapter is a distinction between utilitarian versus retributive punishment goals and how disparate attributions evoke different purposes of punishment. Then, in chapter 5, I provide applications of the theory to everyday problems. The applications are in the context of the school, counseling of marital couples in distress and families with a mentally or physically ill member, organizations, and for aggressive parents and youths. These five chapters are followed by an epilogue that adds a "pleasing symmetry" to the book, providing balance to the prologue by pointing out the major accomplishments of the theory and its shortcomings.

Within the chapters, readers will find 13 experiments that can be performed in a group or class setting. These studies provide concreteness to the abstract discussions as well as adding face validity to the theory inasmuch as the data generated by the readers will replicate the experiments reported in the book. This is a bold statement, but as revealed in the prologue, one of my writing strategies is to be intrepid.

This book is most pertinent to motivational and social psychologists. However, because of the breadth of topics covered, it can be of use to individuals in a variety of disciplines, including clinical, educational, organizational, and personality psychology. It is written primarily for professionals and graduate students but the level of writing is within easy grasp of undergraduates as well. The current work could be used as a text in seminars focusing on attribution theory, social motivation, or social justice. In addition, it may serve as a supplementary source in courses examining aggression, emotion, help giving, impression management, punishment, and other topics that are indicated in the table of contents.

ACKNOWLEDGMENTS

There are many individuals deserving of thanks and gratitude. These include the numerous undergraduates, graduate students, and post-doctoral fellows who have worked with me over the years and contributed to the ideas in this product. Chris Crandall and Nancy Eisenberg provided many important suggestions as reviewers. In addition, I owe a great debt to Chris Williams for his dedicated editing and teaching me important rules of writing. And my wife, Jaana Juvonen, gave valuable advice that resulted in major book revisions. As usual, Jaana and my daughter, Miina, created the positive setting in which this kind of endeavor can reach fruition. This is certainly my final book product, and reaching this goal gives me a great deal of fulfillment and satisfaction.

Prologue

To avoid some of the pitfalls encountered when writing a book, I made a number of decisions at the outset that determined my style of writing as well as defining more clearly the content of this work. These resolutions involved apparently competing polarities.

ADVOCACY VERSUS HONESTY

This book is guided by what might be considered two conflicting or contradictory rules:

Rule #1. To not hide any light under a barrel. To be a salesperson and "put my best foot forward." To be forceful and certain.

Rule #2. To not hide any shortcomings. To be aware of justified criticism. To be realistic and honest, recognizing limitations and shortcomings.

Despite the apparent inconsistency of these rules, I do not regard them as conflicting or contradictory. Quite the contrary. Trained miners can discriminate between fool's gold and genuine gold, and if one is forthright in identifying the fake, then the real is more likely to be accepted.

THEORETICAL VERSUS EMPIRICAL FOCUS

There are other characteristics of this book also captured by apparently contradictory statements. Among them is a distinction between a theory-oriented versus a data-focused approach.

Theory Orientation

This book is primarily about theory. In my lifetime as a motivational psychologist, I have developed two interrelated and overlapping attribution conceptions, one for *intra*personal and the other for *inter*personal motivation. The intrapersonal theory focuses on achievement striving; thoughts and emotions concern the self; and behavior such as striving for success need not involve others. Conversely, the interpersonal theory relates to social behaviors, primarily helping and aggression, and to social justice and punishment, but also addresses other social phenomena including compliance, impression formation and stigmatization. In this theory, thoughts and emotions are about others, and behaviors such as helping, aggression, and punishment are directed toward these others. This book is best described as proposing an attributional theory of interpersonal or social motivation.

This conception is conceived in the tradition of the "grand" theories of motivation proposed by Clark Hull and Kenneth Spence (Drive theorists) and John Atkinson, Kurt Lewin, Julian Rotter, and Edward Tolman (Expectancy × Value theorists) in that there is an attempt to incorporate a wide range of observations with a limited number of constructs. I make a strong distinction between a theory and a hypothesis. Many so-called theories in social psychology and motivation are not theories at all but rather are akin to hypotheses, for there is an absence of a scaffold of interrelated concepts and little attempt at generality beyond the specific phenomenon being studied.

The label "theory" has to be earned, not declared, and I regard the criteria justifying this label to be rather strict—precise prediction across an array of areas with a parsimonious construct system. I believe the attribution theory showcased in this book warrants the "theory" designation. A main goal of my writing is to convince readers this is an unbiased conclusion.

Data Orientation

This book is primarily about data, or empirical observations. These empirical laws must be accepted regardless of their theoretical interpretation(s), and must be amenable to explanation for any pertinent theoretical system to be viable. It is particularly upsetting to me when a claim for a validated theory is made, yet key predictions of the theory cannot be empirically replicated with certainty.

I include in this book the raw material (e.g., questionnaires, surveys, etc.) for 13 experiments relating to core predictions of the proposed attribution theory. These *always* will be confirmed and can be used as demonstration experiments in classroom settings without fear of embarrassment. Readers might contend that the verifications of the predictions are so certain because the hypotheses are trivial, or because the experiments involve role-playing or imaginary rather than actual behavior. These investigations and their criticisms are examined later. For now, it is sufficient to convey that this book is about empirical laws, laws that remain as theories or explanations rise and fall.

In sum, it has been paradoxically suggested that the focus of this book is conceptual analysis as well as that the focus is on empirical laws. As was true for the writing rules of advocacy versus honesty, I do not regard these as inconsistent or contradictory beliefs. It is precisely the reliability of the research predictions that strengthens the proposed attribution theory, and it is the unequivocal predictions of the theory that highlight the importance of the confirming data. Hence, this book is about the connection of theory and data and how each facilitates the other. The readers will find dual representation of theory and data, with equality of importance.

CAUSAL BELIEFS AS DEPENDENT VERSUS INDEPENDENT VARIABLES

In the study of causal beliefs, attributions can be treated as dependent variables, where one is concerned with their determinants, or as independent variables, where one is interested in their effects.

Causes as Dependent Variables

The issues most examined by early attribution theorists, including Fritz Heider (1958), Edward Jones (Jones & Davis, 1965) and Harold Kelley (1967), concern the antecedents or determinants of causal decisions. After Heider, who also considered intentional versus unintentional causality, this was followed by a more specific pursuit: whether an event is better explained with an internal (dispositional) or an external (situational) cause. This question is the focus of concern in studies of "the fundamental attribution error," which is the relative disregarding of situational causality or the over-allocation of dispositional ascriptions. Other well-researched issues within attribution theory also revolve around dispositional versus situational ascriptions. For example, it is contended that actors are more likely to make situational attributions, whereas observers see persons as causal. "I hit him because he provoked me," as opposed to "He hit me because he is aggressive," illustrates one anticipated pattern of causal beliefs supporting an actor/observer difference. Another popular topic guided by attribution theory concerns the so-called hedonic bias, which states that persons tend to take credit for success (internal attribution) but blame failure on external factors. Hence, perhaps the three most studied topics under the rubric of attribution theory: the fundamental attribution error, actor versus observer discrepancies, and hedonic biasing, all ask whether and under what conditions persons are prone to make dispositional as opposed to situational attributions. Related research considers if these attribution tendencies can be altered by, for example, cognitive load, distraction, and the like (see Gawronski, 2003).

Considering attributions as dependent variables and concentrating on dispositional versus situational causation is a very narrow center of attention, ignoring for the most part the psychological significance of causal thoughts and the breadth of issues to which causal attributions are pertinent. The study of attributions can be subsumed under the umbrella of cognitive functionalism, that is, causal thoughts give rise to meaningful actions. Given this theme, attributions are better conceived (or at least also conceived) as independent rather than dependent variables.

Causal Beliefs as Independent Variables

When attributions are independent rather than dependent variables, the psychological questions shift from what determines causal ascriptions to what they affect. For example, one asks what difference it makes when parents ascribe failure of their child to lack of effort as opposed to lack of ability. This is a motivational question, as opposed to one of cognitive inference regarding what parents believe is causing their child's failure and what the antecedents are of this conclusion. It also is a functional query concerning the psychological significance of a causal belief. Answers regarding the consequences of causal thinking require attention to the following issues, which form the heart of this book:

1. Do different causal beliefs have unique consequences, or might causal thoughts possess certain characteristics such that families of causes give rise to similar psychological end states? To foreshadow the answer to this query, causes share a limited number of properties and thus have common effects. However, while sharing some features, they also may differ on others, so for most causal comparisons there are common and noncommon effects. This issue and the brief answer are examined in depth in this book.

2. What do causal beliefs influence? Regarding the tripartite division of psychology into thinking, feeling, and acting (cognition, emotion, and conation), which are affected by causal ascriptions? Does the parental decision that their child is failing because of lack of studying influence subsequent

thoughts about their child, emotional reactions, and/or their behavior? It is intuitively reasonable to conclude that all three are affected, and this also is a central issue explored in the book.

3. Considering now only the consequences on action, is behavior determined directly by causal beliefs (my son did not study; I will reduce his allowance); indirectly by the causal attribution and directly by emotion (my son did not study; I am angry; I will reduce his allowance); simultaneously by both causal thinking and feeling (my son did not study and I am angry; I will reduce his allowance); or by some other configuration or ordering of antecedents? This question raises fundamental issues regarding the sequence of a motivational episode. This query is not amenable to a simple answer, other than, "It depends." In the book I convey on what the answer depends. For example, helping behavior is determined primarily by the heart (i.e., feelings are proximal to acting), whereas aggressive retaliation is directly influenced by both the head and the heart (i.e., thoughts as well as feelings).

4. Are the documented relations uncovered by attribution theory invariant between individuals and cultures, or must individual and cultural differences be considered? That is, within a mediation approach, where motivation is considered a sequential process, are there also moderators that alter the strengths or even the direction of the postulated associations? In this book I examine political ideology as one exemplar moderator of causal relations. I conclude that individual differences in political ideology have significant effects on causal beliefs and therefore on social behavior as well. However, these effects can be captured without alteration of the general theory.

In sum, here I consider the consequences, or results, of various causal beliefs. This makes salient the functional significance of causal thinking, thereby adding richness and vitality to attribution questions.

EXPLANATIONS AS CAUSES AS OPPOSED TO REASONS

The final distinction to be made in this prologue contrasts explanations based on causes as opposed to reasons. If one is asked why he went to Movie X, the likely answers will be what are called *reasons*, such as: "I heard it was good"; "I wanted to get out of the house"; "I was given free tickets"; "It is playing close to my house"; "I love mysteries"; and so on. Similarly, if a student is asked why she enrolled in a particular psychology course, she might say: "I need it for my major"; "I heard the teacher is great"; "It meets at a perfect time for my schedule";

"I like that subject"; "All my friends are taking it"; and so forth. These explanations or justifications make the choice understandable and intelligible. In explaining everyday actions, people focus on reasons, which typically are associated with incentives (costs and benefits) and volitional choice.

Attribution theory as embraced in this book is founded on an analysis of causes. However, inasmuch as everyday explanations invoke reasons, it appears that attribution theory does not capture the thinking of the naïve person (see Malle, 1999). It also has been argued that attribution theory not only neglects reasons, but also has confounded the distinction between reasons and causes (see Buss, 1978).

I agree that reasons must be distinguished from causes and believe the focus of attribution theory is causes. Attribution analyses as discussed in this book begin with an outcome and are invoked to explain end results or consequences rather than actions. Hence, from the perspective of this attribution theory, one does not ask why Jane enrolled in a psychology course, but rather why she succeeded or failed.

Given this perspective, reasons are linked to intentional actions and what appears to be free will. The person has made a free choice and justifies that decision by calling forth reasons. On the other hand, causes apply to some intentional (drug taking) and all unintentional (being blind) end states. One usually does not speak of the "reason" for being blind as opposed to the cause of blindness. The answer to the "why" question for blindness implies an antecedent condition rather than a justification.

In sum, there is a valid distinction between reasons and causes, even though it is murky at times and fraught with philosophical intricacies and quagmires. For present purposes, it is sufficient to note that this book deals with causes, not reasons, and is concerned with folk explanations of outcomes, not actions. A causal rather than a reason analysis limits the range of the theory (as repeated later, the theory of social motivation cannot incorporate why a hungry rat runs down an alleyway for food, which is a central observation for many motivation conceptions). However, this leaves many phenomena that can be embraced within this attributional perspective. In the chapters that follow I turn to some of the main areas of application.

1

A Theory of Social Motivation and Justice: Logic and Development

There are three distinguishable approaches to the study of human motivation. These differ in many ways, particularly in their aspirations or what might be called their pretensions. One approach, previously mentioned, is to build a "grand" theory, that is, create a conceptual system embracing many aspects of human (and perhaps subhuman) behavior. This is the psychological search for the equivalent of Einstein's statement that $E = mc^2$ (with appropriate recognition of the limits and limitations of social science).

One category of theories having very general ambitions characterizes humans as machine-like, needing energy to initiate action and having the goal of reaching homeostasis (equilibrium), thereby (and in contrast to machines) producing feelings of pleasure. Among the theories included within this description are Freud's (1915/1948) psychodynamic view, Hull's (1943) drive theory, and Lewin's (1938) hydraulic vision. These conceptions made significant contributions to the understanding of human motivation. Nonetheless, the reader may note they all appeared relatively early in the history of motivational psychology, implying that this level of aspiration is too grandiose and the development of a "complete theory of motivational psychology" is not a viable goal.

A second avenue in the study of motivation is more modest but nonetheless also is lofty. This is to devise separate theories for each motivational domain. For example, one might attempt to develop a theory of achievement behavior, as did Atkinson (1957), or of aggression, as did Berkowitz (1993). One such theory would attempt to account for all aspects of, for example, achievement, while not aspiring to explain aggressive actions, or vice versa. These conceptions also added in seminal ways to understanding human behavior and, unlike the so-called grand theories, certainly are extant today.

Finally, the most modest approach represented in the science is to understand one determinant of achievement, or of aggression, and eschew any attempt to explain all behaviors within the motivational domain under study. Included here is documenting, for example, that intermediate subjective expectancy of success augments achievement striving, or that aggression is exacerbated in the summer when the weather is hot. This approach characterizes the vast majority of psychological research and may be described as hypothesis testing rather than theory building, although it contributes to conceptual growth by laying the empirical foundation necessary for theory development.

This chapter borrows from the first and third traditions just outlined of generality and specificity, while rejecting the second approach that advocates explanation of an entire motivational area such as achievement or aggression. I believe it is possible to create a general theory of motivation that cuts across motivational domains, that is, a theory able to address, for example, achievement concerns as well as aggression. However, this theory would not explain all aspects of behavior within a domain, such as all of achievement strivings and all of aggression, which was the goal of the second approach previously outlined. Rather, it would account for limited behaviors within those domains, and the same concepts could be used to account for selected aspects of behaviors in other motivational contexts as well. Hence, there is generality across motivational situations, but only a subset of behaviors within any area or field of motivation is addressed.

For example, assume I propose the concept of diffusion of responsibility as the cornerstone for a general theory of motivation. This construct may explain why the likelihood of helping another in need decreases as the number of people available to help increases. Furthermore, it might account for why personal aggression increases with crowd size. That is, aspects of helping and aggression (two motivational domains) are influenced by group size and may be explained, or at least addressed, with the same concept. But this construct does not account for why helping is augmented when one is in a good mood or why aggression is more evident on hot days. Diffusion of responsibility thus clarifies a limited number of helping- and hostility-related behaviors; other empirical observations fall beyond its theoretical reach.

This chapter offers a general theory of motivation at this midrange of generality, identifying determinants of behavior that cut across motivational areas.

This theory incorporates a wide diversity of psychologically meaningful actions. But what constructs should one select to reach this theoretical goal? To find general determinants of behavior that transcend motivational contexts, metaphors proved to be essential guides.

THE ROLE OF METAPHORS

Metaphors (derived from Greek, meaning to carry from one place to another) require us to pretend something is true when it is not. For example, it might be exclaimed that people are sharks. This implies humans share attributes of sharks although, of course, not enough of these characteristics to actually be classified as sharks. This metaphor then acts as a lens or schema and the world is viewed in a new light, illuminating the previously obscure and uncovering new facts. That is, in a metaphor, a familiar concept or image helps us understand something that is not familiar. The shark metaphor, for example, may result in observations of cunningness, aggressiveness, strength, or other associated implications of a shark. In sharp contrast, the metaphor "He is a pussycat" alerts one to an entirely different set of attributes: The person is fun-loving, relaxed, easy to make happy, and so forth.

Metaphors may exist side by side in the explanation of behavior. Thus, Jane might be described as a shark and a rock. The shark metaphor provides some insights to her achievement strivings, aggression, and power seeking. Yet it may not shed light on her helping behavior. Being a rock also helps in understanding her reactions to achievement failure and to the aggression of others, as well as illuminating her attitudes about help giving, yet it is irrelevant to her concerns with power. Hence, diverse metaphors can be applied to the same motivational domain (a shark and a rock apply to Jane's achievement strivings), and a given metaphor may be applicable to different domains but not necessarily to all fields of motivation (a shark characterizes Jane's achievement strivings and aggression but not her helping behavior). This notion of multiple principles, each with limited (circumscribed) generality or applicability, captures the approach to motivation I am advocating.

In sum, metaphors exist side by side, often supported by incommensurable observations. Even Freud acknowledged using metaphors in his scientific discoveries. He wrote (Freud, 1926/1959): "In psychology we can only describe things by the help of analogies. There is nothing peculiar in this; it is the case elsewhere as well. But we have constantly to keep changing these analogies for none of them lasts us long enough" (p. 195). I hope in this chapter to describe a metaphor that will not need continuous changing and will last us "long enough."

The Person Is a Judge

What metaphor provided the foundation for the attribution-based theory of social motivation and justice developed in this book? In searching for the most useful metaphor, one must consider what aspects of behavior the metaphor is likely to capture. The metaphor that the person is a machine proved useful to behaviorists to explain learned actions, and the metaphor that the person is a computer helped cognitive scientists to understand thinking processes. The metaphor I need must address social behavior and justice. "The person is a machine," for example, does not appear useful to capture phenomena incorporated under these rubrics. A metaphor better able to satisfy my goals is "the person is a judge," along with a variant of this theme, that life is a courtroom.

What are the characteristics of a judge? Why be guided by this metaphor? A judge must rationally interpret evidence and reach a decision regarding an alleged transgression of another. It must be decided if the person engaged in a misdeed and is responsible for the action. This requires integration of much information and the imposition of moral standards and cultural imperatives. In addition, the judge has feelings toward the supposed transgressor. These feelings also are likely to determine the imposed sentence. In sum, the judge metaphor includes cognition, affect, and action and transfers well to issues related to social justice and moral conduct.

In a similar manner, life can be considered a courtroom where dramas in regard to transgressions are played out. For example, consider the everyday situation of waiting for your date to appear but he or she does not arrive on time. You wait 10, 15, 20 minutes. During this period you are likely to experience numerous affects—perhaps fear that something dire has happened, concern you are at the wrong place, anger that the person is tardy, and so on. Finally, the awaited other arrives; he or she is 30 minutes late. Unexpected and negative events stimulate causal search, so you immediately ask: "What happened? Why are you so late?" This is the judge seeking evidence regarding innocence or guilt. The transgressor then says: "Oh, it was so nice out I took a round-about path to get here." (This is only for illustration; most criminals do not self-condemn.) This explanation probably arouses great anger and you declare the other guilty. You then pass a sentence—I am leaving and not dating you again. The guilty party then seeks forgiveness and a lesser sentence. He or she states a terrible event occurred ("I just found out I did not get the job I wanted") and time was needed to recover so the date would not be ruined. This mitigator of responsibility is accepted, the sentence is lessened, perhaps totally withdrawn, and the transgressor is paroled (the date continues).

Conceiving the person as a judge and life as a courtroom calls forth an array of thoughts and emotions in an interpersonal setting that shed light on social motivation. It captures the underlying theme of this chapter—social life is moral life and moral concerns pervade social conduct. Hence, judgments regarding fairness, deservedness, fault, blame, and responsibility are the essence of social behavior. Stated somewhat differently, social life is governed by religious principles, which in turn also have guided the law. My task is to document the validity and generality of this approach across motivational fields. It must be remembered, however, that metaphors are neither precisely defined nor exact. Hence, one must be wary of their use. A metaphor is neither an explanation nor a theory; rather, it generates images and broad construals that serve essential functions in the evolution of understanding.

Just as I had to make decisions regarding which metaphor most aids in the development of a useful theory to understand social motivation and justice, choices also were made regarding which aspects of social motivation and justice are best captured by the conception, or what is the focus (the main empirical strength) and range of convenience (the extensity) of the theory (Kelly, 1955). To help in this endeavor, my search was guided by observations in the classroom, which is a microcosm of the social universe. What occurs in a classroom pertaining to social motivation? Perhaps of greatest salience is that teachers are appraising students, determining if they succeeded or failed, if they are "good" or "bad," and what kind of feedback they should be given. Above all in the classroom is achievement evaluation, with the teacher as judge. But also found in the classroom, and certainly in the broader social world, are stigmatization, help giving, compliance with authority, aggression, punishment, and many social and moral emotions. These and other topics are addressed as I advance from the judge metaphor toward a formal theoretical statement to capture the "late date" scenario used earlier.

ACHIEVEMENT EVALUATION

Years ago I was co-author of an investigation concerning judgments of others in achievement contexts (Weiner & Kukla, 1970). This experiment has been replicated on many occasions in many cultures, so the pattern of data may be regarded a "fact" (see Weiner, 1986). Empirical certainty is essential for theory building. This experiment is shown in Box 1.1 for the reader to perform prior to reading further. It is my belief that the data generated by the reader will mirror findings reported by Weiner and Kukla (1970). I regard this as a "bold" empirical claim, not frequently made by those advocating a particular motivation theory. Although this research was conducted almost 35 years ago, near the start of my career, I have spent my academic life trying to explain the findings and have offered numerous interpretations. I always return to this set of data as part of the foundation for my thinking.

In this study, students were described in a questionnaire as experiencing varying degrees of success or failure on an exam. This outcome information was factorially combined with accounts of each student's ability level (high or low) and effort expenditure (high or low), which are the dominant perceived causes of achievement performance (see Weiner, 1986). Thus, for example, in one condition a student was characterized as high in ability, low in effort, and failing an exam (Student #4 in Box 1.1), whereas in a contrasting condition the student was described as low in ability, high in effort, and succeeding (Student #5). Respondents were asked to evaluate (provide feedback to) each of these hypothetical students, where the feedback ranged from +5 (most positive evaluation) to –5 (most negative evaluation).

BOX 1.1   Determinants of Achievement Evaluation

In the following study, eight different pupils are described. They have just taken a test and received either a high (success) or low (failure) score. As the teacher of these children, you know each student's ability level and how much effort has been put into the test preparation. You are now to provide evaluative feedback to the children. Pretend this is in the form of stars: Gold stars are for a good evaluation and red stars for a bad. You can put anywhere from 5 gold stars (represented by "+") to 5 red stars (represented by "–"), but you cannot put both gold and red stars on a paper, so a single decision must be reached.

Student	Ability	Effort	Outcome	Student feedback (Evaluative Judgment) (+5 to –5)
1	High	High	Success	
2	High	High	Failure	
3	High	Low	Success	
4	High	Low	Failure	
5	Low	High	Success	
6	Low	High	Failure	
7	Low	Low	Success	
8	Low	Low	Failure	

Calculations for main effects		Evaluation
Success (lines 1, 3, 5, 7)	=	_____
Failure (lines 2, 4, 6, 8)	=	_____
Difference	=	_____
High effort (lines 1, 2, 5, 6)	=	_____
Low effort (lines 3, 4, 7, 8)	=	_____
Difference	=	_____
Low ability (lines 5, 6, 7, 8)	=	_____
High ability (lines 1, 2, 3 ,4)	=	_____
Difference	=	_____

The data from one investigation reported by Weiner and Kukla (1970) are shown in Fig. 1.1. In Fig. 1.1, the outcomes ranged from excellent through fair, borderline, moderate failure, and clear failure. Figure 1.1 reveals, as expected, that positive outcomes are rewarded more (punished less) than are negative outcomes, holding the causes of those outcomes constant. That is, within any causal configuration, the better the performance, the higher the evaluation. This also can be shown in the calculation for the outcome main effect in Box 1.1 and is an equity principle for distributive justice. That is, what you get is in part determined by the results of your actions. Considering only failure and guided by the judge and courtroom metaphors, one might say "the punishment fits the crime." This is known as the *actus reus* principle of justice. Stated somewhat differently (and again limiting attention to failure), punishment is guided by beliefs in proportionality. This is from an ancient principle of matched retribution stating that justice demands "an eye for an eye, tooth for tooth, and hand for hand" (Exodus 21:24). Hence, the lower the exam score, the worse the received evaluation. This retributive goal of punishment is examined in detail in chapter 4.

In addition, and of greater importance for present purposes, high effort or motivation is rewarded more for success and punished less given failure than is lack of motivation or effort (compare the top versus the bottom two lines in Fig. 1.1). This holds within all levels of exam outcome. That is, the severity of imposed justice additionally depends on whether the student had a "guilty mind." This is known in law as the principle of *mens rea*.

Conversely, low ability is associated with greater reward and less punishment than is high ability within almost all levels of outcome (compare the first

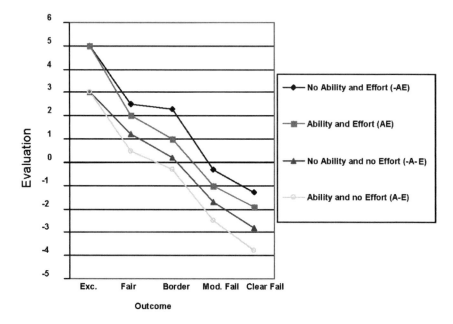

FIG. 1.1.   Evaluation as a function of pupil outcome, effort, and ability. From Weiner and Kukla (1970). Copyright © 1970 by the American Psychological Association. Reprinted with permission.

and third versus the second and fourth lines in Fig. 1.1). This seemingly strange finding occurs because, given this set of information, low ability accompanied by hard work (and especially given moderate success) is particularly rewarded. Indeed, the person overcoming a handicap to succeed is regarded as a cultural hero, divulging key values related to the Protestant ethic held by those in the United States (and in other countries as well). On the other hand, persons not utilizing their capacity and failing because of lack of effort are most punished. They are cultural and moral villains (assuming that in the particular situation, effort is anticipated and regarded an obligation). Because of this configuration of independent variables, lack of ability emerges as a positively valued attribute in terms of its effects on evaluation by others (but not to the same extent as success and high effort). Of course, people do not aspire to have low ability and, because of the relation between ability and outcome, high ability has positive evaluative consequences.

Concentrating on failure outcomes and considering the relation between perceived causality and evaluation, two general principles and motivation sequences that provide a foundation for theory construction emerge from the data reported by Weiner and Kukla (1970):

1. Failure—lack of effort as the cause—high punishment.
2. Failure—lack of ability as the cause—low (or no) punishment.

Although these empirical conclusions are self-evident, their explanation is not.

An Attributional Interpretation

To understand these findings, I detour to an analysis of phenomenal causality. Recall that attribution theory was guided by a distinction between internal versus external causality (or the locus of the cause). But ability and effort are both internal to the actor. Hence, this causal distinction is inadequate to explain these data. To understand the pattern of results, there must be a more detailed understanding of causal beliefs. For this to be accomplished, the properties of causes, or their characteristics and classification within some taxonomy, must be ascertained.

There are, of course, many causes of achievement outcomes in addition to ability and effort, and their identification aids in the construction of a causal taxonomy. Considering negative outcomes, failure may be regarded as due to poor strategy, bad luck, bias of teachers, hindrance from peers, illness, and on and on. Similarly and now shifting to the affiliative domain, social failure (rejection) might be due to poor interpersonal skills, the desired partner already has plans, the other regards you as unattractive, and so on. Note I am speaking about phenomenal causality, that is, perceived causes of achievement failure and rejection, which may or may not be the same as the "real" causes.

These diverse and manifestly different causes have common characteristics or properties; they are genotypically similar despite phenotypic disparities. Hence, although they differ qualitatively, it is possible to compare them quantitatively. To start with our known distinction, in the achievement domain some causes of success and failure—including ability, effort, and strategy—all relate to (are internal to) the person, whereas chance, the biases of teachers, and peer hindrance all describe something about the environment (i.e., these causes are external to the person). As indicated earlier, this distinction provides the basis for much research in attribution theory, in part under the rubric of the "fundamental attribution error," and is essential when considering self-esteem and its maintenance (for self-esteem to rise or fall, attributions must be made to the self by the actor). It therefore may be stated that failure due to lack of math ability and insufficient studying are alike, being internal to the person, whereas they differ from teacher bias and peer hindrance, which are external to the person. The same analysis applies in the affiliative domain, where a person rejected because of unattractiveness implicates an internal cause, while rejection ascribed to the other person being busy is due to an external cause. Note that, with this dimension, causes can be compared and contrasted between motivational contexts. For example, failing math because of low ability and being rejected for a date because of unattractiveness share the property of being internal to the actor. Therefore, phenotypically different causes explaining behavior in disparate motivation domains are comparable and conceptually similar. This cross-domain comparability is essential for the creation of a general theory of motivation from an attribution perspective.

A second causal property of great centrality in this book is controllability, or the degree to which a cause is volitionally alterable. Lack of effort is perceived as controllable or personally changeable—"it could have been otherwise." But this is not the case for the absence of aptitude. A similar distinction is applicable in the affiliative domain. For example, rejection because one is "sloppy" is perceived by others as under volitional control, but this is not the case if one is rejected because of being too tall or too short.

Controllability is logically separable from the causal property of locus, although at times these characteristics are confounded. The oft-used phrase "internal locus of control" illustrates one such confound and creates conceptual confusion inasmuch as causes may be internal but uncontrollable. For example, aptitude is construed internal to a person yet is uncontrollable by that individual. It is not susceptible to change directly by desire or by reason. On the other hand, effort is internal and controllable. Not trying in the absence of mitigating circumstances is a free choice. The property of controllability is perhaps more important than locus when considering the functional consequences of attributions in social contexts because it relates directly to moral judgments, as is documented throughout this book.

As just reasoned, internal causes may be controllable (effort) or uncontrollable (aptitude). This also is true of external causes, but the idea of a controllable external cause requires the shifting of agency, or a change in the perceived focus of agency. In the case of a student failing an exam, all external causes are by definition uncontrollable by that student. But the cause may be controllable by an external agent. For example, peer hindrance is external to the failing student and uncontrollable by him or her, but this behavior is controllable by the peer. In this book, I use the concept of controllability in a "shifting focus" manner. This is essential because an external cause controllable by others is the antecedent for other-blame and anger and has a number of additional social consequences.

There is most likely one (and perhaps only one) further underlying property of causality. This relates to the generality of causal explanation over time and is referred to as *causal stability*. For example, low general intelligence as a cause of math failure is considered stable over time, whereas failure because of bad luck, or having the flu, is regarded as temporary. Causal stability deserves attention inasmuch as it influences beliefs about the future, including expectancy of success, which is accepted as one of the most important determinants of motivated behavior. The property of causal stability is examined in detail in chapter 4 when considering the goals of punishment.

There is substantial evidence that locus, controllability, and stability are the only replicable properties of phenomenal causality (see review in Weiner, 1986), although one can argue for causal generality ("globality") across situations as an additional causal dimension, which the learned helplessness camp has done (Peterson, 1991). I chose not to (strongly) support this contention because the global property does not emerge in empirical studies of causal properties (see Weiner, 1986), although it has intuitive appeal. In addition, this work has almost entirely been conducted in America so cross-cultural substantiation of a declaration of three or four basic causal properties is badly needed.

Why there are only three (or four) causal dimensions is unknown. It has been argued that causality, just as time and space, is a basic category of human thinking, inborn and "ready" for use. This might be the case for the dimensions of causes as well, although there is no compelling evidence documenting this explanation as opposed to learning the categories over time on the basis of particular experiences (e.g., when infants reach to attain objects they may come to learn effort is a controllable cause, whereas when some objects are out of reach they learn that in some instances causality is uncontrollable). But these conjectures roam far from the topic of this book and it is sufficient for present purposes to propose that three properties of phenomenal causality are locus, controllability, and stability, and controllability can be regarded from the viewpoint of the actor or an external agent.

With this discussion in mind, I return to data from Weiner and Kukla (1970) and the finding that failure caused by lack of effort elicits punishment from the teacher, whereas this is not so given lack of ability as the cause. In what ways do lack of effort and lack of ability differ? Table 1.1 shows these two causes and their underlying properties. It is evident from Table 1.1 that ability and effort are both internal to the actor. Hence, causal locus cannot account for evaluative differences associated with ability versus effort as causes of failure. On the other hand, the two causes differ in their controllability, with insufficient effort perceived controllable, whereas diminished ability is generally thought of as uncontrollable (here considering ability akin to aptitude rather than a learned skill). In addition, effort is usually regarded as unstable or temporary, whereas ability (aptitude) is permanent. (A weaker version of this statement is effort is considered more unstable than ability.)

TABLE 1.1

Causal Properties of Ability and Effort

Causal Property	Ability	Effort
Locus	Internal	Internal
Controllability	Uncontrollable	Controllable
Stability	Stable	Unstable

Hence, evaluative disparities given lack of ability compared to the absence of effort as causing failure can be due to differences in either the controllability or stability of these causes.

But it is relatively easy to demonstrate that controllability, rather than stability, is the main determinant of the inequalities in evaluative feedback these causes generate. It can be specified that effort is stable (the student is always lazy) or unstable (the student did not work hard on this occasion), and ability is stable (the student is of low general intelligence) or unstable (the student had not yet developed the required skills). When such variations are introduced, effort-related causes are punished more for failure than are ability-related causes, whether stable or unstable. That is, being lazy has more negative evaluative consequences than lack of intelligence (both stable causes), and not trying at one particular time or occasion is more negatively evaluated than lacking skill (both unstable and temporary causes). Hence, the key attribution difference producing evaluative disparities is causal controllability, or whether the student could or could not have volitionally changed behavior and the linked outcome.

Given this conclusion, the evaluative or motivational principles previously described may be supplemented to include the control dimension of causality:

1. Failure—lack of effort (controllable causality)—high punishment.
2. Failure—lack of ability (uncontrollable causality)—low or no punishment.

It can then be reasoned that any cause subject to volitional change by the agent that gives rise to failure promotes punishment or condemnation, whereas any uncontrollable cause does not evoke reprimand. For example, in the affiliative domain others criticize a person for being rejected because of personal sloppiness ("you can dress better"), whereas condemnation of that person is highly unlikely when rejection is due to unattractiveness. Hence, a more general statement regarding the relation between causality and sanction given a negative achievement (or other-domain) outcome is:

1. Failure—controllable causality—negative evaluative reaction from other.
2. Failure—uncontrollable causality—absence of negative evaluative reaction from other.

Lack of effort, therefore, is only one cause among many that augments punishment because it is characterized as controllable. Note I have not examined the possibility that uncontrollable failure may evoke positive responses from others (e.g., sympathy and help giving). This position is elaborated in later discussions. In addition, I have not addressed fully why one rewards or punishes. This issue is considered in chapter 4. Nor have I recognized circumstances that may mitigate the punishment meted out for not trying; this is examined in chapter 3.

Fairness of Evaluative Rules.   It has been established that individuals take controllability into account in deciding how harshly to judge others in achievement settings. But is this "fair?" After all, it might be contended that effort expenditure and inferences about personal control should not be considered in achievement evaluation because a refusal to try does not result in a transgression against another. It is a victimless crime. In addition, it could be asserted that the only thing that matters is the "bottom line," that is, the outcome (or what is known as "strict liability" in the law).

To explore the issue of perceived fairness, a colleague and I (Farwell & Weiner, 1996) directly examined fairness judgments in situations of achievement evaluation. Readers may partake in this experiment, some of which is shown in Box 1.2.

In the investigation by Farwell and Weiner (1996; as well as in Box 1.2), pupils were described as failing an exam (committing a transgression) either because of the absence of effort (personal controllability) or lack of ability (an uncontrollable cause). This information was paired with the teacher's evaluations, which ranged from −1 to −5. The evaluations were varied in a factorial manner so that, for example, at times the pupil failing because of lack of ability received feedback of −1, whereas the lack-of-effort student received −5 (see #3 in Box 1.2). In other conditions, both received feedback of −5 or −1 (#2 and #4), and in yet another condition the pupil failing due to lack of ability was evaluated −5, whereas the student performing poorly due to lack of effort received feedback of −1 (#1). We asked our respondents to judge the fairness, as well as the strictness, of the paired teacher evaluations on a scale from +3 to –3.

BOX 1.2 Fairness and Strictness of Teacher Evaluations

Imagine two students in a classroom, and both do poorly on an exam. In addition to exam score, the teacher provides evaluative feedback to the students in the form of red stars when there is a poor performance. One student failed because of low ability, the other failed because of not trying. The teacher gives from 1 to 5 red stars (or from –1 to –5). Below are a number of different evaluations. Rate how fair and how strict (hard) these are. Give your ratings in the spaces provided. The ratings can go from +3 (very fair, very strict) to –3 (very unfair, not strict).

	Lack of ability (Red Stars)	Lack of effort (Red Stars)	How fair? (+3 to –3)	How strict? (+3 to –3)
1.	–5	–1		
2.	–5	–5		
3.	–1	–5		
4.	–1	–1		
5.	–4	–2		
6.	–4	–4		
7.	–2	–2		
8.	–2	–4		
9.	–4	–1		
10.	–1	–4		
11.	–1	–1		
12.	–4	–4		

Calculations for ratings when:	Fairness
Ability > Effort by 4 = (Line 1)	
Ability > Effort by 3 = (Line 9)	
Ability > Effort by 2 = (Line 5)	
Ability = Effort (Lines 2, 4, 6, 7, 11, 12)	
Ability < Effort by 2 = (Line 8)	
Ability < Effort by 3 = (Line 10)	
Ability < Effort by 4 = (Line 3)	

I am quite sure the responses of the readers will again be similar to those of typical college students who serve as research participants in most of these investigations. As shown in Fig. 1.2 (which gives both the fairness and the strictness ratings), evaluations rated as fairest occurred when the negativity of the feedback given for failing due to lack of effort was greater than for lack of ability. The fairest pattern (the highest negative number) evaluated the lack-of-effort student –5 and the lack-of-ability student –2, or the lack-of-effort student –4 and the pupil low in ability –1. Conversely, the evaluations judged most unfair occurred when lack of ability resulted in harsher feedback than lack of effort. Strictness was associated with the total degree of negativity of the feedback in the paired causal groupings, rather than being determined by differences in the evaluations.

The centrality of fairness in achievement contexts again demonstrates that achievement evaluations are also moral judgments. In his classic book, *The Protestant Ethic and the Spirit of Capitalism,* Weber (1904/1958) pointed out the association between achievement strivings and morality. He argued that it is a moral duty to put forth effort and strive for success. That is, achievement is intertwined with ideas about ought, should, and obligation, and is part of a larger moral duty. As Feather (1999) pointed out, in achievement contexts success without effort is not perceived as "deserved" and elicits feelings of injustice. The metaphor "the person is a judge" therefore fits comfortably into the study of achievement strivings and judgments about others in achievement settings. Also, as illustrated in the chapter, this metaphor and the ability/effort distinction are applicable in the affiliative and other domains as well.

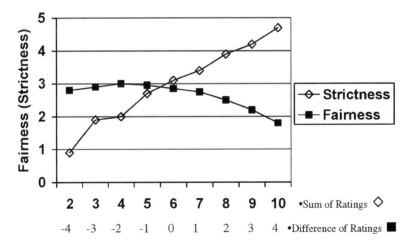

FIG. 1.2.   Strictness and fairness of negative allocations as a function of feedback to low ability versus low effort students. Data from Farwell and Weiner (1996).

REACTIONS TO THE STIGMATIZED

I now turn attention to a different social domain—stigmatization and reactions to the stigmatized. Let me begin again with a very simple study, one not classroom-related, and then report another set of findings that pertains to a school setting. In this illustrative investigation, along with two colleagues (Weiner, Perry, & Magnusson, 1988), I examined the relations between a number of the most common stigmatizing conditions and thoughts about, as well as affective reactions toward, individuals with those stigmas, including beliefs related to responsibility and blame and feelings of liking, anger, and sympathy. The procedure was quite straightforward and readers are invited to take part in a similar study now, which is shown in Box 1.3.

The stigmas examined, and the reported reactions, are shown in Table 1.2. There is a division within the table, with the top part including stigmas from Alzheimer's disease to paraplegia, while the lower section of the table ranges from AIDS to obesity (alcoholism was not included in the experiment). The stigmas included in the top half of the table elicit little responsibility and blame and relative liking, high pity, and little anger. For the bottom portion of Table

---

BOX 1.3 Reactions to the Stigmatized

Please fill in the responses with numerical values that represent your opinions. For each question, 1 = very low (e.g., not controllable, not responsible, no anger, no sympathy); 7 = very high (e.g., highly controllable, etc.). For each stigma and judgment, use any number from 1 to 7.

Stigma	Controllability	Responsibility	Anger	Sympathy
AIDS				
Alcoholism				
Alzheimer's disease				
Blindness				
Cancer				
Child abuser				
Drug abuser				
Heart disease				
Obesity				
Paraplegia				

Data Sheet: Sum of the data, five stigmas in each category

Stigma Classification	Controllability	Responsibility	Anger	Sympathy
Controllable stigmas (AIDS, alcoholism, child abuser, drug abuser, obesity)				
Uncontrollable stigmas (Alzheimer's disease, blindness, cancer, heart disease, paraplegia)				

TABLE 1.2

Mean Values on Responsibility-Related Variables

Stigma	Responsibility	Blame	Liking	Pity	Anger
Alzheimer's disease	0.8	0.5	6.5	7.9	1.4
Blindness	0.9	0.5	7.5	7.4	1.7
Cancer	1.6	1.3	7.6	8.0	1.6
Heart disease	2.5	1.6	7.5	7.4	1.6
Paraplegia	1.6	0.9	7.0	7.6	1.4
AIDS	4.4	4.8	4.8	6.2	4.0
Child abuser	5.2	6.0	2.0	3.3	7.9
Drug abuse	6.5	6.7	3.0	4.0	6.4
Obesity	5.3	5.2	5.7	5.1	3.3

Note. Data from Weiner, Perry, and Magnusson (1988), p. 740.

1.2, the data markedly differ: There is responsibility and blame, little liking or pity, and anger.

How can this empirical division be explained? Here again, attribution theory provides some answers. Stigmas, just as causes, have particular properties and can be classified on the bases of these characteristics. For example, stigmas vary according to medical seriousness, whether they are concealable or not, permanent or temporary, and, most importantly in this context, if their origins are biological or behavioral (see Jones et al., 1984).

The data shown in Table 1.2 suggest that individuals with somatically (genetically, biologically) originated problems, such as Alzheimer's disease and blindness, elicit less negative reactivity than persons with behavioral problems, such as being a child abuser or obese. The absolute as well as relative negativity of responses toward others with behavioral-based problems including AIDS, obesity, alcoholism, and drug addiction is reported in many investigations, and just as the achievement evaluation data, these attitudinal findings can be considered "facts" (see review in Weiner, 1995). The reader should examine Box 1.3 to see if a similar pattern is expressed.

Returning to the classroom for a set of related data, it has been documented that children generally do not accept peers having nonnormative characteristics, such as being socially withdrawn, unattractive, handicapped, and so on (see Hartup, 1983; Juvonen, 1991). However, peer reactions differ according to the type of deviance. Children exhibiting aggressive, antisocial, or hyperactive behaviors are rated low in liking, whereas the mentally and physically handicapped are among the more preferred deviant groups (see Juvonen, 1991; Sigelman & Begley, 1987). These disparities are summarized in Table 1.3 (which specifies reprimand as the behavioral response).

It might be contended that these groups elicit different reactions because hyperactive and aggressive children interfere with others, whereas those with physical and mental handicaps do not create interpersonal problems for the nonstigmatized. However, among children, the obese are most rejected and disliked (Richardson, Hastorf, Goodman, & Dornbusch, 1961), even though they do not necessarily interfere with others. It therefore appears that the characteristic distinguishing relatively accepted (not reprimanded) from rejected (reprimanded) individuals is whether or not the stigmatizing condition is biological or behavioral in origin (see Table 1.3).

In sum, the principles and motivation sequences derived from studies of stigmatization may be summarized as follows:

TABLE 1.3
Evaluation of School-Related Stigmas

Stigma	Classification	Reprimand
Hyperactivity	Behavioral	High
Braggart	Behavioral	High
Aggressive	Behavioral	High
Physical handicap	Somatic, genetic	Low
Mental handicap	Somatic, genetic	Low
Unattractive	Somatic, genetic	Low

1. Stigmatizing condition—behavioral origin—reprimand.
2. Stigmatizing condition—biological origin—no reprimand.

It also is believed stigmas of behavioral origin are controllable. That is, they are brought about by "choice." One "need not" overeat, take drugs, drink too much, engage in promiscuous sex, and so on. "Just say no" is the phrase called forth. On the other hand, stigmas of biological origin are not perceived subject to the will of the actor. After all, one does not choose to have Alzheimer's disease, nor can its severity be greatly influenced by volitional choice. Thus, these relations can be further depicted as:

1. Stigmatizing condition—behavioral origin (controllable)—reprimand.
2. Stigmatizing condition—biological origin (not controllable)—no reprimand.

These principles can be further refined. Some stigmatizing conditions appear to be of biological origin, say heart disease, yet they may be brought about by dysfunctional behaviors, such as not exercising and smoking. Lifestyle choices are being increasingly invoked as determinants of illness. On the other hand, other stigmas appear to be of behavioral origin, say obesity, yet may have perceived biological underpinnings, such as a defective thyroid condition. In these examples, perceived controllability determines behavioral reactions to the person, so the individual with lifestyle-linked heart disease is likely to be reacted to more negatively than the individual obese due to a thyroid dysfunction (see Weiner et al., 1988). Hence, the relations between stigmatizing conditions and behavioral reactions can be more accurately depicted as:

1. Stigmatizing condition—controllable—reprimand.
2. Stigmatizing condition—not controllable—no reprimand.

Recall that, when considering achievement evaluation, persons who overcome lack of ability and succeed because of extra exertion are highly evaluated. In a related judgment process, individuals stigmatized because of controllable actions who overcome or "erase" their stigmas, presumably through great moral efforts, also are valued highly (see Sniderman, Piazza, Tetlock, & Kendrick, 1991). The recovered alcoholic, the contributing citizen who formerly was a drug addict, and the marathon runner who was obese because of overeating are often perceived to be "cultural heroes." Perhaps paradoxically, they are admired more than those who never drank, took drugs, were obese, and so on. Indeed, they are sought as counselors to serve as role models for nonrecovered individuals.

Welfare Recipients Versus the Poor. Among stigmatized groups, a distinction is made between individuals on welfare as opposed to the poor, although these are overlapping populations. Persons described as on welfare (which, at its inception, was targeted to assist widows) are reacted to more negatively than individuals described as poor (see Henry, Reyna, & Weiner, 2004). In contrast to the poor, welfare recipients are regarded as in control of their problems. More specifically, they are perceived to be not working. On the other hand, the poor are thought to be working but not receiving sufficient wages to provide a decent life.

Examples of these contrary stereotypes exist in the political rhetoric that surrounds welfare and poverty issues. In two different speeches given in 1999, then Republican presidential candidate George W. Bush reinforced these different images of welfare recipients versus the poor. With respect to welfare, in a speech given in Texas, Bush warned, "Those who remain on welfare … if you refuse to help yourself, then Texas cannot help you" (Bush, 1999a). Regarding poverty, he stated in a later address, "We will rally the armies of compassion in our communities to fight a very different war against poverty" (Bush, 1999b). This conjures a contrasting image of the helpless and uncontrollable poor.

Democrats have also reinforced these stereotypes, which are based on causal beliefs regarding controllability. Former President Clinton strategically named his welfare policy the "Personal Responsibility and Work Opportunity Act" (see Clinton, 1996), noting, "Our welfare reform proposal will embrace two simple values: work and responsibility" (Clinton, 1995). This sentiment implies that the new American welfare policy will no longer be handouts to the immoral (the lazy).

It is thus again evident that moral concerns play a major role in judgments of others. Persons with stigmas are regarded as sick or as sinners. The sick are not morally culpable or morally deficient. They are blind, or have Alzheimer's disease, or are poor. It is not their fault. Sinners, on the other hand—the drug takers, the obese, the consumers of too much alcohol—are blamed, faulted, and punished. They are moral failures in that their transgressions are preventable by themselves. Free will, which is discussed later, is assumed by the judge and is necessary for a judgment of sin.

A THEORETICAL INTEGRATION

A specific fact in and of itself is of less interest than what that evidence more broadly represents. For example, it is of great importance that lack of effort elicits more punishment than lack of ability given achievement failure. But it is of greater significance to realize that causal controllability, which is substantiated or materialized by lack of effort, generates more punishment than causal uncontrollability, which is embodied within low aptitude. This importance becomes apparent when it is recognized that behavior-generated stigmas, which elicit negative reactions, are considered caused by controllable factors (e.g., sexual behavior as a cause of AIDS; overeating as a cause of obesity; laziness as a cause of welfare), and thus they differ from somatic stigmas, which elicit more positive reactions and are construed as personally uncontrollable (e.g., the aging process or a genetic deficit as a cause of Alzheimer's disease; low wages as a cause of poverty). Hence, the two sets of phenomena respectively related to achievement evaluation and reactions to the stigmatized can be embraced within the same conceptual framework:

1. Achievement failure; stigma—controllable causality—reprimand.
2. Achievement failure; stigma—uncontrollable causality—no reprimand.

In sum, two empirical laws have been joined and a property of causality has made explanatory generalization possible. Furthermore, metaphors have been used—the person is a judge and life is a courtroom—that provide direction to a principle (the "sentence" imposed in part depends on personal controllability, or *mens rea* in legal language) enabling between-context comparability. The judge and courtroom metaphors and the derived principles do not allow for a complete understanding of achievement evaluation or for a complete understanding of reactions to the stigmatized. After all, for example, reactions to the stigmatized also are influenced by personal fear and physical characteristics of the stigmatized other. However, the metaphors and the rules or ideas they generate are applicable in both the achievement and stigma domains, and that is the goal for which I am striving.

Now two social phenomena: Punishment for lack of achievement-related effort (and no punishment for lack of ability) and punishment for behavioral-based stigmas (and the absence of punishment for biologically based stigmas) have been embraced under a single conceptual framework. However, achievement appraisal and reactions to the stigmatized do not represent the core of social behavior. They receive scant attention in introductory textbooks in motivation or social psychology. When considering social motivation, three other areas are of significance in that they are closer to the center of motivation and social psychology. They are helping (altruism), or going toward others; power and compliance, or given noncompliance, going away from others; and aggression, or going against others. I next turn to these three motivation domains, guided by the interpretations of achievement evaluation and reactions to the stigmatized. As might be imagined, however, new theoretical hurdles are faced.

HELP GIVING

Can help giving be placed within the theoretical structure developed thus far? To answer this question, let me turn to an investigation I conducted that relates to helping in the classroom (see Weiner, 1980b). As before, readers are given the opportunity to undertake the experiment and I express great confidence their data will mirror what is reported here. This experiment is given in Box 1.4.

The participants in this study were to assume that a classmate asked to borrow their class notes (see Box 1.4). Then the cause of this need was varied. In one condition, the fellow student stated the notes are needed because of eye problems—he is having difficulty seeing and had to consult an eye doctor. To make this more believable, the student was described as wearing an eye patch.

BOX 1.4   Helping in an Achievement Context

The following stories concern a fellow student's attempt to borrow your class notes. In each instance, the story will describe this event and indicate why he is seeking help. Afterwards you will be asked to relate your thoughts and feelings about the person involved and what you might do.

At about 1:00 in the afternoon, you are walking through campus and a student comes up to you. He says that you do not know him but that you are both enrolled in the same class, where he happened to notice you. He asks if you would lend him the notes from the classes last week. He indicates that he needs the notes because he was having difficulty with his eyes; a change in glasses was required and during the week he had difficulty seeing because of eye drops and other treatments. You note that he is wearing a patch over one eye.

Please answer the following questions about the incident:

1. How much anger and annoyance do you feel toward this person?

1	2	3	4	5	6	7

A great deal of anger   No anger
and annoyance   and annoyance

2. How much sympathy do you have for this person?

1	2	3	4	5	6	7

A great deal of sympathy   No sympathy

3. How likely is it that you would lend your class notes to this person?

1	2	3	4	5	6	7

Definitely *would*
lend the notes

Definitely would *not*
lend the notes

4. How controllable is this person's reason for not taking notes? That is, is the reason that he does not have the notes subject to personal influence? One might think that he should have been able to control the amount that he was affected by the problem or that he could not control this.

1	2	3	4	5	6	7

Under personal
control

Not under
personal control

At about 1:00 in the afternoon, you are walking through campus and a student comes up to you. He says that you do not know him but that you are both enrolled in the same class, where he happened to notice you. He asks if you would lend him the notes from the classes last week. He indicates that he needs the notes because he skipped class to go to the beach and "take it easy."

Please answer the following questions about the incident:

5. How much anger and annoyance do you feel toward this person?

1	2	3	4	5	6	7

A great deal of anger
and annoyance

No anger
and annoyance

6. How much sympathy do you have for this person?

1	2	3	4	5	6	7

A great deal of sympathy

No sympathy

7. How likely is it that you would lend your class notes to this person?

1	2	3	4	5	6	7

Definitely *would*
lend the notes

Definitely would *not*
lend the notes

8. How controllable is this person's reason for not taking notes? That is, is the reason that he does not have the notes subject to personal influence? One might think that he should have been able to control the amount that he was affected by the problem or that he could not control this.

1	2	3	4	5	6	7

Under personal control

Not under
personal control

In the second condition, the student said notes are needed because he went to the beach instead of class. Participants were then asked the likelihood they would lend the notes. Other reactions also were assessed, including controllability of the cause of the need and how much anger and sympathy they feel toward the needy classmate.

Selected data from this investigation are shown in Table 1.4. The data reveal the person needing notes because of going to the beach instead of class is perceived in need because of a controllable cause. This arouses (is associated with) little sympathy, much anger, and a weak tendency to lend the notes. On the other hand, the student desiring the notes because of eye problems is in need because of an uncontrollable cause. This elicits (is related to) sympathy, little anger, and help giving. This experiment and variants of it have been replicated on many occasions (see Barnes, Ickes, & Kidd, 1979; review in Weiner, 1995) and quite likely as well in the responses given in Box 1.4.

Focusing on the behavioral consequences regarding help giving, the experimental findings may be represented as:

1. Need class notes—went to the beach—no help.
2. Need class notes—eye problems—help.

It is evident that going to the beach is closely associated with lack of effort as a cause of failure. That is, the cause of the need is internal and controllable by the person. Conversely, an eye problem may be considered a somatically originated stigma and is conceptually similar to lack of ability as a cause of achievement failure (internal and uncontrollable). Hence, consistent with the prior analyses and as documented in Table 1.4, the findings may be depicted as:

TABLE 1.4

Mean Judgments and Standard Deviations in the Two Helping Conditions

	Condition			
	Beach		Eye Problem	
Variable	M	SD	M	SD
Control	6.75	2.63	3.84	2.88
Sympathy	.63	1.05	5.52	1.91
Anger	4.57	2.77	1.20	1.96
Lend	2.07	2.66	5.58	2.49

Note. Data from Weiner (1980b), p. 679.

1. Need for help—controllable causality—help withheld.
2. Need for help—uncontrollable causality—help given.

Such help-giving contexts therefore can be conceptualized within the same structure imposed on achievement evaluation and reactions to the stigmatized. Individuals who have "made their own bed" must "sleep in it" and do not deserve aid. On the other hand, those with uncontrollable needs "ought to be" helped. Consistent with achievement evaluation and reactions to the stigmatized, a within-domain theory (in this case, of help-giving) is not being proposed. After all, the determinants of help include fear and distress, the number of people available to help, genetic relatedness, and on and on. Rather than describing a complete theory of helping, in the present analysis one determinant of helping behavior has been isolated and identified, and this antecedent (inferred controllability) also affects achievement evaluation and reactions to the stigmatized, although other variables influence these reactions as well.

To summarize the conclusions thus far, in instances of achievement evaluation, reactions to the stigmatized, and where aid is sought, the judge and courtroom metaphors highlight that perceived control is an essential cognition regulating social reactions and mediates between an event or state and the reaction it elicits. These social behaviors have their roots in theology, law, and other sources of moral thinking.

COMPLIANCE WITH OTHERS IN POWER

Imagine a principal informs a teacher that a student is the son of a significant donor and that giving him a high evaluation, regardless of his actual performance and its cause, will result in a salary increment. Bribes and other influence attempts are rare in school but they certainly occur in various forms, and of course they are prevalent out of the classroom as well. Would this change the behavior of the teacher and, if so, how would that teacher be judged?

In this example, a potential change in behavior had its origin in another person. An individual's power is considered the relative ability to shape, alter, or influence the behavior of others (see French & Raven, 1959). Social power—that is, the degree to which one can influence others—can be traced to six fundamental sources: information, reward, coercion, expertise, reference, and identification (French & Raven, 1959; Raven, 1965). Before discussing these further, readers are invited to complete the experiment in Box 1.5, which asks about reactions to others who comply with a request to do something unethical, influenced by the various bases of power. In this experiment, the label of responsibility replaces that of control because it is more appropriate (as will soon be elaborated).

BOX 1.5   Compliance Given Different Power Sources

Imagine the following situation. A doctor asks a nurse to give an experimental drug to a patient, one that has not been officially authorized to be dispensed. After some reluctance and indication that she did not want to comply, the nurse complies with the request. As a result of this, the patient gets worse, is admitted to an Intensive Care Unit, and a few days later dies. In the following, you will read of the doctor's communications to the nurse that resulted in the compliance with the request. You are to read these messages and then make judgments regarding the responsibility of the nurse, your feelings of anger and sympathy toward her, and what your behavioral reaction would have been had you the authority to punish the nurse. The messages that the doctor delivered were one of the following:

1. "I will help you with a promotion if you do what you are told." (reward)

2. "You will be fired if you refuse to follow directions." (punishment)

3. "As the private doctor, I have the right to tell you which medicine should be administered." (legitimacy)

4. "We have always seen things eye to eye. Let's keep things that way." (reference)

5. "Put your trust in my expert knowledge and do what you have been asked." (expertise)

6. "I will show you such compelling evidence about the value of the new medication that you will convince yourself that this was the right thing to do." (information)

Now answer the following questions for each message (ratings from 1 to 7):

1. How responsible do you hold the nurse?
   (1 = not responsible; 7 = very responsible)

2. How much anger would you feel toward the nurse, if this patient was a friend of yours?
   (1 = not angry; 7 = very angry)

3. How much sympathy do you feel toward the nurse?
   (1 = no sympathy; 7 = very sympathetic)

4. How great a punishment or reprimand should the nurse be given?
   (1 = least possible; 7 = most possible)

For example, in Row 1 the nurse is told that she will get a promotion (reward) if she does what she is asked. The nurse complies. The ratings capture the degree to which the nurse is regarded as responsible, the reader's anger and sympathy, and the recommended punishment (all on a 7-point scale).

Sources of Power	Responsibility	Anger	Sympathy	Punishment
1. reward				
2. punishment				
3. legitimacy				
4. reference				
5. expertise				
6. information				
Means, Group 1 (1 + 4 + 6)	———————	———————	———————	———————
Means, Group 2 (2 + 3 + 5)	———————	———————	———————	———————

In the compliance experiment just completed, the six bases of power are represented. Reward (receive a promotion) and coercion or punishment (be fired) are readily recognized. The remaining four bases of power are labeled legitimacy (the doctor has the right to tell me), reference (we have always seen things the same way), expertise (put your trust in expert knowledge), and information (the doctor showed me compelling evidence). These have been considered distinct and qualitatively different, although there have been attempts to cluster the power strategies into meaningful classifications.

Rodrigues and his colleagues (e.g., Rodrigues, 1995; Rodrigues & Lloyd, 1998) documented that causal beliefs provide one framework in which types of power can be classified so that phenotypically different power bases may be regarded genotypically similar (in the same manner that distinct causes of achievement such as ability and effort have been shown to be similar in some fundamental ways and different in others). Rodrigues (1995) found that compliance generated by reward, information, and reference sources of power is considered more internal to and controllable by the person being influenced than compliance elicited by coercion, legitimacy, and expertise. Specifically, for example, if a nurse complies with an illegal request from a doctor because of an anticipated reward, then her behavior is considered due to an internal and controllable cause. On the other hand, if there is compliance because of fear regarding punishment, then the behavior is seen as due to an external and uncontrollable cause (this comparison is examined in detail in chap. 4). Similarly, if one complies because of reference power, which is determined by similarity and shared experiences, then this cause of influence is considered internal and controllable by the complying individual, whereas compliance because the other is authorized to give commands (legitimacy) is generated by an external, uncontrollable cause.

To test these ideas and examine the effects of attributional classification on the reactions of others, Rodrigues and Lloyd (1998) gave their participants a variant of the scenario included in Box 1.5. A nurse was described as complying with the request of a doctor to unethically give experimental medicine to a patient, with the results positive in one condition (the patient recovered) and negative in the other (the patient died, as in Box 1.5). In addition, the social influence attempt of the doctor was based on the six sources of power.

In their analyses, Rodrigues and Lloyd (1998) combined the data from the reward, information, and reference power bases (the internal controllable causes, called Group 1 power sources) and the data from the coercion, legitimacy, and expertise power bases (the external uncontrollable causes, labeled Group 2). The data from one of their investigations, in which nurses were the respondents, are given in Table 1.5, which shows in both the good and bad outcome conditions, Group 1 causes (e.g., reward) are rated more internal to and controllable by the nurse than Group 2 causes (e.g., punishment). In addition,

TABLE 1.5

Means for Group 1 and Group 2 Power Bases
(Study 1: Behavior of the Nurse Viewed by Practicing Nurses)

Variables	Group 1	Group 2
A. Good-outcome condition		
Internality	5.15	3.72
Controllability	6.62	4.96
B. Bad-outcome condition		
Internality	5.46	3.89
Controllability	6.76	4.29
Anger	6.16	4.67
Punishment	5.38	4.30

Note. Data from Rodrigues and Lloyd (1998), p. 987.

and here considering only the negative outcome, internal and controllable causes elicit greater anger as well as more severe recommended punishment of the nurse than do external uncontrollable causes.

Guided by the prior discussions of achievement evaluation, reactions to the stigmatized, and help giving, these data suggest the following conceptual analysis (again considering only the negative outcome and only the control dimension of causality):

1. Compliance—based on reward, information, or reference power—punishment.
   Compliance—based on coercion, legitimacy, or expertise power—(relatively) no punishment.
2. Reward, information, and reference power = controllable causality.
   Coercion, legitimacy, and expert power = uncontrollable causality.
3. Compliance—controllable causality—punishment.
   Compliance—uncontrollable causality—(relatively) no punishment.

Hence, the argument being made can be extended to yet another domain, one embracing compliance and the reasons a social influence attempt was realized. In the psychological literature, achievement evaluation, reactions to the stigmatized, help-giving, and compliance have not been discussed under the same conceptual scaffold. Indeed, I believe no pairing has been placed within the same theoretical structure. But using an attribution (and in this case moral) framework makes it evident these areas can be brought together under a common umbrella.

AGGRESSION

I now turn to yet another area of psychological study, that of aggression, to ascertain if it also can be incorporated into the emerging theoretical structure. In discussing aggression, I deviate from my prior practice by not presenting a simple experimental questionnaire that readers can also complete. The picture being drawn is now obvious and an experiential component is no longer needed in this section. On the other hand, theoretical stretching is required in comparison to the ease with which achievement evaluation, reactions to the stigmatized, help giving, and compliance to transgress were brought together.

One pertinent set of investigations bearing on an attributional or causal approach to aggression adhered to a deception paradigm. In these experiments, a subject received an aversive stimulus (e.g., shock, a loud noise) from an experimental partner (who may have been a confederate or did not actually exist but was thought to be in an adjoining room). Information was conveyed that the partner did or did not know of the effects of her action, was or was not aware of the level of aversive stimulation she had administered, and the like. For example, in one study following the shock administration, it was revealed to the victim that the shock machine had been incorrectly labeled, so when a high shock was selected by the presumed fellow participant the subject actually received a low shock and vice versa. After undergoing this shock-receiving experience, in conjunction with the additional information, the subject was provided the opportunity to respond aggressively toward the person believed to have administered the shock (see Dyck & Rule, 1978; Epstein & Taylor, 1967; Nickel, 1974). In this manner, the magnitude of the shock received and the experimentally manipulated inferences of personal intent were independently related to behavioral aggression (retaliation).

This research has consistently found that the overt aggression of the subjects matches the intensity of the aversive stimulation they believe their partner *intended* to administer, rather than the level of shock or noise actually experienced (see Dyck & Rule, 1978). These data can be depicted as:

1. High aversive stimulation received—intended—retaliation.
   High aversive stimulation received—not intended (low was intended)
   —no retaliation.
2. Low aversive stimulation received—intended—no retaliation.
   Low aversive stimulation received—not intended (high was intended)
   —retaliation.

A second literature more pertinent to the classroom contains an individual difference or correlation component as well as some experimental manipulations. Here, attention of researchers has been on the belief of aggressive children that others provoke them "on purpose," which justifies retaliation (see also chap. 5). Indeed, even among nonaggressive individuals, persons believing another acted with malicious intent feel justified in endorsing aggressive retaliation. Hence, if some persons generally perceive that others act with such intent, then they are likely to be aggressive.

In one of the original studies guided by this line of research, Dodge (1980) identified aggressive and nonaggressive boys based on teacher and peer ratings. The children, who were tested individually, were given a puzzle-assembly task to complete with the possibility of winning a prize. During the middle of the task, they were interrupted and taken into an adjoining room where they could view a puzzle supposedly being worked on by another child. At that time, they "overheard" a bogus intercom system conveying this other child was examining their partially completed puzzle. The child was then heard destroying the puzzle. Two experimental conditions conveyed that the damage was done either purposely or accidentally. In a third condition, the cause of damage was ambiguous and could be interpreted as purposeful or accidental. After receiving this information, the subject was left alone in the room to observe if he would retaliate by damaging the other child's puzzle.

In the overheard hostile intent condition, aggressive and nonaggressive children responded with retaliatory aggression. Conversely, in the listened-to accidental damage condition both groups acted with restraint. But in the ambiguous condition where the cause was uncertain, aggressive children inferred greater intent and behaved more aggressively than nonaggressive children. Similar findings have been reported by Graham, Hudley, and Williams (1992) and others (see review in Crick & Dodge, 1994).

In sum, laboratory research using a retaliatory shock paradigm and individual difference research examining the tendency to attribute hostile intent to others are consistent in documenting intent–retaliation linkages. Aggression, therefore, seems amenable to the analysis that has been proposed. But in the examination of achievement evaluation, reactions to the stigmatized, help giving, and transgression compliance, reported relations were between perceived control and some dependent variable. The concept of intentionality was not mentioned. Thus, an essential question is: Can aggression be included within the same framework as these other phenomena given this disparity? Is there a connection or similarity between attributions of control and perceptions of intent? How might these two concepts be incorporated within the same conceptual framework?

Are Causal Control and Intentionality Equivalent?

There are many reasons to contend that controllability and intentionality are distinct concepts. Among their differences is that controllability, in this context, refers to a causal property. For example, effort is considered a controllable cause of failure, not exercising is a controllable cause of heart problems, and the like. On the other hand, intention refers to the motives or goals of a person and the reason for an action—one did or did not intend to (desire to, want to) harm another. Malle and Knobe (1997) have shown that intention includes beliefs as well as desires, and the conditions for acting intentionally include awareness of purpose. This is distinct from the concept of causal controllability, for causes need not involve goals and beliefs about the likelihood of goal attainment (see Malle, Knobe, O'Laughlin, Pearce, & Nelson, 2000). In addition, one may not intend to fail, but nonetheless the cause of failure is controllable (e.g., lack of effort). Thus, control is not equivalent to intent, which creates a barrier to bringing aggression within the scaffold developed thus far. However, further inspection of the concepts of control and intent or intention reveals a property they do share—both are antecedents to or components of a more encompassing inference, that of personal responsibility (the label used in Box 1.3 and Box 1.5).

INCLUDING RESPONSIBILITY AND DIFFERENTIATING IT FROM CONTROL AND INTENT

The essence of responsibility is moral accountability, whether through an act of omission or commission. A person must "answer" to others regarding an outcome, particularly when that outcome is aversive (from the Latin *repondere*, to answer). Because one must address others, issues of responsibility arise in social contexts.

Responsibility for an outcome implies one has caused that outcome. In addition, inferences of responsibility require that the causal agent have freedom of choice, or free will (see Fincham & Jaspers, 1980; Shaver, 1985; Weiner, 1995). Hence, a person failing because of lack of effort is deemed personally responsible inasmuch as one can choose to expend or not expend effort, which is controllable by that individual. Conversely, this is not the case when failure is due to lack of aptitude. Lack of aptitude as a cause of failure, therefore, does not result in a judgment of personal responsibility.

Similar to control, intention also is a crucial antecedent or determinant of perceptions of responsibility. It has been firmly established that one is held more responsible for an intentional rather than an accidental occurrence. The greater punishment meted out for intended death (murder) than for unintended killing (manslaughter) captures this distinction (see Malle & Knobe, 1997). An intentional more than an accidental occurrence reveals a "guilty mind."

In sum, although controllability and intention or intentionality are distinct, they share a role as determinants of responsibility judgments. The perception of both control and intent typically augments inferences of responsibility, just as lack of control and the absence of intent decrease judgments of responsibility. In addition, controllability and intentionality can be distinguished from responsibility in another manner. This is observed in the many instances in which causal controllability and/or intentionality is not accompanied by a judgment of responsibility and reprimand. For example, one is not reprimanded for failure to put forth school-related effort if there was a need to take care of a sick parent.

This justification (the act serves a higher moral goal) is a mitigating circumstance freeing the person from responsibility, even though not expending effort is controllable (see Weiner, 1995). Similarly, an individual who cannot distinguish right from wrong by virtue of age, mental state, different cultural norms, and so on is not held responsible for an intended aggressive transgression (see Morse, 1978, 1985). When a child kills another "on purpose," the child is not tried for murder. Hence, as already stated, both control and intent are distinguishable from responsibility, although they contribute to this more encompassing judgment. Full responsibility inferences require internal and controllable causality, intention, and the absence of mitigating circumstances.

A PRELIMINARY THEORY OF SOCIAL CONDUCT

The foregoing discussion provides the background for a preliminary attempt at the construction of a general theory of social motivation and justice. This theory is shown in Fig. 1.3, which incorporates the disparate social phenomena of achievement evaluation, reactions to the stigmatized, help giving, compliance, and aggression.

Returning to the achievement domain, which serves as my prototype, examination of the top row of that figure shows an achievement-related failure caused by lack of effort. Lack of effort is a controllable cause and therefore, in the absence of mitigating circumstances, the actor is held responsible for the transgression of failure. A judgment of responsibility, in turn, produces antisocial behavioral reactions including reprimand, condemnation, neglect, and/or retaliation. This same analysis holds for reactions to the aggressive action of another when that act was intended because, as already indicated, intent also is an antecedent of personal responsibility.

On the other hand, going down to the bottom half of Fig. 1.3, it is reasoned that achievement failure due to lack of ability is not controllable and therefore the actor is not responsible for this outcome. Nonresponsibility results in prosocial actions such as withholding of reprimand, no condemnation, help giving, and an absence of aggressive retaliation. This analysis also is applicable to aggressive actions by another when those acts were not intended (e.g., accidental).

This theory, therefore, can be described as having a temporal sequence that progresses from thinking to doing, where causal thoughts generate inferences about the responsibility of a person, which then determines action. It also may be described as a rational theory, with behavior directly linked to moral beliefs. Hence, the theory addresses how we psychologically represent sin versus sickness and the motivation process to which these construals are linked. But the theory has a significant void.

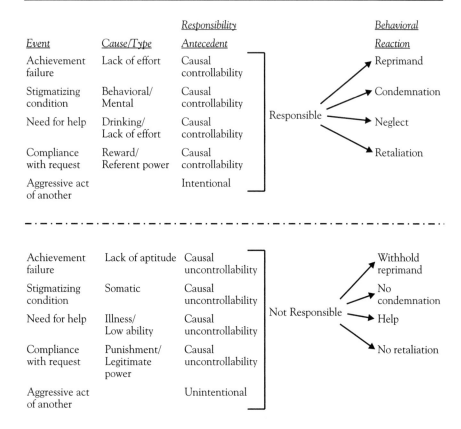

FIG. 1.3. Preliminary theory of motivation differentiating paths according to the responsibility of the actor.

THE ROLE OF EMOTION

In Fig. 1.3 a number of key cognitions that influence social behavior are identified. Yet it is a "cold" theory inasmuch as feelings or emotions play no part in motivated behavior. But motivation surely is determined by affects. A fault with many current approaches to motivation, exemplified in self-efficacy theory, goal theory, intrinsic motivation theory, and many other conceptualizations, is they are devoid (or nearly devoid) of affects. Virtually all of the "grand" theories at the very least postulated that behavior could be traced to the pleasure–pain principle: We desire to maximize good feelings and minimize bad ones, with actions guided by a cost–benefit analysis and hedonic desires.

Responsibility and Anger

More specific or discrete emotions than pleasure and pain influence the motivation process as well. To understand this process, first consider what thoughts might promote some specific emotions. Imagine, for example, your feelings when your child is doing poorly in school because of a refusal to do homework, or when an athlete on your favorite team is loafing. The readers are asked to turn to Box 1.6 and report when the specific emotions of anger and sympathy are experienced.

An examination of the responses in Box 1.6 are expected to reveal that inferences of controllability, intentionality, and personal responsibility in situations of transgression evoke anger. You are mad at the rebellious child and lackadaisical athlete. Anger is an accusation or value judgment following from the belief that another "could and should have done otherwise" (see Averill, 1982, 1983; Frijda, 1986; Reisenzein & Hoffman, 1990; Roseman, 1991; Weiner, 1995). In the mental health field, there is a huge literature documenting "expressed emotions," or EE (see chap. 5), which captures the anger that relatives of mentally

---

BOX 1.6   Emotional Reactions

1. Think of a time when you felt angry at another person. Tell about that situation and what caused it.

2. Think of a time when you felt sympathy for another person. Tell about that situation and what caused it.

ill persons (e.g., with schizophrenia and depression) experience toward these individuals because of the belief that their illness and behavior is under personal control (see, for example, Lopez, Nelson, Snyder, & Mintz, 1999; Weisman & Lopez, 1996).

There is an abundance of additional research supporting the position that anger follows judgments of responsibility. Averill (1983), for example, asked persons to report recent events that made them angry. In his research, more than 50% of the incidents were considered "voluntary," that is, the harm doer was fully aware of the consequences of the action and the act was perceived by the victim as unjustified. The next largest category of situations producing anger (30%) was associated with avoidable harm not necessarily intended but perceived as subject to volitional control, such as injury resulting from another's negligence or carelessness. Hence, nearly 80% of the contexts eliciting anger involved ascriptions regarding controllable actions for which the other person would be held responsible. Anger therefore may be regarded as a moral emotion (see Tangney & Fischer, 1995 and chap. 3).

In spite of the certainty regarding the linkage between responsibility for a negative plight and elicitation of anger, difficult questions remain that are beyond the scope of this book. For example, when one kicks the car for failing to start, is this evidence of anger in the absence of controllable causality and inferences of responsibility? Perhaps—but then again, the emotion may be frustration or unhappiness rather than anger. Or this might be a "pretend" response that accompanies the metaphoric assignment of human qualities to machines. And can one who is intentionally harmed by another not experience anger? I think the answer to this is "yes"; one can "turn the other cheek." The intentional harm–anger relation describes ordinary people in ordinary situations and does not account for the behavior of saints or other extraordinary individuals exhibiting extraordinary acts.

In sum, if another is regarded as the cause of a negative state that impacts on the self, then an overwhelming number of individuals react with anger. That one can be "talked into" or "out of" anger reveals its close connection to thoughts, or appraisals, about the causes of an event. And it follows logically that if the harmed person communicates anger, the information conveyed in this message is that the other is responsible for the untoward event (as is further discussed in chaps. 3 and 4).

The Absence of Responsibility and Sympathy

In contrast to the linkage between responsibility and anger, an absence of responsibility given the personal plight of another is associated with sympathy and related emotions of pity and compassion, as should also be revealed in Box l.6. A person confined to a totalitarian state (external causality), athletic failure because of a physical handicap (internal, uncontrollable causality), and school failure because of the need to care for a sick mother (a mitigating circumstance) are predicaments eliciting sympathy inasmuch as the person is not held responsible for his or her plight.

In one investigation documenting this linkage (Weiner, Graham, & Chandler, 1982), college students recalled instances in their lives when pity or sympathy was experienced. The most frequently reported situations were observing others with handicaps and personal interactions with the very aged. More broadly conceived, Wispé (1991) summarized, "One will sympathize more with a brave sufferer, in a good cause, in which one's afflictions are beyond one's control" (p. 134). Sympathy, then, follows when another is not responsible for a negative state or event. Similar to anger, it also logically follows that one can be "talked into" or "out of" a sympathetic reaction (e.g., "Don't feel sorry for him. It was his fault."). In addition, if another communicates sympathy, this indicates that the recipient of this message is not perceived responsible for his or her current state (again, see chaps. 3 and 4).

Emotions and Action

In addition to being elicited by thoughts about responsibility or nonresponsibility, anger and sympathy are stimuli for subsequent action (see Averill, 1983; Frijda, 1986), thereby having motivational significance. That is, emotions provide bridges between thinking and conduct. Anger often directs the typical experiencer of this emotion to "eliminate" the wrongdoer, to go toward that person and retaliate with aggressive action, or go away from that person and withhold some positive good. Anger typically is a "goad" or a stimulus that "pushes" the person to undertake self-protective and/or retaliatory actions that even the scales of justice. Hence, anger has functional and evolutionary significance.

Sympathy, on the other hand, directs the person to increase prosocial behaviors such as help giving and decrease antisocial conduct including punishment (Eisenberg, 1986). Sympathy also is a motivator, but unlike anger, the motivation is to undertake prosocial rather than antisocial acts. Sympathy is a critical social force, and compassion is an essential step toward social justice.

Many other emotions are linked backward to causal thinking and forward to behavior, as is documented in chapter 3. But it is anger and sympathy, the key moral emotions, which provide the bridges needed to expand the "cold" conceptual structure in Fig. 1.3.

A MORE COMPLETE THEORY OF SOCIAL BEHAVIOR

When emotional reactions to responsibility appraisals as well as behavioral reactions to emotions are included within the motivation sequence, the conceptual system for social motivation and justice may be represented as follows:

1. Event → Cause → Causal Property → Responsibility → Affect → Response
(Achievement (Lack of (Controllable) (Responsible) (Anger) (Punish)
Failure) Effort)

That is, a person has failed an achievement-related task. Guided by a variety of evidence not considered here, others ascribe the failure to lack of effort. Effort is a controllable cause and, in the absence of mitigating factors, the person is held responsible for the failure. Responsibility for a negative, self-related outcome arouses anger. Anger, in turn, provokes a retaliatory reaction. This sequence contrasts with the following exemplar:

2. Stigma → Cause → Causal Property → Responsibility→ Affect → Response
(Alzheimer's) (Genetics) (Uncontrollable) (Not Responsible) (Sympathy) (Help)

In this example a negative state, Alzheimer's disease, is considered caused by a genetic dysfunction. One's genetic heritage is not controllable by the self and one is not held responsible for being in this state. Lack of responsibility for a plight arouses sympathy, which elicits a prosocial reaction of help giving.

The full theory capturing these sequences is shown in Fig. 1.4. As depicted, the theory includes the fundamental assumption that the motivation process progresses from thinking to feeling to action or, more specifically, from causal understanding and perceptions of intent to inferences about personal responsibility, and then to the emotions of anger and sympathy, which generate social reactions involving reprimand, help, aggression, and so forth. As later elaborated, I regard this as the "deep structure" or "universal language" for motivated action.

Of course, other motivation orderings are conceivable. The one most likely to compete with a thinking–feeling–acting sequence specifies that thinking gives rise to feelings as well as actions, so thoughts and emotions have equal causal status (both are proximal) in guiding behavior. And one might posit that emotions precede thoughts. Empirical tests of these and other sequential theories are presented next in chapter 2 within the context of help giving and aggression.

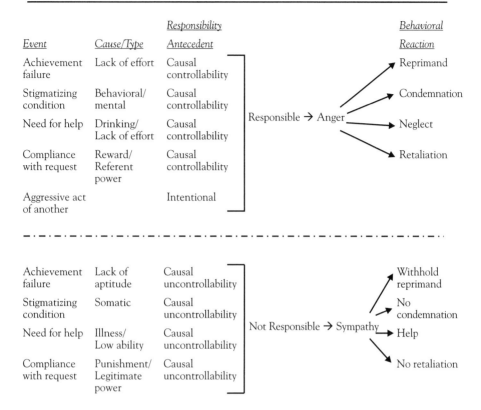

FIG. 1.4. Final theory of social motivation and social justice, including affects as bridges between thinking and behavior.

ADDITIONAL COMMENTS ABOUT RESPONSIBILITY AND EMOTIONS

It is evident that responsibility and emotions are core elements within this theory. I therefore end this chapter by elaborating two key issues related to their use: the relation of responsibility beliefs to the free will versus determinism debate, and conceiving emotions as "push" rather than "pull" determinants of behavior, which relates to the issue of immediate versus ultimate determinants of action.

Acceptance of Free Will and Determinism

Scientific psychology has always accepted determinism; this is a *sine qua non* if there is a desire to predict the future. But this stance is perhaps even truer today, with the growing influence of evolutionary theory and neuroscience in psychology. Given an evolutionary perspective, behavior is a product of a long history where current actions are undertaken because they have been successful in solving prior problems. Just as a rat "must" hunt for food during the night, and a moth "must" fly toward light, humans "must" engage in certain actions. In a similar manner, given certain patterns of neural activation, particular actions must follow. Determinism reigns supreme.

On the other hand, the attribution approach to social motivation and social justice assumes that humans are regarded as responsible for many of their actions, which are freely chosen and volitionally undertaken. This assumption provides the foundation for theology and the legal system. Is the deterministic position incompatible with an acceptance of free will, and is attribution theory remiss in leaving the deterministic camp? That is, can humans be held morally responsible for their actions when behavior is linked to deterministic laws?

My position is that attribution theory accepts determinism, yet perhaps paradoxically one of the incorporated determinants of action is the subjective belief that others have freedom of choice. That is, attribution theory bases predictions on thoughts ordinary persons have about free will. Free will is part of naïve psychology, and it is accepted that individuals can freely adhere to a chosen course of behavior. Perceived freedom produces judgments of responsibility, emotions such as anger and sympathy, and linked action. Stated somewhat differently, attribution theory embraces a deterministic system that includes the belief in free will among the antecedents of behavior. This might be considered a distant variant to what is known as the compatibilist approach to the free will–determinism issue (see Frankfurt, 1988).

Discrete Emotional Determinants Rather Than Ultimate Springs of Action Are Primary

A number of distinctions are embraced within this comparison. Many theories of motivation presume an "ultimate" spring of action. Three "final goals" are dominant. The oldest postulated principle is, "Organisms strive to maximize pleasure and minimize pain." Attaining positive and avoiding negative emotions is postulated to provide the common goal of all motivated action, which serves to fulfill hedonic goals. Behavior, therefore, is not driven by emotions, but rather by the anticipation of emotions. This is a hedonism of the future.

This approach at times is associated with the metaphor "The person is a machine." That is not because machines have or anticipate feelings, but rather because pleasure–pain is linked to homeostasis and the desire to return to a state of equilibrium (e.g., we eat when hungry, drink when thirsty, and the like, which produce good feelings and initiate a rest period). It also is the case that Expectancy × Value theorists have pleasure–pain as the root of all behavior, even though they typically do not include homeostasis among their governing concepts.

The second proposed ultimate determinant of behavior is understanding, or mastery of self and the environment. Perhaps this can be traced back to Buddhism and the search for self-enlightenment. Attribution theorists focusing on causal inferences and antecedents of causal decisions are associated with the metaphor that persons are scientists, seeking to understand themselves and the world in which they live (see Heider, 1958; Kelley, 1967). This belief is incorporated within the theory presented here. Understanding may be considered functional and in service of hedonic goals, but this need not be the case.

Finally, a third ultimate determinant of behavior, associated with evolutionary theory and sociobiology, is "individuals are motivated to preserve and enhance their self and/or their genetic pool." All organisms are believed to have this ultimate aim and all behavior is construed as instrumental to genetic enhancement.

Ultimate springs of action are neither provable nor disprovable. At best, instances in which these presumptions are upheld (or disconfirmed) can be collected so one can better infer whether the ultimate principle is reasonable to maintain. Theories declaring ultimate goals might outline proximal or immediate determinants of behavior as well. For example, while Drive theory traces behavior back to homeostasis and hedonism, it also postulates that the immediate determinants of behavior are drive and habit. This is, of course, a more testable proposition.

The attribution theory of social motivation contrasts with these approaches in a number of ways. First, the pleasure–pain principle is conspicuous by its absence. In its place are immediate determinants of action—specifically causal inferences, responsibility beliefs, and the emotions linked with these thoughts. Second, emotions are conceived as goads urging and pushing organisms to action. The anticipation of affective end states is not motivational, but rather currently aroused affect brings about action. This is a push rather than a pull conception of how emotions function to instigate behavior. Furthermore, the pushing is done by discrete emotions rather than by diffuse affective states labeled pleasure (happiness) or pain (unhappiness). The disparate emotions are elicited by distinct thoughts, or what are known as cognitive appraisals.

In sum, the theory proposed here has proximal, discrete emotional determinants that provoke persons to action. This contrasts with the ultimate, diffuse emotional determinants that pull individuals toward a goal in the most prevalent pleasure–pain formulations of motivation. Attribution theory does include an ultimate goal—mastery of the environment—but it plays a secondary role.

Are there any advantages to the present formulation as opposed to the contrasting grouping? Perhaps, in that a fuller range of human emotions, as well as complex thinking-to-feelings links, can be incorporated into the motivation process. Furthermore, the principles of behavior are subject to empirical confirmation or nonconfirmation and are less encumbered by untestable ultimate assumptions.

On the other hand, there also are serious shortcomings of the attribution approach (a statement I examine again later in the book). Attributions as defined here require that an action has occurred; that is, the theory starts with an already completed deed or state, such as a person failing or asking for help. There is no mechanism to account for why an individual seeks another to harm or initiates activities to find others in need of help. The theory is, for the most part, reactive rather than proactive, with most proactive actions unaccountable because there are no pertinent ultimate motivation goals or principles often incorporated into "reasons." In addition, this approach, guided by the judge metaphor, assumes a thinking person using information and directed by higher order moral rules. Whether this is a valid view of human behavior is certainly subject to argument.

SUMMARY

What conclusions can be reached about the determinants of social motivation and social justice, given an attribution perspective?

1. The causes of events are crucial determinants of action.

2. Causes can be classified into three fundamental properties or characteristics: locus, controllability, and stability. The first two particularly are linked to moral beliefs.

3. This causal assessment, along with other information concerning mitigating circumstances and inferences of intent, gives rise to responsibility inferences about the person. The perception of free will is incorporated into the conception.

4. Cognitive appraisals of personal responsibility are linked with anger and sympathy.

5. Affects are the proximal determinants of action, promoting pro- and antisocial reactions. These affects push rather than pull the organism. Causal thinking (beliefs about responsibility) and linked feelings (anger and sympathy) are significant determinants of achievement evaluation,

reactions to the stigmatized, help-giving, responses to power-induced compliance, and aggression. Hence, inferences of responsibility provide a broad framework for the understanding of social motivation and justice. However, behaviors are influenced as well by factors unrelated to the attribution process.

6. The metaphors of the person as a judge and life as a courtroom provide the background for this analysis. These metaphors produce vivid images that further understanding of social behavior and link this theory to law and theology. That is, what is fair, just, and deserved is the lens through which social life is perceived and enacted from this attribution scaffold. Moral beliefs are the foundation and conceptual glue for a general theory of social motivation and justice in that behaviors undertaken in many contexts are based on beliefs regarding sickness versus sin, or good versus evil.

2

Testing the Theory and Incorporating Cultural and Individual Differences

In chapter 1, the logical development of an interpersonal theory of social motivation and social justice was presented. The proposed theory has a number of essential components, especially causal beliefs and their underlying properties. In addition, temporal associations are specified between causal understanding and responsibility judgments, responsibility inferences and emotions, and emotions and behavior. Finally, proximal versus distal sequential associations are stipulated between thinking, feeling, and acting. But evidence regarding the complete motivation sequence was not presented. That is the first task of this chapter. A number of questions related to the motivation sequence also were raised in chapter 1, with one of central concern in this chapter: Do causal beliefs have a direct link to action, or are they distal, with emotions proximally related to behavior? That is, what is the order of a motivation episode? In addition, recall that to validate a general conception of motivation, it was contended that the formulated theory must be applicable to numerous fields of motivation. Thus, not only are attribution theory and the sequential issue put to empirical test here, but verification is across two domains of motivation—help giving and aggression.

A second issue examined in this chapter, which was ignored in chapter 1, concerns how cultural and individual differences can be incorporated within the conception. As presented thus far, it appears that the proposed theoretical relations are universal, invariant across cultures and persons. Is this the case?

44

And does this imply that the conception cannot deal with or handle such differences when they occur?

Finally, some general characteristics of the theory are examined, featuring a contrast between a mediation- versus moderator-based conception. Other characteristics are considered as well to compare this theory with other conceptions of motivation and to highlight its essential qualities.

THE MOTIVATION SEQUENCE

At a macro level, the theory developed in chapter 1 suggests that the motivation sequence progresses from thinking to feeling to acting. That is, emotions provide the bridge between cognition and behavior, being determined by thoughts and giving rise to action. Also, as already indicated, many other motivated sequences can be postulated. For example, perhaps emotions give rise to thoughts ("I am angry; that person must be responsible for the need") and thinking produces action ("It is his fault; I will not help"). Or perhaps thinking generates both emotions and behavior, so that affects are epiphenomena regarding their relation to behavior. That is, emotions are concurrent with action, rather than producing it. And these are just a few conceivable permutations, particularly if bidirectional associations are accepted; that is, the linkages go right-to-left as well as left-to-right (which is documented in chap. 4).

Some of the numerous possible motivation sequences are shown in Fig. 2.1 in the context of help giving. In Fig. 2.1, Model 1 has been championed thus far; Model 2 includes thoughts as proximal determinants of action; Model 3 shows that the two affects are interconnected; Model 4 has affective interrelations as well as a direct path from thinking to action; and Model 5 includes a direct relation between the situation and behavior circumventing the attribution process. Once again, these are only a few of the possibilities that can be suggested.

Current statistical advances permit one to choose between these various alternatives by use of path analytic techniques. Using this methodology, within a complex theory consisting of many constructs and associations, relations between variables can be portrayed holding all other associations constant. Hence, for example, if emotions are the most proximal or nearest determinant of action, then even if there is an association between a causal belief and behavior, taking emotion from this relation statistically could reduce it markedly, perhaps to zero. Imagine one is judging another who failed because of lack of effort while having ingested a chemical that takes away all feelings. Would the lazy person still be negatively evaluated, or does an unfavorable evaluation require the arousal of anger? If an association between the outcome and the negative evaluation remains in the absence of anger, then thoughts directly relate to behavior. On the other hand, if the relation is reduced to zero given the affect-inhibiting drug, then it would be revealed that affect, not thought, directly elicits the negative reaction.

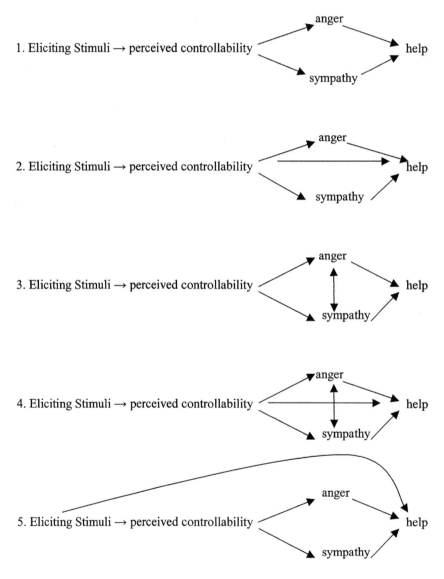

FIG. 2.1.   Some possible motivational sequences (paths) between stimulus onset and a final behavioral response (in this case, helping).

META-ANALYSES OF HELP GIVING
AND AGGRESSION

To conduct the types of analyses that permit an answer to the sequence issue, a large sample must be tested. One efficient way to accumulate data is to conduct meta-analyses. In this methodology, findings from all known pertinent studies are collected, data are combined, and the hypotheses and/or larger theoretical structures proposed are examined to see if they can account for ("fit") the data. This methodology minimizes problems created by using only data gathered by the involved theorist, who may have inadvertently biased his or her findings. In addition, the collected investigations differ in many ways, so it is unlikely any positive overall results are due to a particular methodological quirk or restricted to a particular population. Furthermore, some crucial moderator variables might be identified that influence the magnitude of the observed relations. Along with other colleagues (Rudolph, Roesch, Greitemeyer, & Weiner, 2004), I have undertaken such analyses.

Two meta-analyses, one for helping and one for aggression, and an exploratory comparison of the results of these separate analyses follows. In contrast to the most common use of meta-analysis, which focuses on determining the magnitude of association between two variables, my main interest here is detecting causal relations between motivational variables and examining the motivation sequence proposed by attribution theory. A comprehensive account of methods for exploring causal mediating processes is given in Cook et al. (1992) and Shadish (1996).

When considering the present theoretical account from a methodological point of view, causal beliefs and emotions have the status of *mediators*, or intermediate constructs; that is, they are "the generative mechanisms through which the focal independent variable is able to influence the dependent variable of interest" (Baron & Kenny, 1986, p. 1173). In this context, the outcome (e.g., failure), event (e.g., transgression), or state (e.g., stigma) is an independent variable, whereas subsequent perceptions of controllability, inferences of responsibility, and emotions of anger and sympathy are mediators that influence behavioral outcomes (e.g., helping and aggression).

As Shadish (1996) pointed out, mediators are often confused with *moderators*, which represent "a qualitative (e.g., sex, race, class) or quantitative variable (e.g., level of reward) that affects the direction and/or strength of the relations between an independent or predictor variable and a dependent or criterion variable" (Baron & Kenny, 1986, p. 1174). In addition to analyzing the proposed causal thought–emotion–behavior sequence using meta-analytic procedures, we also examined several potential moderators. Because attribution theories of motivation occasionally are criticized for restricting themselves to data from thought experiments instead of "real" data (for example, see Enzle & Shopflocher, 1978), we were particularly interested in including type of investigation as a potential moderator. For generalizability, it is crucial that the pattern of results not be limited to a special paradigm, for example, to simulation data obtained by thought experiments. This is true because thought experiments perhaps elicit controlled processes, where logical reasoning is fostered. On the other hand, perhaps motivated behavior is guided by immediate or automatic processes not as rational as the sequence captured in the theory and fostered by thought or simulation experiments (see Lerner, 2003). Inasmuch as several studies incorporated in the meta-analyses provide data about behavior in "real" contexts, it proved possible to test whether there are differences between simulation data on one hand and real event data on the other.

For both of the following meta-analyses regarding helping and aggression, the same procedure and type of analysis was conducted. I present the methodology only as applied to helping, except when specific details regarding the aggression analysis are needed.

Criteria for Inclusion

There were three criteria for inclusion in the reported meta-analyses: (a) the study required an attribution variable (i.e., controllability, responsibility); (b) the study required at least one emotion and/or behavioral variable, with anger and sympathy as possible emotions and some help- or aggression-related variable as a possible behavior; and (c) first-order or raw correlations between at least two of these variables were available. When other kinds of statistics were reported, the principal author of the study was contacted to obtain the first-order correlations.

Literature Search

Our search for relevant studies included three steps. First, a comprehensive set of keywords and combinations of keywords was developed to conduct a computer scan of the PsycLit database. For both help giving and aggression, three groups of pertinent variables exist, namely, cognitive, emotional, and behavioral. For help giving, the respective keywords included responsibility and controllability for the cognitive variables, anger and sympathy for the emotion measures, and help, help giving, and social support for the behavior variables. Thus, studies where helping is a duty and is independent of the characteristics of the person in need, or responsibility is associated with one's role rather than with causal beliefs, were not included because they did not fall within the range of this theory. For the aggression domain, the key words aggression, retaliation, and violence were used for the behavior measures; for the cognitive and emotion variables, the same keywords were used as for help giving. All possible combinations between at least two groups of variables were searched (e.g., by combining "controllability" and "help," or "responsibility" and "retaliation").

A second step toward locating appropriate studies was to examine citations provided within the reports and reviews identified by the PsycLit search. About 1,800 papers were identified with this method. The abstracts were searched manually to extract relevant studies. By this method, the number of potential investigations was substantially reduced. Less than 20 % of these publications were empirical contributions; the others were theoretical pieces containing no original data. Finally, all principal authors of papers and studies identified by these first two steps were contacted and asked for pertinent unpublished or submitted manuscripts.

As a result of this search process, 39 studies were retrieved that met the aforementioned criteria for help giving and 25 studies were obtained for aggression. The total number of participants involved in investigations of help giving was 7,945, with an average of 204 participants per study. In regard to aggression, the number of participants was 4,598, with an average of 184 participants per study. Thus, the data of more than 12,000 respondents were included in the analyses.

Study Categorization

In the helping and aggression meta-analyses, five descriptive variables were coded and used in a moderator analysis: (a) type of culture, contrasting independent cultures (e.g., the United States, Germany) with interdependent cultures (e.g., Japan, Nigeria); (b) type of investigation (simulation, recounting, participation in a real event); (c) type of sample (children, community, students); (d) year the study was conducted (based on a median split); and (e) publication status (published, unpublished). The detailed classifications for these moderator variables are presented in Tables 2.1 and 2.2, along with the raw correlations for each individual study. For the helping meta-analysis, one additional moderator was proposed: group in need of help (stigmatized, nonstigmatized).

Two path models were focused on and compared when examining relations specified by the theory as predicting Help Giving and Aggression (see Fig. 2.2). In Model 1, direct paths from Controllability/Responsibility (hereafter referred to as Control) to Sympathy and Anger were specified (the key variables are now given in capital letters). In addition, direct paths from Sympathy and

TABLE 2.1

Overview of the Helping Studies Included in the Meta-Analysis

No.	Authors	Study	Status	N	Subjects	Eliciting Stimulus	Measure of Help Giving	C—S	C—A	C—H	S—H	A—H	S—A
1	Meyer & Mulherin (1980)	1	1	80	Canadian students	8 causes for being in need for money	Self-reported intention	-.37	.64	-.14	.37	-.65	.37
2	Weiner (1980a)	3	1	28	U.S. students	Drunk vs. ill person in subway	Self-reported intention	-.77	.55	-.37	.46	-.71	-.17
3	Weiner (1980b)	2	1	116	U.S. students	Needing class notes	Self-reported intention	-.54	.36	-.41	.59	-.49	
4	Reisenzein (1986)	1	1	138	U.S. students	Class notes, Subway	Self-reported intention	-.49	.51	-.44	.45	-.43	-.71
5	Schmidt & Weiner (1988)	1	1	496	U.S. students	Needing class notes	Self-reported intention	-.64	.35	-.29	.47	-.58	
6	Weiner, Perry, & Magnusson (1988)	1	1	59	U.S. students	10 different stigmas (kinds of illness)	Self-reported intention	-.55		-.39	.63		
7	Weiner & Graham (1989)	1	1	370	U.S. citizens (5 to 95 years old)	Various situations with controllable vs uncontrollable reasons for needing help	Self-reported intention	-.56	.52	-.26	.38	-.35	
8	Betancourt (1990)	1	1	156	U.S. students	Problem in school	Self-reported intention	-.40		-.43	.45		
9	Betancourt (1990)	2	1	61	U.S. students	Problem in school	Self-reported intention	-.33		-.15	.39		
10	Sharrock, Day, Qazi, & Brewin, (1990)	1	1	34	U.S. medical staff	Helping behavior toward patients	Self-reported intention	-.31	-.23	.29			

11	Graham & Weiner (1991)	1	1	370	U.S. community sample	Waiting in line situation	Self-reported intention	-.56	.52	-.26	.38	-.40	
12	Karasawa (1991)	1	1	180	U.S. students	Falling behind in school	Self-reported intention	-.51	.33		.32	-.34	
13	Kojima (1992)	1	1	112	Japanese students	Lending class notes	Self-reported intention	-.71	.61	-.47	.51	-.61	-.70
14	Matsui & Matsuda (1992)	1	2	100	Japanese students	Lending class notes	Self-reported intention	-.51	.61	-.52	.53	-.52	-.36
15	Matsui & Matsuda (1992)	2	2	80	Japanese students	Lending class notes	Self-reported intention	-.42	.57	-.38	.54	-.65	
16	Zucker & Weiner (1993)	1a	1	122	U.S. students	Personal financial help in case of poverty	Self-reported intention	-.31	.44	-.28	.60	-.45	-.44
17	Zucker & Weiner (1993)	1b	1	122	U.S. students	Welfare decision in case of poverty	Self-reported intention			-.39	.43	-.34	
18	Zucker & Weiner (1993)	2a	1	47	U.S. students	Personal financial help in case of poverty	Self-reported intention	-.53	.17	-.61	.77	-.19	-.26
19	Zucker & Weiner (1993)	2b	1	47	U.S. students	Welfare decision in case of poverty	Self-reported intention			-.56	.79	-.32	
20	Betancourt, Hardin, & Manzi (1995)	2	1	126	U.S. students	Needing help at school	Self-reported intention	-.20	.06		.40	-.09	
21	Menec & Perry (1995)	1	1	249	Canadian students	Various stigmas (kinds of illness)	Self-reported intention	-.46	.78	-.35	.34	-.31	-.22
22	Sunmola (1994)	1	1	414	Nigeria comm. sample	Offer help to government	Self-reported intention	-.29	.27	-.27	.31	-.35	-.27

(continued)

TABLE 2.1 (continued)

No.	Authors	Study	Status	N	Subjects	Eliciting Stimulus	Measure of Help Giving	C–S	C–A	C–H	S–H	A–H	S–A
23	Menec & Perry (1998)	1	1	133	Canadian students	Various stigmas (kinds of illness)	Self-reported intention	-.60	.62		.46	-.19	-.25
24	George (1997)	1	2	279	U.S. students	Academic problem of friend	Actual behavior	-.26	.45	-.16	.25	-.09	-.21
25	Menec & Perry (1998)	2	1	137	Canadian students	Various stigmas (kinds of illness)	Self-reported intention	-.31	.63		.51	-.13	-.18
26	Dagnan, Trower, & Smith (1998)	1	1	40	U.S. health care staff	Persons with learning disabilities	Self-reported intention	-.42	.52	-.25	.25	-.53	-.40
27	George, Harris, & Price (1998)	1	1	537	Community sample	Academic problem of friend	Actual behavior	-.29	.49	-.19	.32	-.05	-.22
28	Dijker & Koomen (2003)	1	2	143	Dutch students	Various stigmas (kinds of illness)	Self-reported intention	-.57	.63	-.58	.56	-.47	-.34
29	Steins & Weiner (1999)	1	1	281	U.S./German students	Infection with HIV	Self-reported intention	-.39	.21	-.20	.51	-.15	-.32
30	Watson & Higgins (1999)	2	2	217	Canadian students	Various stigmas (kinds of illness)	Self-reported intention	-.38	.59	-.20	.33	-.06	-.26
31	Yamauchi & Lee (1999)	1	1	171	Japanese students	Moral dilemmas	Self-reported intention	-.27	.40	-.11	.27	-.13	-.28
32	Zucker (1999)	1	1	161	U.S. community	Unwanted pregnancy	Self-reported intention	-.23	.20	-.05	.37	-.15	-.33

#	Study			N	Sample	Task	Outcome						
33	Rudolph & Greitemeyer (2001)	1	2	766	German students	Autobiographical recall of helping	Recalled behavior	−.15	.27	−.11	.35	−.04	−.03
34	Rudolph & Greitemeyer (2001)	2a	2	210	German community	Autobiographical recall of helping	Recalled behavior	−.32	.58	−.19	.35	−.20	−.26
35	Rudolph & Greitemeyer (2001)	2b	2	210	German community	Autobiographical recall of helping	Recalled behavior	−.36	.63	−.15	.34	.01	−.32
36	Greitemeyer & Rudolph (2003)	1	2	204	German students	Being in need of help in various social vs. achievement settings	Self-reported intention	−.32	.61	−.16	.40	−.22	
37	Greitemeyer & Rudolph (2003)	2a	2	150	German students	Strangers being in need of help in various social vs. achievement settings	Self-reported intention	−.29	.35	−.01	.39	−.12	−.12
38	Greitemeyer & Rudolph (2003)	2b	2	150	German students	Family members being in need of help in various social vs. achievement settings	Self-reported intention	−.48	.71	−.29	.47	−.35	−.42
39	Greitemeyer et al. (2003)	1	2	649	German students	Personal help following a car accident	Self-reported intention	−.42	.60	−.11	.54	−.02	−.30

Note. Study indicates which experiment in the publication is included. For (Publication) Status, 1 = published, 2 = unpublished or submitted. C = controllability/responsibility; S = sympathy; A = anger; H = helping/prosocial behavior. Reported here are 1st-order correlation coefficients. Data from Rudolph et al. (2004), p. 824.

TABLE 2.2

Overview of the Aggression Studies Included in the Present Analysis

No.	Author(s)	Study	Status	N	Subjects	Eliciting Stimulus	Measure of Help Giving	C–S	C–A	C–V	S–V	A–V	S–A
1	Zumkley (1981)	1	1	75	German students	Intention to retaliate	Self-reported intention		.34				
2	Johnson & Rule (1986)	1	1	100	U.S. students, males only	Reactions on an insult by a coworker	Self-reported intention					.27	
3	Vala, Monteiro, & Leyens (1988)	1	1	258	Portuguese students	Perception of violence	Self-reported intention			.48			
4	Betancourt & Blair (1992)	1	1	154	U.S. students	Perception of a stone-throwing competition	Self-reported intention	–.33	.27	.32	–.44	.47	–.35
5	Graham, Hudley, & Williams (1992)	1	1	88	U.S. children	Perception of ambiguous events by aggressive/unaggressive children	Self-reported intention		.51	.33		.41	
6	Graham & Hoehn (1995)	3	1	86	U.S. children	Perception of ambiguous events	Self-reported intention	–.44	.28	.27	–.51	.63	–.51
7	Higgins & Watson (1995)	1	2	56	U.S. students	Intention to retaliate	Self-reported intention		.51	.31		.39	
8	Ho & Venus (1995)	1	1	203	U.S. community sample	Reactions to a battered woman who killed her spouse	Recalled behavior			.48			
9	Stiensmeyer-Pelster (1995)	1	2	465	German students	Intention to retaliate by aggressive versus nonaggressive school children	Self-reported intention		.52	.62		.59	
10	Thompson, Medvene, & Freedman (1995)	1	1	130	65 U.S. couples	Cardiac patients and their wives/husbands	Recalled behavior					–.39	

#	Study			N	Sample	Dependent variable	Measure						
11	Feather (1996)	1	1	220	Austral. comm. sample	Reactions to penalties	Self-reported intention	-.33				.50	.46
12	Feather (1996)	2	1	181	Austral. comm. sample	Reactions to penalties	Self-reported intention	-.32				.74	.31
13	Allred, Mallozi, Matsui, & Raia (1997)	1	1	132	66 U.S. same-sex dyads	Negotiation performance in employer versus employee role	Self-reported intention	-.50	.50	-.03			
14	Byrne & Arias (1997)	1	1	132	66 U.S. couples	Marital satisfaction and marital violence	Recalled behavior			.45			
15	Graham, Weiner, & Zucker (1997)	1	1	177	African Am. & Whites	Reactions to O. J. Simpson	Self-reported intention	-.42	.12	.49	-.50	.15	-.30
16	Graham, Weiner, & Zucker (1997)	2	1	166	U.S. students	Reactions to O. J. Simpson	Self-reported intention	-.45	.57	.55	-.52	.47	-.21
17	Stiensmeyer-Pelster & Gerlach (1997)	1	1	219	German children	Intention to retaliate by aggressive versus nonaggressive children	Self-reported intention		.57	.39		.46	
18	Rodrigues & Lloyd (1998)	4	1	190	U.S. students	Compliance after a good versus negative achievement outcome	Self-reported intention		.48	.37			
19	Wingrove & Bond (1998)	1	1	23	English students	Angry reactions to failure on a cooperative game	Actual behavior		.50			.37	
20	Watson & Higgins (1999)	1	2	217	Canadian students	Four kinds of stigmas	Self-reported intention	-.15	.82	.45	.01	.46	-.04

(continued)

TABLE 2.2 (continued)

No.	Author(s)	Study	Status	N	Subjects	Eliciting Stimulus	Measure of Help Giving	C—S	C—A	C—V	S—V	A—V	S—A
21	Rudolph & Greitemeyer (2001)	1	2	56	Austrian students	Autobiographical recall of aggressive events	Recalled behavior	-.42	.39	.34	-.42	.58	-.43
22	Rudolph & Greitemeyer (2001)	2	2	766	German students	Autobiographical recall of aggressive events	Recalled behavior	-.06	.57	.43	-.07	.52	-.06
23	Greitemeyer & Rudolph (2003)	1	2	204	German students	Intention to retaliate in a social versus achievement situation	Self-reported intention	-.24	.72	.68	-.34	.76	-.22
24	Greitemeyer & Rudolph (2003)	2a	2	150	German students	Intention to retaliate concerning strangers	Self-reported intention	-.68	.77	.77	-.69	.85	-.73
25	Greitemeyer & Rudolph (2003)	2b	2	150	German students	Intention to retaliate concerning family members	Self-reported intention	-.56	.65	.57	-.47	.77	-.52

Note. Study indicates which experiment in the publication is included. For (Publication) Status, 1 = published, 2 = unpublished or submitted. C = controllability; responsibility; S = sympathy; A = anger; V = violence/aggression. Reported here are 1st-order correlation coefficients. Data from Rudolph et al. (2004), p. 828.

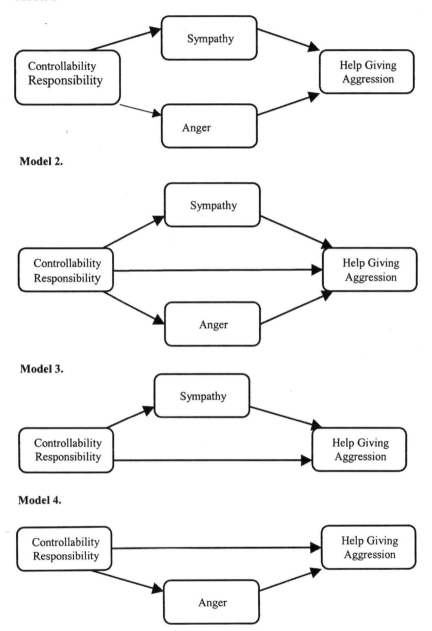

Model 1.

Controllability
Responsibility

Sympathy

Anger

Help Giving
Aggression

Model 2.

Controllability
Responsibility

Sympathy

Anger

Help Giving
Aggression

Model 3.

Controllability
Responsibility

Sympathy

Help Giving
Aggression

Model 4.

Controllability
Responsibility

Anger

Help Giving
Aggression

FIG. 2.2.   Four models tested regarding the determinants of helping and aggression
Adapted from Rudolph, Roesch, Greitemeyer, and Weiner (2004), p. 833.

Anger to Help Giving (or Aggression) were hypothesized. Model 1 has been championed in the book thus far. Model 2 is identical to Model 1 except this model includes a direct path from Control to Behavior. The necessity of this path was evaluated by comparing the fit of Model 1 to the data versus the fit of Model 2. A nonsignificant difference between the fits of the two suggests the models are equally valid. Hence, the more parsimonious model (Model 1, in this case, without the Control–Behavior path) would be the "best-fitting" model (see Bollen, 1989) because it has fewer specified relations between constructs. On the other hand, if a significant difference results, then the model with the better statistical fit would provide a more accurate representation of the data. I also included two other models, each with only one of the affects, as in a number of studies both emotions were not assessed. Data pertinent to these models are included here, but not discussed further. We also considered three additional nonpredicted models starting with emotions to test alternative explanations of the data (e.g., emotion–thought–behavior, or, more specifically, anger and sympathy–controllability and responsibility–help giving). Finally, after the initial path analyses, all models were examined at levels of the moderator variables described earlier.

Results for Helping

The means of the correlation coefficients between Control, Sympathy, Anger, and Help Giving, as calculated from the data provided in Table 2.1, as well as the Confidence Intervals (CI) for these correlations, are given in the top half of Table 2.3. The table shows that when a need is Controllable, then Sympathy decreases ($r = -.45$), Anger increases ($r = .52$), and Helping is reduced ($r = -.25$). Furthermore, Sympathy is positively related ($r = .42$), and Anger negatively related ($r = -.24$), to Help Giving. Hence, Helping is associated with less Control, more Sympathy, and less Anger. I refer to this configuration as the *Predicted Data Pattern* inasmuch as it completely conforms to theoretical predictions.

The fits of Models 1 and 2 and paths were evaluated next. The path coefficients or magnitudes of associations for these models are presented in the top half of Table 2.4. Both Model 1 and Model 2 fit the data very well. The Control–Sympathy path coefficient is negative ($\beta = -.45$) and the Control–Anger path is positive ($\beta = .52$) in the two relevant models. That is, more Control is associated with less Sympathy and more Anger. In addition, the Sympathy–Help Giving path is positive (average $\beta = .38$) and the Anger–Help Giving path is negative (average $\beta = -.08$) in the two relevant models. That is, more Sympathy and less Anger are associated with more Help Giving. Finally, the Control–Help Giving path, revealing that more Control resulted

TABLE 2.3

Overall Weighted Correlations Among Controllability, Sympathy, Anger, and Behavior
for Help Giving and Aggression

	Sympathy			Anger			Behavior		
	r	CI	N	r	CI	N	r	CI	N
Help Giving									
Controllability	−.45	−.43/−.46	7416	.52	.50/.54	7140	−.25	−.23/−.27	6840
Sympathy				−.39	−.37/−.42	5484	.42	.40/.44	7382
Anger							−.24	−.22/−.26	6800
Aggression									
Controllability	−.35	−.32/−.39	2509	.61	.59/.63	4448	.49	.47/.52	3719
Sympathy				−.31	−.28/−.35	1976	−.44	−.41/−.47	2377
Anger							.56	.54/.58	3458

Note. High scores on the variables reflect more controllability, sympathy, anger, and behavior (help giving, aggression). All correlations are significant at $p < .001$. CI = confidence interval. Data from Rudolph, Roesch, Greitemeyer, and Weiner (2004), p. 835.

TABLE 2.4

Path Coefficients for Help Giving and Aggression Models

	Model 1	Model 2	Model 3	Model 4
Help Giving Models				
Control-Sympathy	−.45*	−.45*	−.45*	—
Control-Anger	.52*	.52*	—	.52*
Control-Help Giving	—	−.05*	−.08*	−.15*
Sympathy-Help Giving	.39*	.37*	.39*	—
Anger-Help Giving	−.09*	−.07*	—	.17*
Aggression Models				
Control-Sympathy	−.35*	−.35*	−.35*	—
Control-Anger	.61*	.61*	—	.61*
Control-Aggression	—	.17*	.38*	.24*
Sympathy-Aggression	−.30*	−.27*	−.31*	—
Anger-Aggression	.48*	.38*	—	.42*

Note. — is not part of target model; * indicates $p < .05$. Data from Rudolph, Roesch, Greitemeyer, and Weiner (2004), p. 836.

in less Help, is negative in Model 2 ($ß = -.05$). That path coefficient is smaller in magnitude than Sympathy–Help Giving and Anger–Help Giving associations in both models.

A test was then conducted to determine whether dropping the Control–Help Giving path results in a decrement in overall model fit. To accomplish this, the fit of Model 1 was compared to the fit of Model 2. It was found that eliminating the Control–Help Giving path did not result in a significant decrement in model fit. That is, statistically taking away the relation between Control and Help Giving did not weaken the ability of the model to predict the data. Model 1 therefore is more parsimonious and hence "better." In sum, both models meet theoretical expectations, but because Model 1 is simpler or more parsimonious, requiring fewer paths than Model 2, that model is judged as the better of the two (see Rudolph et al., 2004, for more detail regarding these comparisons). As indicated previously, this choice reflects a basic criterion of theory evaluation: The fewer the number of associations postulated, the more acceptable the theory (with all else being equal).

The fits of three other nonpredicted models initiating with emotions also were examined. All provided a poor fit with the data; that is, a motivation sequence capturing these data does not place emotion before thought.

Moderator Analysis.   The two target models were then tested at each level of the moderator variables (i.e., type of culture, type of investigation, type of sample, year the study was conducted, publication status, and group in need of help). No differences were found. The path coefficients for these models are similar to those in the overall models previously presented. As indicated earlier, the moderator analysis for type of investigation is especially instructive. As can be seen from Table 2.5 (top half), no differences are obtained between the paths as a function of the type of investigation (simulation vs. recounting or participation in a real event). Additionally, for both simulation and real-event data, the direction and magnitudes of the coefficients are in accord with the theory of social conduct shown in Model 1. Therefore, the confirming results are not limited to simulation data or "thought experiments," but apply as well to the analysis of real events. Further examination of help giving follows the presentation of the findings related to aggression.

Results Related to Aggression

Correlations between Control, Sympathy, Anger, and Aggression are presented in the bottom half of Table 2.3. All correlations conformed to the Pre-

TABLE 2.5

Path Coefficients for Help Giving and Aggression (Model 1)
for Moderator Type Investigation

Help Giving	Simulated Level	Real Event Level
Control-Sympathy	−.47*	−.37*
Control-Anger	.54*	.45*
Control-Help Giving	−.07*	.01
Sympathy-Help Giving	.40*	.28*
Anger-Help Giving	−.04*	−.12*
Aggression		
Control-Sympathy	−.40*	−.28*
Control-Anger	.63*	.56*
Control-Aggression	.19*	.18*
Sympathy-Aggression	−.31*	−.13*
Anger-Aggression	.34*	.42*

Note. * $p < .05$. For help giving (Model 1), there were 25 studies including simulation data and six studies including real event data. For aggression (Model 1), there were 15 studies including simulation data and six studies including real event data. Data from Rudolph, Roesch, Greitemeyer, and Weiner (2004), p. 837.

dicted Data Pattern. That is, greater amounts of Aggression are associated with more Control ($r = .49$), less Sympathy ($r = −.44$), and more Anger ($r = .56$).

Using the correlations from the bottom half of Table 2.3, the fits of Models 1 and 2 and the paths of both models were tested. The path relations for these models are in the bottom half of Table 2.4. Model 1, with no path from Control to Aggression, fit well, as did Model 2 with this path. To test whether dropping the Control–Aggression path results in a decrement in overall model fit, Models 1 and 2 were compared. In contrast to the results for help giving, eliminating the Control–Aggression path produced a significant decrement in model fit. Model 2, with the additional path from thinking to behavior, therefore better fit the data.

As in the help giving meta-analysis, we also evaluated three other models previously specified as beginning with emotions that might explain the relations among Control, Sympathy, Anger, and Behavior (Aggression). None fit well.

In sum, the results reveal that the attributions of Control, as well as the emotions of Anger and Sympathy, are all proximate determinants of Aggression (see Model 2). In addition, Control is directly related to Anger and Sympathy and thus also indirectly associated with Aggression through these two emotion variables. That is, Control influences Aggression directly and indirectly.

Moderator Analysis. The two target models were tested at each level of the five moderator variables and again no differences were found. The path coefficients for these models are similar to those in the overall models previously presented. For the moderator-labeled type of investigation (simulation vs. recounting or participation in a real event), the path coefficients are presented in the bottom half of Table 2.5. The relation strengths other than for Sympathy–Aggression are very similar. Therefore, as was the case for the helping studies, the findings are not limited to imagined courses of action. Rather, strong support was found for the proposed attribution theory of social conduct using "real" behavior as a dependent variable.

Comparing the Helping and Aggression Models

It appears that both pro- and antisocial behavior can be explained with the same conceptual framework. Some philosophers also have made this contention. It has been reasoned that failure to help an injured other, and injuring another, leave both in the identical state (see Waldron, 2003). Hence, these actions should be subject to the same rules. To what extent do the data support this assertion and the related query that helping and aggression can be conceptualized in the same manner? The answer to this is: It depends. It depends on how molar versus molecular an analysis is considered, or if the focus is on the most general law as opposed to modified specific instances of the general law.

At the most molar level, it can be concluded that behavior is a function of cognition and affect. This provides one (among many) alternative to the equally broad statement associated with Lewin (1935) that behavior is a function of the person and the environment. A somewhat more precise formulation of this general law is: Thinking is a distal determinant of motivated or goal-seeking behavior, whereas emotion is proximal. This principle was partially supported—emotions are indeed proximal in accounting for both help giving and aggression. However, thoughts (i.e., perceptions of causal control and responsibility inferences) are distal determinants of help giving, whereas they proximally affect aggression. Another way of stating these findings is that aggression has more immediate attribution determinants than does help giving, with hostile responding a direct product of both the head and the heart, whereas helping directly involves only the heart. Guided by these findings, one would be most effective when attempting to collect charity funds by eliciting sympathy (from "bleeding hearts") and reducing anger, whereas aggression may be hindered by directly appealing to reason and/or emotion (see Lerner, Goldberg, & Tetlock, 1998). This intimates that it is easier to talk one out of aggression than out of prosocial reactions.

Why might this be the case? One can offer only speculations and, as stated again later, one must be very guarded in the certainty or generality of the claim that help giving and aggression are associated with disparate motivational sequences. It may be that most help giving or social support has relatively minor consequences for the self (with the occasional exception of extreme personal sacrifice). Driving a friend to the airport, lending $10, or carrying a package for someone does not greatly hinder personal well-being. On the other hand, even weak aggressive retaliation might come with great cost. After all, the target could strike back with severity, which may be likely inasmuch as a hostile action already was engaged in by that individual. Thus, having thoughts as proximal determinants in hostile contexts is functional in terms of personal survival.

Another issue of importance concerns the magnitudes of the relations exhibited in the two motivation domains. Given an attribution perspective, what is more predictable, help giving or aggression? That is, which area is "better suited" for an attribution explanation? To examine this issue (and taking some liberties with statistical requirements), the fits for the equally valid Models 1 and 2 from the help-giving meta-analysis were compared to the fit for Model 2 from the aggression meta-analysis. The findings revealed the indices for Model 2 in the aggression meta-analysis provided a better fit than Model 1 and Model 2 in the help-giving meta-analysis. This suggests that Model 2 better represents aggression than either Model 1 or Model 2 represents (accounts for) help giving.

It can be reasoned, therefore, that help giving has more determinants outside the attribution–emotion framework than does aggression. When another is approached for help, surely attribution questions are elicited, such as "Why does she need help?" In addition, however, a number of non-attribution-related uncertainties also come to mind, including "Is this person a relative of mine?" "Do I have the extra money to help?" "How great is the need?" That is, nonattribution factors appear to play a major role in help giving. On the other hand, when one is attacked, it is likely that subsequent behavior is strongly guided by attribution-related queries such as: "Why did he hit me?" "Was it on purpose?" That is, inferred harmful intent, along with the anger this generates, are likely to be salient or encompassing influences on aggressive retaliation, more so than the corresponding attributions and attribution-linked emotions associated with helping. Of course, any number of other speculative explanations can be proposed; why helping and aggression have somewhat different attribution interpretations obviously awaits more research and theoretical insight.

Finally, in spite of the extremely large number of research participants, the diversity of the investigations, and the intuitive logic of the arguments supporting the findings, I urge caution in reaching premature conclusions regarding these very complex issues. Closure has not been reached. Finding direct versus indirect causation may depend on numerous undetermined variables (indeed, I introduce one of these later in the chapter).

It was indicated previously that there are many determinants of helping and aggression falling beyond the range of attribution theory. These also may exert some of their effects through perceptions of controllability and/or the emotions of anger and sympathy. Of course, one must be modest about such claims, and it is not my contention that all (or even much of) help giving and aggression accounted for by these other variables can be linked to concepts advanced by attribution theory. Nonetheless, this possibility does provide food for thought. For example, considering help giving, it is known that genetic relatedness increases proneness to help. It may be that relatives are held less responsible for an untoward state or event than nonrelatives, which explains the greater help giving exhibited toward relatives in need (see Greitemeyer, Rudolph, & Weiner, 2003). Similarly, it has been documented that positive mood increases help-giving. Perhaps helping is facilitated by positive mood because perceptions of responsibility are biased in a favorable direction, so others are perceived as less responsible for their plights. Similarly, regarding aggression, there is abundant evidence that aggression is greatest in summer. Perhaps on hot days individuals overestimate the negative intents of others and/or are prone to experience anger, which accounts for the temperature–aggression relation. One could go about this reinterpretation game (i.e., looking for attribution-linked mediators) for much (but surely not all) of the helping and aggression literatures. However, as already indicated, this is suggested with caution and without the belief that these other variables will be rendered merely distal antecedents within an attribution–affect–action sequence.

A central issue remaining is whether the full theory advocated here and its sequential arrangement can be applied to and tested in other fields of motivated behavior. The most obvious place to search is the achievement domain, where attribution theory has played a major role in understanding reactions to the success and failure of others. Unfortunately, unlike the voluminous data addressing help giving and aggression, there is not an adequate empirical literature including all stages in the proposed motivation sequence to test this possibility. There are numerous studies capturing one or two linkages—for example, lack of effort is perceived as more controllable than lack of ability; lack of effort elicits more anger and less sympathy as a cause of failure than lack of ability; and lack of effort is evaluated more negatively when causing failure than is the absence of ability (see Weiner, 1985a, 1986, and chap. 1). Thus, although studies including attributions, affect, *and* evaluative reactions have not been conducted in situations of success and failure, it is not unreasonable to believe that research would produce the same pattern of relations shown in Tables 2.3 and 2.4 (with uncertainty regarding the need for a control–behavior path; see Van Overwalle, Mervielde, & De Schuyter, 1995).

CULTURAL DIFFERENCES

Few (if any) psychologists or educators formulate a theory and limit its applicability to particular cultures, ethnicities, or historical periods. Perhaps because of cognitive development, a theory might not be expected to apply to younger children (e.g., one would not think a theory of prejudice is pertinent to infants). And perhaps one might even specify that the theory holds for only one of the genders (e.g., early achievement theory implicitly excluded females, in part because the measurement of achievement needs did not appear to be valid for them). But for most theories with which I am familiar, demographic or sociocultural constraints are ignored, not specified, and/or not anticipated. Even in the recent past, when the motivation research subjects were white rats, there was little recognition of generality issues. Is this as it should be? Do theories of human motivation, and particularly the attribution theory with which I am associated, require basic modification to incorporate diverse ethnicities and cultures?

For example, suppose I advocate that motivation is determined in part by the expectancy of goal attainment. Hence, I predict one will not undertake activities for which the subjective expectancy of success or the likelihood of goal attainment is zero. I might think this principle irrelevant for very young infants, inasmuch as they may lack the cognitive abilities to formulate means–ends relations and expectations. But I would be unlikely to say my position holds only for White males, to the exclusion of African Americans, Asians, females, and others not included in the White male category. Similarly, if I believe learning is maximized by Socratic methods, then it is unlikely I would limit this position to a particular race or social class. Neither did Socrates, as he engaged in a Socratic dialogue with Meno's lower SES Greek slave. But perhaps life is more complex for attribution theorists, and I have failed to recognize the diversity in cultural, environmental, and personal histories when I blindly and blithely apply this conceptual system.

My position regarding whether this theory fits diverse cultures (and individuals) can be summarized as follows. The basic structure of the theory—

that is, the concepts and their sequential ordering—are so entrenched in my mind as to make them nearly inviolable. This conception hopefully captures universal "deep structures." On the other hand, culture, demographics, personal history, and the like determine the specific operational definitions of the concepts, such as what defines a positive or negative outcome. In addition, culture may influence what information is used to determine causality, which causes are salient, where a cause is placed in dimensional space, and so on. Hence, antecedents (determinants) of constructs may differ between cultures and individuals. Attribution theory embraces phenomenology, and constructs have a subjective definition and meaning. For example, in one culture success is defined as a good crop of yams; in another, it is attaining corporate leadership. Similarly, for one individual a B at an exam is defined as a success, whereas for another it is regarded as a failure. In some cultures and for some individuals, the search for causality starts with internal causes; for others, the search for understanding starts externally. In some instances, the cause of a positive event or outcome is thought to be a favor from God; for others, the main perceived cause of success is innate ability. In sum, attribution content is specific. However, the attribution process and the structure of the theory are general and transcend the specific instance.

In addition to affecting the antecedents or operationalizations of any particular construct, culture and personal history at times also act as moderators between the specified associations in the theory. For example, as already discussed, lack of effort is under personal control, so failure due to this factor results in anger followed by reprimand and punishment. But some cultures (e.g., Japan) regard achievement outcomes as more controllable than do other cultures (e.g., America), and more endorse effort as a determinant of success. Hence, Japanese teachers may stress effort and punish lack of trying to a greater degree than do American teachers. That is, individual idiosyncrasies and/or group beliefs are also recognized within the theory as functioning as moderators of particular relations. But the presence of moderators does not alter the structure of the general theory.

Ethnic Differences in Reactions to Obesity

To illustrate these points, consider the following cultural difference regarding reactions to obesity. Studies document that Mexicans react less negatively to obesity than Americans (Crandall & Martinez, 1996). That is, being overweight is stigmatized less and is less "sinful" for Mexicans than for Anglo Americans. Crandall (1995) even reports that some Americans with a conservative ideology withhold money for college to punish their daughters for being overweight. This cultural difference may be addressed by any number of conceptual systems. Here I consider how attribution theory approaches this cultural disparity, guided by the sequential logic of the theory.

For Americans, obesity is perceived as caused by overeating and/or exercising too little (see Table 1.2); it is a lifestyle illness. These are controllable causes in that one can choose to eat less and exercise more. That is, the causes as well as the outcome of obesity "could have been otherwise." Perceptions of controllability give rise to inferences that the overweight other (e.g., daughter) is personally responsible for her "failed" condition. This, in turn, evokes anger. Anger along with responsibility inferences (either directly or indirectly) result in an antisocial response such as some form of punishment (withholding college tuition). This analysis is captured in the top half of Fig. 1.4. (Other interpretations of lack of financial support certainly are possible, including those not involving moral reactions. For example, perhaps it is believed the obese will not succeed, so withholding funds is expectancy mediated rather than morality mediated. I ignore these and other possible data interpretations here).

But Mexicans do not react as negatively to obesity as do Americans. According to attribution theory, why might this be the case? More generally, how does attribution theory handle cultural diversity and differences in responses between ethnic groups? Here are some possible answers, again progressing sequentially through the proposed theory:

1. Mexicans do not regard obesity as a "failure." That is, thinness does not represent a goal for which they strive and/or the definition of obesity starts at a higher weight than it does for Americans. Therefore, among Mexicans, the attribution process is not activated by a "heavy" daughter and responsibility judgments, negative emotions and their linked behaviors do not follow.

2. Mexicans regard obesity a "failure," but the perceived causes are external and/or uncontrollable rather than internal and controllable. For example, the perceived cause may be poverty, lack of education regarding the adverse consequences of being overweight, lack of time to engage in exercise and other healthy activities, and on and on. Because the cause is considered external to the obese person, assignment of responsibility, anger, and reproach do not follow.

3. Despite the same perceived causes as Americans (eating too much and exercising too little), these are regarded by Mexicans as less controllable than they are by Americans, with the same consequences as indicated before.

4. Controllable causes among Mexicans are less likely to arouse anger and other negative emotions than among Americans. That is, even given the identical causal analysis, their emotional reactions are more muted.

5. Given anger, Mexicans are less likely than Americans to react with punitive responses that impede education. Perhaps their anger is more directly physical or verbal. That is, the direction or avenue through which anger is expressed differs between cultures. Or, perhaps given the identical degree of anger, subsequent aggression among Mexicans is generally less intense than among Americans.

Culture, then, not only alters the operational definitions of constructs in the theory, but also acts as a moderator between some linkages in the theory. To repeat, the overall conception does not vary across ethnic groups: There are outcomes, causal antecedents, selected causes, dimensional placement, further cognitive inferences regarding perceived responsibility, elicited affect, and behavioral responses among both ethnic groups. But nonetheless there is cultural and personal diversity that are captured within the theoretical framework as moderators of proposed relations.

I started this section by exclaiming few theorists limit applicability of their theories to a particular culture, or time, or place in history, or gender. I am among those who might be faulted for this shortsightedness. Skinner derided theorists for their tendency to force data into their prevailing theories even when the fit was unclear. I may have been one of his targets (assuming he was aware of attribution theory, which is probably an unreasonable assumption).

I believe attribution theory, that is, the theory as a set of interrelated constructs, does not need alteration to incorporate cultural differences. But one must be careful in the assumptions being made when contrasting ethnic groups, cultures, genders, and such. Success for one may be failure for another; causal information for one may go unnoticed for another; causes salient to one group may be in the far background for the other; and so on. The theorist must be alert for differences between cultures. However, one must be equally alert to convert phenotypic disparities into genotypic similarities and to discover the general laws of behavior. That is the theoretical goal guiding my thinking.

INDIVIDUAL DIFFERENCES

Just as there are differences in responses to an event, outcome, or state because of culture, there also are disparities in reactions between individuals within a culture. And just as differences elicited by obesity in American versus Mexican cultures are incorporated within the theory and explainable without conceptual modification, differences between individuals within a culture also can be included within the theory without theoretical alterations.

The first issue needing attention is what individual differences might act as moderators within the proposed sequence of event (outcome)–attribution–affect–action. Perhaps one starting point is to identify demographic variables recognized as affecting achievement evaluation, reactions to the stigmatized, help giving, compliance, and/or aggression, and then look for attributions, beliefs about responsibility, and/or emotions linked with the demographic categories. For example, there is a vast literature documenting that females (with a few exceptions) are more likely than males to help those in need (see, for example, Eagly & Crowley, 1986). Here, a demographic variable affects a behavior addressed by attribution theory. The theory suggests females make more uncontrollable attributions, regard the needy as less responsible for their plights, and/or react with more sympathy and less anger to those in need than males. These differences in mediating variables account for the behavioral (helping) disparities between the sexes. That is, gender acts as a moderator within the conception, altering the magnitudes of component variables and/or influencing the strengths of mediating associations within the theory. There is some literature supporting these anticipated gender differences (see George, Carroll, Kersnick, & Calderon, 1998; MacGeorge, 2003). Hence, organizing this section of the book around gender would be a fruitful endeavor. However, the reported findings are not extensive (see MacGeorge, 2003), so this moderator is not examined in detail to illustrate how individual differences are incorporated within the theory.

A second possibility is to search for an established trait and then determine if this trait might act as a moderator within the attribution framework. For example, it is accepted that individuals labeled high in authoritarianism, or having an authoritarian personality, strongly believe that the conventions of society should be upheld. Perhaps persons with this personality structure also hold others highly responsible given a transgression, react with heightened anger and little sympathy, and are predisposed to respond with aggression and withhold help in pertinent situations. Individual differences associated with authoritarianism, including racism and religiosity, might be amenable to a similar attribution analysis. However, for these individual differences, data that can be neatly imposed on the attribution constructs also are not readily available.

Another individual difference relevant to judgments of responsibility is derived from the just world hypothesis, which states that people have a need to believe their environment is a just, orderly place where good is rewarded and bad is punished (Lerner & Miller, 1978). A Just World Scale exists that measures individual differences in the tendency to blame victims. This could be a reasonable starting point in the search for individual differences to include as moderators within the theory. But I also elected not to focus on just world concepts, in part because of the inconsistency in the reported data (see, for example, Zucker & Weiner, 1993).

In short, there are numerous individual difference moderators pertinent to attribution theory, although the examples presented thus far are rejected for further discussion because of the relative paucity of data. In contrast to the just-mentioned moderators, an individual difference clearly documented to be related to concepts within attribution theory is political ideology. Political ideology (liberal versus conservative orientation) has some association to authoritarianism, racism, religiosity, and just world beliefs. However, it differs from these and has generated a separate, extensive, and systematic literature.

The main justification guiding selection of political ideology as an exemplar moderator is that, similar to gender disparities, there are documented differences in helping exhibited by liberals as opposed to conservatives. As summarized by Skitka (1999), "Support for public compassion, or for using collective resources to help the less fortunate members of our society, appears to depend largely on … ideological … differences. Liberals generally favor, whereas conservatives oppose, increased spending on social programs (Feather, 1985; Kluegel, 1990; Kluegel & Smith, 1986; Sniderman & Tetlock, 1986; Williams, 1984)" (p. 793). Furthermore, according to Skitka (1999), differences in endorsement of public spending (helping the needy) are mediated by distinct attributional beliefs about the cause of the need (poverty) held by the two ideological groups. Thus, her position may be summarized as follows:

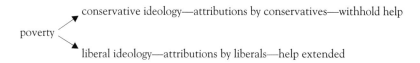

Previously, support was provided for the classification of causes according to their controllability, linking controllable causality and responsibility, and specifying that emotions mediate between perceptions of causation and helping behavior. Thus, the analysis by Skitka (1999) may be elaborated to the following:

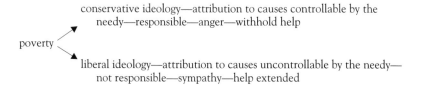

These sequences can be combined to form a general motivation statement:

ideology

↓

need (poverty)—cause—causal controllability—responsibility—emotion—behavior

Given this conceptual analysis, ideology moderates the relation between a need and the causal attribution for the need. That is, political ideology influences the perception of social reality, or the type and strength of the attribution made for poverty. However, given either ideology, attributions of control, responsibility inferences, and emotions mediate the relation between need (poverty) and the elicited behavior. Of course, it might be the case that political ideology also acts as a moderator between, for example, the attribution and perceptions of responsibility (given the same attribution, there nonetheless are differences in responsibility inferences as a function of ideology). Similarly, ideology may moderate the relation between responsibility and emotion (given the same level of responsibility, there are differences in the magnitudes of emotional experience) and/or moderate the relation between emotion and behavior. Here I confine my analysis to the hypothesis that the need–attribution link is moderated by ideology, and anticipated differences regarding responsibility, emotion, and action are solely traceable to the disparity in attribution-related beliefs.

To provide evidence for the analysis just given, it first must be shown that ideology does relate to attributions (here focusing only on attributions for poverty). Following this documentation, I present two exemplar investigations illustrating the role of political ideology within the full motivation sequence. My aim here is not to present a complete literature review regarding these associations, but rather to depict how individual differences can be incorporated within the theory.

Political Ideology and Attributions for Poverty

There have been a number of descriptive studies examining people's perceptions of the causes of various events or outcomes, such as the causes of achievement failure, mental illness, crime, and so forth (see review in Weiner, 1986). Included in this list are investigations of the perceived causes of poverty. Feagin (1972) was the first to address this issue systematically and develop a taxonomy or classification system for these causes. On the basis of free response measures, Feagin determined there are eleven primary perceived causes of poverty. He categorized these into three types: individualistic explanations such as laziness and self-indulgence, which place responsibility for poverty on the poor themselves (internal and controllable); structural explanations such as no available jobs and low wages, which hold economic and social factors responsible (external and uncontrollable by the poor but controllable by those in government); and fatalistic explanations including fate and bad luck (external and uncontrollable by anyone).

Although most Americans ascribe poverty to individualistic factors and endorse the possibility of "The American Dream," patterns of explanation vary greatly across a number of demographic variables (see Kluegel & Smith, 1986). Cross-cultural comparisons also reveal disparities in causal endorsement, while the three types of causes identified by Feagin remain in evidence (see, for example, Feather, 1974).

Having established that individuals supply causes for poverty, that the causes fit within a tripartite classification system, and that there is great variability in the perception of causation, I turn to whether one of the determinants of this variability is political ideology. But first, why should this be? What is it about political ideology that might elicit different causal ascriptions for poverty? A few explanations have been proposed. One interpretation, articulated by Lane (1962), includes the supposition that "at the roots of every ideology there are premises about the nature of causation, the agents of causation, and the appropriate ways of explaining complex events" (p. 318). Conservatives, who are resistant to social change and value the capitalistic system in America, are not expected to attribute poverty to the existing system, or what previously were labeled structural causes. This attribution suggests that modification of the system is needed. Conversely, at the heart of a conservative ideology is the belief that hard work gets one ahead, and individuals are responsible for their outcomes in life. Hence, conservatives are likely to blame poverty on the poor themselves, which was identified an individualistic cause. This causal ascription also is a justification for social inequities in America between the rich and the poor ("It's their own fault").

Liberals, on the other hand, do not share this Horatio Alger construal of causality. They favor altering the existing system and place causality for poverty on society. This promotes social change and supports their belief that current social inequities between the "haves" and the "have nots" are undeserved and unjustified. Thus, just as conservatives, liberals endorse causes that preserve their own value systems.

A somewhat different explanation for ideological differences in causal beliefs has been offered by Lakoff (1996). Lakoff relates conservative and liberal philosophies respectively to the metaphors of father as a strict disciplinarian and mother as a source of unconditional love and comfort. The father (conservative ideology) expects hard work and places responsibility for outcomes on the children themselves, rewarding positive behavior and disciplining harshly for any transgressions. In contrast, the mother (liberal ideology) offers solace and comfort when things go wrong, regardless of the cause. These overriding "resonances" (see Skitka & Tetlock, 1993b), or syndromes that include beliefs and affects, in part define what it means to be a liberal or conservative (also see Skitka & Tetlock, 1993a).

And still another, more speculative, hypothesis regarding an ideology–attribution link is that people vary in their general tendencies to make dispositional versus situational attributions (see Skitka, Mullen, Griffin, Hutchinson, & Chamberlin, 2002), perhaps because of early childrearing experiences. This, in turn, attracts them to different ideologies such that dispositional attributors are drawn to a conservative ideology, whereas situational attributors embrace liberal doctrines.

In sum, there are logical reasons supporting the hypothesis that liberals and conservatives will reach opposing decisions regarding the causes of poverty, as well as exhibiting different reactions (e.g., help giving) to people in this state. The question now is, do the data confirm that liberals and conservatives vary in their attributions for poverty? The answer is an unequivocal "yes." Consider, for example, two early studies examining this issue. In one investigation, Williams (1984) had college participants read a story about a person whose welfare was being terminated. In one condition, the reason for the termination was structural (external and uncontrollable by the poor but controllable by others in society). The specific cause given was budget cutbacks. In a second condition, the cause was left ambiguous. Participants, classified according to political ideology, were asked questions regarding responsibility of the welfare recipient for this loss. Even when the cause was structural, conservatives ascribed more responsibility to the welfare person than liberals, endorsing blame because of their character as well as their behavior.

In a prior study conducted by Pandey, Sinha, Prakash, and Tripathi (1982), Indian students classified according to political ideology (neutral, right, left) were asked their attributions for poverty. Four types of causes were identified: self (or individual), fate, government's policies (structural), and economic factors (structural). Table 2.6 shows the participants' responses. It is clear from Table 2.6 that self and (unexpectedly) fate were perceived more causal by conservatives (right), whereas liberals (left) regarded structural factors (policies and economic factors) as more important determinants of poverty than conservatives.

These illustrative studies, conducted in two disparate cultures, with one assessing responsibility beliefs and the other examining specific causes, document that ideology affects causal perceptions, or social reality, in the generally

TABLE 2.6

Perceived Causes of Poverty as a Function of Political Ideology

Perceived Cause of Poverty	Political Ideology		
	Neutral	Right	Left
Self	5.63	5.76	3.96
Fate	4.40	4.86	2.96
Government's policies	6.50	7.26	8.56
Economic factors	7.23	6.76	8.96

Note. Data from Pandey, Sinha, Prakash, and Tripathi (1982).

anticipated manner. Conservatives fault the poor for poverty (i.e., blame the victim), whereas liberals place the fault with society.

Political Ideology and the Motivation Sequence

As indicated earlier, there are also research investigations that explicitly consider emotional as well as thought processes that might mediate between political ideology and decisions regarding help for the impoverished. In one of these investigations, Skitka (1999) examined reactions of individuals to a national disaster—the flooding of a Midwestern community. Although an uncontrollable event, individuals could have purchased flood insurance or constructed antiflood devices to limit damage. Thus, there were ambiguous issues regarding the cause(s) of the financial needs of flood victims.

In a random national telephone survey, respondents revealed their political identification, perceived responsibility of flood victims for their current plights, emotions of anger and sympathy toward the victims, and whether victims deserved aid. The latter was used as an indicator of help giving (although it is not the best variable to assess help or intended help because it is closely related to the meaning of responsibility).

Figure 2.3 shows the path diagram of reactions toward individuals who did not purchase flood insurance. First, political orientation (conservatives are given the higher numerical values) is associated with perceptions of responsibility such that conservatives hold victims more responsible for their plights than do liberals. Increased responsibility, in turn, significantly lessens sympathy (positive affect) and augments anger (negative affect); sympathy, but not anger, relates to ratings of deservedness of aid. In addition to these findings, there is a strong direct path from political orientation to deservedness, with conser-

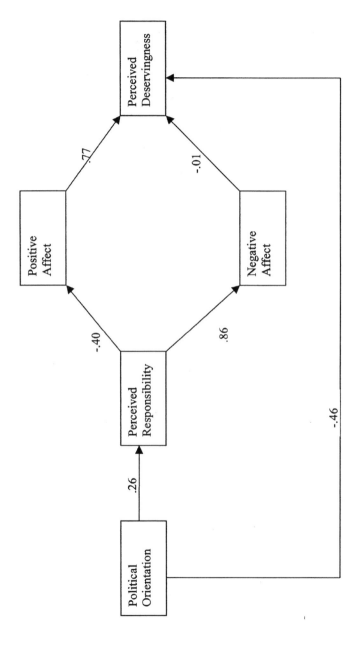

FIG. 2.3. Path diagram relating political orientation to perceived deservingness of aid. Adapted from Skitka (1999), p. 803.

vatives regarding those in need as less deserving than do liberals. Hence, some differences in help giving due to ideology are not mediated by attributions and emotions. This is consistent with other data showing, for example, that abortion attitudes are influenced directly by the perceived cause of the need for abortion as well as by political ideology (conservatives are against abortion), which directly affects attitudes because of the personal or symbolic meaning of abortion (see Zucker, 1999).

In sum, political/ideological orientation relates to causal beliefs. In addition, ideology both directly and indirectly (via attributions and emotions) influences beliefs related to helping. This is consistent with the idea that political ideology moderates the relations between poverty and behavior, and ideology has (part of) its effects mediated by responsibility inferences and affects.

Rather similar albeit more complex results were reported earlier by Zucker and Weiner (1993). We gave our college participants the 13 causes of poverty identified by Feagin (1972) and asked about their importance as contributors to this plight. Then, in addition to determining political orientation, we assessed causal controllability, blame (which, at the time, we regarded as interchangeable with responsibility), pity, and anger regarding those in poverty. In addition, two judgments were made related to help giving, one concerning willingness to provide personal help and the second regarding assistance with welfare. Although these appear equally valid indicators of a desire to benefit the needy, they are distinguishable in important respects. Foremost among the differences is that welfare is less personally involving than personal help. A distinction between types of help as a function of personal involvement was not introduced when examining prior tests of the theory, but may be one source of variance between studies when considering strengths of the paths from attributions and emotions to help giving.

Table 2.7 shows the correlations between the variables (for ease of explanation I substitute the concept of responsibility for blame, with knowledge this is taking questionable liberties). Following the top row of the table, it can be seen that conservatism correlates positively with individual causes (#8; $r = .19$) and negatively with social causes (#9; $r = -.39$). These findings support the prior contention that political ideology moderates the association between poverty and perceptions of causality, with conservatives endorsing individual causes whereas liberals perceive society as causing poverty. In addition, perceived controllability and responsibility are highly positively correlated ($r = .65$) and responsibility, in turn, relates negatively with pity ($r = -.61$) and positively with anger ($r = .66$). This strongly supports the cognition–emotion linkages championed in this book. Finally, responsibility, pity, and anger correlated in the expected manner for both indicators of help

TABLE 2.7

Correlations Between Political Ideology, Attributional Variables,
and Two Indices of Help Giving

	1	2	3	4	5	6	7	8	9	10
1. Conservatism	—	.21	.24	−.36	.20	−.30	−.37	.19	−.39	−.10
2. Controllability		—	.65	−.31	.44	−.28	−.39	.36	−.19	−.18
3. Blame (Resp.)			—	−.61	.66	−.46	−.45	.45	−.42	−.14
4. Pity				—	−.44	.60	.43	−.22	.43	.16
5. Anger					—	−.45	−.34	.33	−.07	−.13
6. Help						—	.58	−.20	.26	.23
7. Welfare							—	−.30	.38	.27
8. Individual Causes								—	−.06	.12
9. Social Causes									—	.26
10. Fate Causes										—

Note. From Zucker and Weiner (1993), p. 939.

giving, with pity positively associated (average r = .51) and responsibility and anger negatively correlated (respectively, absolute average r = −.45 and −.40) with helping. Again, this is in accord with prior theorizing. Furthermore, among the expected determinants of help giving, the positive emotion of pity is most highly related to intentions to aid. All of this should sound familiar and redundant.

Figure 2.4 displays the path models for these data. The figure shows that political ideology (again conservatism is the higher value) moderates the association between need (poverty) and its perceived cause. Perceptions of responsibility and emotions then mediate between the causal attribution and decisions to help, as already noted in the correlation data.

There is another interesting aspect of the data not pertinent to the issue of moderator variables but related to conclusions reached previously regarding direct versus indirect determinants of helping. The figure shows two immediate determinants of personal help—pity (sympathy) and anger, with pity the stronger of the two. That is, personal help giving is directly a matter of the heart. On the other hand, there are three direct determinants of welfare decisions—political ideology (conservatives give less), perceptions of responsibility, and pity. That is, in contrast to personal aid and the prior conclusions regarding help giv-

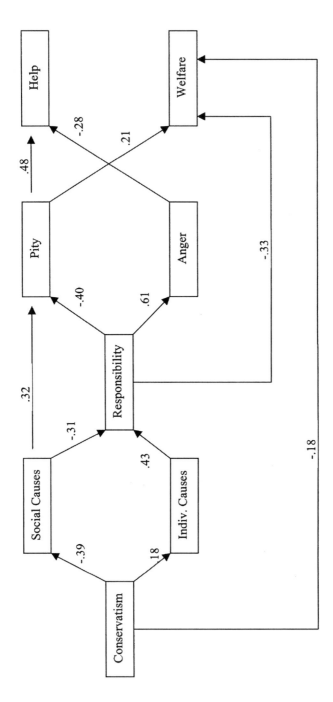

FIG. 2.4. Path diagram relating conservatism to two indicators of help giving: personal help and welfare. Adapted from Zucker and Weiner (1993), p. 937.

ing, impersonal help giving (welfare decisions) is directly influenced by ideology and thoughts about responsibility. As already indicated, the issue of the proximity of thoughts versus emotions as determinants of behavior is not closed, despite the extensive meta-analysis already presented. Just one among many possible factors influencing the motivation sequence is the personal involvement of the actor in the behavior to be undertaken. The more personal involvement, the greater may be the contribution of feelings to action or, conversely stated, the less personal involvement, the greater may be the role played by cognitions in determining action. Another way of thinking about this is that personal help is more guided by automatic processes, whereas impersonal help is more directed by controlled processes (an argument previously suggested to differentiate simulation from "real" experiments).

In sum, political ideology acts as a moderator between the cause of a need and the decision to help or to neglect. However, regardless of ideological orientation, identical mediation variables are involved in the motivation process; the proposed theory is not in need of alteration to include individual differences.

CHARACTERISTICS OF THE THEORY

Thus far I have presented the logic underlying the development of an attribution theory of social motivation and social justice; tests of the theory within domains of help giving and aggression; and how cultural and individual differences, as illustrated in studies of obesity and political ideology, are incorporated as moderators within the theory. I now identify some broader features or characteristics of the conception, in part to compare this approach with other theories of motivation. I wish to convey what is distinct about this conceptual system as well as the essential or most meaningful characteristics of the theory. Some features of the theory, including its reliance on causal explanation rather than reasons, acceptance of determinism and free will, and conceptualization of emotions as push rather than pull variables, already have been examined. Here I focus on features particularly related to conceiving motivation as a temporal process.

A Mediator-Based Rather Than a Moderator-Based Theory

The theory of social motivation and justice presented here can be characterized as mediational. Attributions of causality, inferences of responsibility, and the linked emotions of anger and sympathy mediate between an outcome such as achievement failure, or a state such as being stigmatized, and a behavioral reaction. A mediational approach presumes general laws can be found that transcend cultural and individual differences, as illustrated in reactions to obesity by Mexicans versus Americans and judgments regarding aid for the needy expressed by conservatives and liberals. Cultural and individual differences are of secondary importance and only play a role in refining the generalizations that have been discovered. The theory, therefore, is viable with or without these components.

This position is identical to that articulated by many prior social and motivation psychologists. For example, Festinger (1980) stated:

> Too much concern with individual differences could create a mask that [hides] the underlying dynamic processes. These underlying processes [have] to be discovered.... It would be hopeless to have tried to discover the laws concerning free-falling objects by concentrating on measuring the different rates of descent of stones, feathers, pieces of paper, and the like. It is only after the basic dynamic laws are known that one can make sense of the individual differences. (p. 246)

Berlyne (1968) earlier voiced the same position. He wrote:

> It is perfectly obvious that human beings are different from one another in some respects but alike in other respects. The question is whether we should first look for statements that apply to all of them or whether we should first try to describe and explain their differences. The behavior theorist [which Berlyne was] feels that research for common principles of human and animal behavior must take precedence.... Until we can see what individuals of a class or species have in common, we cannot hope to understand how their dissimilarities have come about or even to find the most fruitful way to describe and classify their dissimilarities. (p. 640)

In contrast to the opinions of Festinger and Berlyne, which I strongly share, contemporary conceptions of motivation, and particularly theories in the achievement domain, often begin their theory building with a search for individual differences. That is, they center their conception on moderators. The different groups of identified individuals then are often described with disparate processes. For example, what is broadly known as goal theory has a large impact on current thinking about achievement motivation. Under this conceptual umbrella, persons are characterized as task- versus ego-focused, learning- versus performance-oriented, entity versus incremental theorists, and the like (see review in Pintrich & Schunk, 2002). The first and essential step in the closely related goal theories is to differentiate individuals. The theories are not viable and cannot exist without their individual difference components. This contrasts with the attribution theory presented here, which is maintained in the face of, or in spite of, individual differences.

Among other obstacles, goal theories fall prey to all the pitfalls associated with trait generality. For example, just as persons are not equally motivated to achieve success in all situations, they are not ego- or task-focused in all situations. Rather, subtle discriminations are made between situations. Furthermore, persons are not one or the other of the two contrasting types—one may be focused on doing better than previously as well as desiring to outperform others, or be motivated to maximize learning as well as performance, and so on. Reliable findings, I believe, are infrequently reported, with one confirmed hypothesis often followed by a disconfirming investigation proposing yet a further situational or personal moderator to explain the lack of replicability.

At an earlier and bolder period of my life (Weiner, 1986), I issued the following challenge: "I would like to ask theorists of these persuasions, What experiment are you willing to wager on as yielding differences between your designated groupings of people?" (p. 11). I still offer this bet and believe a motivation theory must be created on the basis of mediators and not individual difference moderators. Moderators are better introduced after general laws have been discovered. For example, I am sure persons perceived responsible for a stigma are reproached more than those perceived not responsible, so having lung cancer caused by excessive smoking elicits less sympathy than lung cancer caused by unknowingly living in a contaminated area. I certainly am prepared to bet on that statement. Indeed, it would be difficult to find situations in which this type of prediction is not upheld, or to identify individuals who do not exhibit the expected pattern of data (as is elaborated later in this section). I also expect persons with a conservative ideology to be less sympathetic to these two stigmatized groups than those with a liberal ideology (see Farwell & Weiner, 2000). However, my wager will be much smaller, the observed emotional and behavioral differences between ideologies will not be as great as between stigmatized groups, and the between-person disparities will be traced to underlying inferences about responsibility, which returns one to a mediational approach.

An Historical Rather Than an Ahistorical Approach

An historical (sequential) rather than an ahistorical (nonsequential) characterization is strongly related to the previous discussion regarding mediators and moderators. Many prominent theories of motivation are ahistorical, guided by Lewin's (1935) dictum that motivation psychologists need only specify how the psychological situation is perceived at the immediate "moment in time." Current perceptions are sufficient for predictions and it is irrelevant how these perceptions came about. Ahistorical theories are represented in the Expectancy × Value conceptions proposed by Lewin (1935), Atkinson (1957), and Rotter (1954), as well as in the Drive × Habit approach of Hull (1943) and Spence (1956). The ahistorical theorists had two primary goals: First, isolate the determinants of behavior, and second, specify the mathematical relations between these determinants. Thus, mathematical models were proposed, with the primary statistical procedure in their studies the analysis of variance. This allowed investigators to document whether a proposed determinant actually affects behavior and whether theoretical components relate additively or multiplicatively (as indicated by the absence or presence of interactions).

Newer statistical approaches in psychology involve regression analyses and path models, as illustrated earlier in this chapter in the helping and aggression meta-analyses and examination of the role of political ideology in help giving. These techniques permit one to determine if the constructs in the theory influence one another so that causal sequences can be uncovered. A core issue discussed in this chapter concerns temporal or sequential relations among thinking, feeling, and acting. An ahistorical analysis does not allow examination of this issue, nor can it explore the effects of the variables on one another. Action is depicted "at a moment in time" rather than unfolding as part of a process. This sequence or process is a fundamental issue for the field of motivation.

"Deep" Rather Than "Surface" Structures

Similar to the "deep structures" that underlie the grammar of language, the theory developed here attempts to identify the deep structures of motivation (see Ickes, 1996). The language of motivation is represented as a thinking–feeling–behavior episode or, to add specificity to the thinking component, an attribution–affect–action sequence. One might label this an AAA theory (not to be confused with any commercial enterprise). This temporal sequence is meant to capture all content areas within motivation and thus offers a general structure for motivated behavior.

This approach contrasts with a theory of "surface structures," in which the terms or language of the theory are specific to the content domain under consideration. One might propose, for example, that health recovery is a function of the degree of social support from others. This "theory" (hypothesis is a better characterization) is stated at the level of the phenotype (the phenomenon being studied, or the visible properties being measured), rather than at the level of the genotype (the underlying meaning or essence of the terms shared by other phenotypes and conceptually inferred).

It would be more than foolhardy to imagine this attribution conception is equivalent to a general law of physics, with $E = mc^2$ at the pinnacle. But it would be reasonable to proclaim that the scientific goals in the natural and the social sciences are equivalent in that there is a search for general laws that transcend specific contexts or phenomena. It is evident that the content domains embraced by this theory of social motivation and social justice are modest in number, yet in my mind these are not trivial.

A Strong Rather Than a Weak Theory

The distinction between a strong and a weak theory, articulated by Eysenck (1993), also relates to the contrast between theories based on mediators versus moderators. According to Eysenck (1993):

> For weak theories, positive results are much more important than negative results, because a positive result from testing a deduction from the theory suggests both hypotheses and [assumptions] are correct.... For strong theories, negative results are much more important, as the role of [assumptions] has been much reduced. (p. 245)

Given the attribution theory of social motivation and justice, little is now learned if, for example, an investigation reveals that lack of effort is punished more, given failure, than an absence of ability; if cancer caused by smoking is reacted to with less sympathy than cancer caused by living in a contaminated area; or if one is punished more for an intentional rather than an accidental harmful act. The conceptual framework in support of these observations, and their frequent replicability, reduces the likelihood of any additional gain when these hypotheses are once again confirmed. On the other hand, if a culture or a group or a situation can be found in which these relations are not upheld, then a great deal would be revealed. Can the reader envision a situation where, given failure at an achievement task, the person without aptitude is reprimanded more than the individual who did not try? Are there individuals or cultures in which this might be the case? And what would it mean? It is perhaps time to search for these contradicting conditions and atypical individuals.

Associated with a strong theory, or perhaps with the very meaning of this phrase, is that empirical deductions from the theory can be replicated with certainty. A strong theory provides the opportunity for demonstration experiments to be conducted in front of a classroom without disappointment. This is true for the natural sciences—mixing two parts of hydrogen and one of oxygen will have a demonstrable (and wet) result. One reason, I believe, for the temporary ascendance and popularity of Skinnerian psychology was that the frequency of a response designated instrumental to reward reliably increased over time given that reward. Similarly, Drive theory as developed by Hull (1943) and others was buoyed by unfailing observations of hungry rats running mazes faster than sated rats; Lewinian (1935) theory grew in stature with the documentation that incomplete rather than completed tasks elicit approach behavior; and Rotter's (1966) social learning theory could rely on skill compared to chance tasks producing greater increments in expectancy of success following positive outcomes and greater decrements in expectancy following negative outcomes.

On the other hand, many theories are deficient regarding the reliability of key predictions, and these often are moderator-based conceptions. For example, Atkinson (1964) hypothesized that individuals classified as high versus low in achievement needs exhibit opposing risk preferences when confronted with tasks differing in difficulty. This central prediction is not reliably found (see Weiner, 1992b). Similarly, differences in expectancy shifts between people internal versus external in locus of control (as opposed to differential shifts between skill versus chance tasks) cannot be demonstrated reliably, although this is a prediction of Rotter's (1966) social learning theory. I believe the same general conclusion will be reached for any theory having individual differences as the *sine qua non* of the theory. This is a rather strong declaration and some readers will heatedly disagree.

One cannot build a viable theory without an unequivocal empirical core. The attribution conception has a firm foundation of replicable empirical generalizations (e.g., lack of effort is punished more, given failure, than the absence of aptitude; persons perceived responsible for a stigmatized state are reacted to more negatively than those held not responsible; and so on). Hence, the theory is "strong" rather than "weak," and this is due partly to its characterization as mediational and historical rather than based on moderators and ahistorical thinking.

SUMMARY

What can be said about the validity of the theory of social motivation and social justice developed in chapter 1?

1. Two meta-analyses, one for help giving and the other for retaliatory aggression, confirm attributions, inferences of responsibility, and affects mediate between a personal plight or a hostile action and the reactions they elicit. That is, the theory can be applied across motivation domains, accounting for some, but not all, of the determinants of behavior within help-

ing and aggression. The theory is presumably generalizable to other areas of motivation as well.

2. Help giving is likely to have more nonattributional determinants than retaliatory aggression and appears to be proximally influenced only by aroused affects, particularly sympathy. This is more probable given personal rather than impersonal involvement in the help giving, which could be more governed by automatic than controlled processes. On the other hand, aggression is directly influenced by responsibility beliefs and affective reactions, particularly anger. The broadest principle of the theory, that behavior is a function of thinking and feeling, is upheld. However, direct versus indirect influence of these factors differs across areas and situations (although emotion consistently appears to be a proximal influence on behavior).

3. The theory can incorporate cultural and individual differences as moderator variables. Political ideology, one such moderator, alters the perceived causes of an impoverished need state, with conservatives faulting victims (e.g., lazy, self-indulgent), whereas liberals blame society (e.g., no available jobs, low wages). For both groups, their causal beliefs support or are consistent with their underlying philosophies. In addition, for both groups, once a cause is selected, the linked responsibility inferences and affects follow, so the theory need not be altered as a function of the moderator.

4. Among the main features or characteristics of this attribution approach are that it is: (a) mediator- rather than moderator-based (that is, cultural and individual differences are secondary to the search for general laws); (b) historical or sequential rather than ahistorical; (c) based on a conception of a "deep structure" for motivation that progresses from thinking to feeling to acting; and (d) strong rather than weak, so empirical disconfirmations are more informative than confirmations. Related to this description is that the central empirical findings are replicable, as illustrated in the experiments provided for readers to undertake.

3

The Moral Emotions and Creating Positive Moral Impressions

Emotions are considered intrapsychic phenomena. They are subjective or private experiences having a positive or negative quality. Attesting to the personal quality of emotions are their antecedents and methods for identification and measurement. Among the many determinants of feeling states are particular thoughts and/or hormonal conditions, while among their numerous indicators are patterns of physiological activity and/or facial characteristics. Emotions are thus studied at the level of the individual, and it seems difficult to disagree with that position.

On the other hand, an argument can be made that emotions are social phenomena. Of course, this does not characterize all emotions (consider fear of heights). But love and sadness, for example, two among the most prevalent emotions, typically involve social experiences: "We broke up," "We got together," and "My heart is broken" reveal a metaphor for love is merging distinct entities into one social unit. On the other hand, sadness often follows the permanent or even temporary loss of another—we are sad when a loved one departs. Love and sadness, then, can be considered social rather than (in addition to) personal emotions, with their antecedents and indicators found at the social level (e.g., joining or leaving), outside a particular person. Other emotions also arise in social contexts and, as regulators of behavior, have social consequences. Sympathy promoting help giving and anger producing aggression, as discussed in chapters 1 and 2, are two social emotions that play essential roles in the attributional approach to emotions.

Included among the social emotions are so-called moral emotions. These involve a consideration of right and wrong, good and bad, and ought and should. Thoughts about controllability, volition, and responsibility are among their essential determinants. Hence, they are thoughtful emotions; one may be talked into or out of these feelings. As discussed here, they are part of the more general appraisal approach to emotions—feelings are determined by thoughts. This is, of course, a controversial issue that remains the subject of argument, and certainly the antecedents of all emotional reactions cannot be consciously identified.

In this chapter, I examine moral emotions and expand on the contentions that social life is deeply intertwined with moral concerns, that moral judgments are integral to social relationships, that a distinction between sin and sickness pervades a great deal of psychological life, and that religious and judicial rules guide what we feel. The judge metaphor is not confined to rational thinking but incorporates emotions as well.

IDENTIFYING THE MORAL EMOTIONS

Which are moral emotions? From the prior chapters it is evident anger and sympathy have this label. But there are many others as well. As is later defended, those deserving this label include:

1. Admiration
2. Anger
3. Envy
4. Gratitude
5. Guilt
6. Indignation (resentment)
7. Jealousy
8. Regret
9. Schadenfreude (joy at the suffering of others)
10. Scorn (contempt)
11. Shame (humiliation)
12. Sympathy (pity)

These are well-known, frequently experienced feelings, manifestly playing large and integral roles in our affective lives. Other theorists have proposed additional emotions, including disgust, as moral emotions (see Rozin, Lowery, Imada, & Haidt, 1999). The criteria I use to define a moral emotion will soon be evident and reveal why I do not consider disgust in this category.

From Description to Taxonomy

Science has been described as having three phases or stages. The first is description. Many scientific articles begin with a descriptive statistic, such as X million people have a certain health problem. This is the lowest, or perhaps I should say the initial, stage in developing a scientific analysis. It is science because it involves gathering data. In this book, I also began with a description, specifying a number of causes of success and failure, including ability and effort. And now I identified 12 moral emotions. This beginning scientific stage would be further enhanced if numerical evidence had been provided that, for example, X percent of our emotional life consists of moral emotions.

The next stage in scientific growth incorporates taxonomies; entities are grouped and compared and contrasted on basic characteristics. For example, I contend causes have three properties: locus, controllability, and stability. Qualitative distinctions, such as between ability and effort, can be transformed to allow for quantitative comparisons on these continuous properties. It might be concluded, for example, that effort is more controllable and less stable than ability but they are the same in locus.

Can a taxonomy also be created for the listed moral emotions? This has not previously been attempted, so such a system is offered with caution and recognition that others can easily disagree with the assumptions made, as well as with the definitions of the included emotions. One dimension emerging in this attempt relates to the fact that some of these emotions—specifically guilt, regret, and shame—are inner-directed and associated with something the self has or has not done. One says, for example, "I feel guilty (or ashamed) because I ..." On the other hand, contrasting moral emotions such as anger and sympathy pertain to other individuals and are outer-directed, as illustrated in statements such as: "I am angry *at him*"; "I feel sympathy *for her*"; "I am grateful *to her.*"

There are other principles for classification of moral emotions but one stands out because it can be subsumed within Fig. 1.4, which represents the theory of social motivation and justice under examination in this book. Recall that the development of this theory was guided by a distinction in the achievement domain between ability and effort as determinants of success and failure. Moving to the taxonomic stage, ability (aptitude) is considered uncontrollable, whereas effort expenditure is controllable. This causal dimension resulted in responsibility being identified as a key mediator between the cause of an achievement-related outcome and achievement evaluation.

The ability (no control/no responsibility) versus effort (control/responsibility) differentiation also is applicable to moral affects. As previously documented, this distinction elicits contrasting emotional reactions following another's failure—sympathy (given no causal control) versus anger (given causal control). But sympathy and anger are not the only affects tied respectively to ability and effort, although they have been the sole emotions seriously considered in this book. I suggest that envy, scorn, and shame also are linked with perceptions of ability and uncontrollability. On the other hand, in addition to anger, affects of admiration, gratitude, guilt, indignation, jealousy, regret, and Schadenfreude are associated with beliefs about effort or volition. Thus, ability versus effort linkages (the control property of causality) provides a second dimension (along with direction of experience or target locus) to characterize moral emotions. It thus follows that disgust, for example, is not a moral emotion (given this viewpoint) because it often is not elicited by cognitive appraisals regarding ought and should and is not linked to ascriptions of controllability. On the other hand, if disgust is used synonymously with anger ("I am disgusted about what he has done"), then indeed it has a moral quality. But this is not the case when one is "disgusted by the smell of that spoiled food," which is the more typical use.

The goals of this chapter are to elaborate these ideas and document their veracity. My first tasks are to provide an overview of ability-linked emotions and then emotions tied to effort construals. The readers are likely to find these pages speculative and controversial. I do not examine these associations in detail but rather convey the essence of my arguments. Then I propose a more complete taxonomy of moral emotions. After that, I consider impression management strategies that facilitate positive moral (emotional) evaluation and minimize moral condemnation (negative affective reactions). These strategies are examined given both success and failure. In situations of success, inferences about arrogance and modesty also are linked with moral feelings; thus, these personality inferences are discussed. In situations of failure, impression formation strategies including excuse giving and confession are analyzed. In addition, a discussion of forgiveness is included.

The Ability (Uncontrollability)-Linked Emotions

Within the prior listing of moral emotions, four are associated (albeit not exclusively) with beliefs about ability. These are discussed throughout the chapter and include:

1. *Envy.* Envy is aroused when a person desires the advantages of another. This superiority may lie in material goods—a new house or fine car—

and be unrelated to thoughts about ability. However, the desired advantage also may be associated with uncontrollable qualities such as beauty and intelligence (see Feather, 1989; Smith, Parrott, Diener, Hoyle, & Kim, 1999). One does not associate envy with hard work, a controllable quality, because all can exert effort. But others typically are unable to become beautiful or intelligent, and individuals with these qualities are targets of envy. In short, envy is, in part, an ability-linked feeling. Envy often leads to dislike because the other has what one wants and is unable to obtain. This is not an invariant consequence—one may envy the high ability of a friend. However, it is a frequent occurrence.

2. *Scorn.* Scorn, or contempt, connotes the other "cannot"; for example, he or she does not have ability or is perceived as not capable. This emotion is said to occur when "one needs to feel stronger, more intelligent, more civilized, or in some way better than another" (Izard, 1977, p. 328), which then elicits disdain. Others might be scorned or held in contempt because of their actions, but these behaviors likely are ascribed to their character, which I suggest drives this emotional reaction.

3. *Shame.* Shame involves a belief that the self is uncontrollably "flawed" and that this deficiency in character has been displayed to others. Being clumsy, unattractive, or of low intelligence evokes shame, which produces behaviors such as helplessness and withdrawal (see Tangney & Fischer, 1995).

4. *Sympathy.* This affect was examined in detail in chapters 1 and 2. There it was contended, and empirically supported, that sympathy (or pity) is experienced when the plight of another is due to an uncontrollable cause. This cause may be external to the individual, such as living within a totalitarian society, but often is internal to the distressed person, including lack of ability. One typically is sympathetic toward those who are unable, such as the physically and mentally handicapped. It has been suggested that if the difference between the experiencer and the target of the emotion is more qualitative than quantitative (e.g., the target is blind or mentally incapable as opposed to having temporary eye problems or marginal intelligence), then the emotional experience is more akin to pity than sympathy. However, in this book I use these two emotions synonymously.

In sum, a subset of moral emotions (envy, scorn or contempt, shame, and sympathy or pity) is associated with uncontrollable qualities and is ability-linked. These emotions manifestly are not equivalent, and their differences can also be represented in moral terms. One inequivalence between these emotions is the behaviors they generate. Sympathy gives rise to prosocial behavior including helping (going toward), whereas envy and scorn produce antisocial actions (going against), and shame leads to withdrawal (going away from). Furthermore, if others were to judge these emotional experiences (we do praise and criticize others for the emotions they feel), it would be found that sympathy is regarded as more moral, correct, suitable, and appropriate given uncontrollable causality than are envy, scorn, and shame. That is, emotions, just as behavior, are considered "right" or "wrong." There is an absence of data to support this position, for pertinent research has not been undertaken. However, readers can put these ideas to personal test by completing Box 3.1. In addition, Box 3.1 examines the perceived morality of emotion-linked actions and the consistency between what one feels and does.

The presumptions regarding the perceived fairness of some moral emotions are put forward because individuals failing due to an uncontrollable cause do not "deserve to be" the target of negative emotions, either from the self (shame) or from others (scorn). After all, one is not responsible for an uncontrollable cause (e.g., lack of ability) inasmuch as there is no volitional choice regarding its presence or absence. It also follows that one is not accountable for the effects (e.g., failure) of these causes. In a moral sense, neither shame nor

---

BOX 3.1   Appraisal of the Emotional and Behavioral Reactions of Others Given to Failure Due to Lack of Ability (Aptitude)

Imagine a situation where a person failed a test in your class because of low ability (aptitude). Other individuals react with various emotions and behaviors. Evaluate or appraise how just, appropriate, and/or fair are the emotional responses and behaviors. In addition, rate how consistent or rational are the reacting individuals when considering the relation of the emotional reaction to their behavior. Evaluation ratings vary from 1 (very just, appropriate, and/or fair) to 7 (very unjust, inappropriate, and/or unfair) as do the consistency ratings (1 = consistent and rational, 7 = inconsistent and irrational)

Emotional Reaction	Evaluation	Behavior	Evaluation	Consistency
Contempt (Scorn)	_____	Go Away From	_____	_____
Sympathy	_____	Help	_____	_____
Contempt (Scorn)	_____	Help	_____	_____
Sympathy	_____	Go Away From	_____	_____

scorn is an "appropriate" emotional reaction to uncontrollable failure; these might be labeled "immoral emotions" because they are undeserved. On the other hand, a prosocial reaction of sympathy is "correct" given an uncontrollable plight. As argued in chapters 1 and 2, in moral teaching reactions to sickness (an uncontrollable negative state) should be prosocial.

Envy, in contrast to scorn and shame, is associated with positive rather than negative outcomes of others. Nonetheless, envy also may be considered an antisocial emotion one "ought not" feel. After all, a person should not be reacted to negatively or disliked (feelings that are often elicited by envy) for being smart or beautiful or for the benefits these nonvolitional characteristics bring.

In sum, envy, scorn, shame, and sympathy are associated with causal beliefs regarding ability and its uncontrollability. Because lack of ability is "sickness" rather than "sin," emotions of scorn and shame are undeserved and "immoral." Similarly, envy is an inappropriate or immoral reaction to a successful other. Among the ability-tied emotions, only sympathy is considered a justified or deserved reaction. Furthermore, behaviors elicited by emotions other than sympathy, such as rejection and neglect, are not in accord with principles of justice or rules of conduct governed by "right" and "wrong." They therefore are appraised negatively. Readers might now return to Box 3.1 to examine if these conclusions are upheld by data they reported, as well as if there is a perceived emotion–behavior consistency. I believe this will be the case.

The Effort (Controllable)-Linked Emotions

There are eight listed feelings associated with appraisals related to effort and perceptions of causal control. They are briefly introduced here and also discussed throughout the chapter. The eight emotions are:

1. *Admiration.* When a positively valued, controllable behavior like hard work results in success, the outcome is perceived as deserved (see Feather, 1991). Deserved success elicits admiration (see Frijda, 1986; Hareli & Weiner, 2000; Ortony, Clore, & Collins, 1988). Admiration, in turn, evokes positive behavioral responses from others, including social acceptance. As is documented later, however, admiration is not solely linked to effort ascriptions and also is elicited by perceptions of ability.

2. *Anger.* Anger was discussed in prior chapters so I devote little space to it here. Recall there the argument was developed, based on agreement among many emotion theorists, that anger is generated by a judgment of personal responsibility for a transgression. Anger is a value judgment following from the belief that one "could and should have done otherwise."

Lack of effort as a cause of failure, which elicits judgments of responsibility, thus arouses anger.

3. *Gratitude.* Gratitude connotes a thankful appreciation for received favors (Guralnik, 1971). It is derived from the Latin root *gratia*, meaning grace or graciousness (see Emmons & McCullough, 2003). Gratitude tends to follow when a personally positive outcome is due to purposive and intentional actions of another. If an individual accidentally or unintentionally benefited another, then gratitude would not be experienced (see Tesser, Gatewood, & Driver, 1968). Gratitude is associated with moving toward others and positive reciprocation that evens the scales of justice, being experienced when the favor received is valued by the recipient and costly to the benefactor (see review in Tsang & McCullough, 2004). But, as soon discussed, it is a complex emotion with both negative and positive implications for the self.

4. *Guilt.* Inasmuch as guilt is a self-directed emotion, it has been relatively ignored in this book, particularly in contrast to anger. The moral aspect of guilt can be considered in the context of anger, for if communicated anger is "accepted" by the perceived wrongdoer, indicating acknowledgment of personal responsibility, then the recipient of this message will feel guilty (see Graham, 1984; Weiner, 1986; and chap. 4). Like anger, guilt is the subject of voluminous writing and speculation. In general, guilt follows volitional acts (or their omission) that violate ethical norms and principles of justice. Hence, guilt has lack of effort rather than lack of aptitude as an antecedent. In opposition to shame, guilt is associated with action rather than character and controllable rather than uncontrollable causality, and the motivated consequences include making amends rather than withdrawal and helplessness (see Tangney & Fischer, 1995; Weiner, 1986).

5. *Indignation.* For some emotions, particularly indignation, the experiencer of the emotion need not be personally involved in the social transgression (see Dwyer, 2003). For example, we may feel indignant at the bad treatment of B by A. Consistent with the prior discussion, if the bad treatment of B by A was unintended, accidental, et cetera, then indignation or resentment is inappropriate (see Dwyer, 2003). That is, indignation (sometimes used synonymously with resentment) is in part based on the controllability of harm and requires perceived responsibility on the part of the harm-doer. This reaction is difficult to trace to self-interest or personal hedonic gains. Thus, the emotion appears to be generated only by moral concerns, with "virtue as its own reward" (see Turillo, Folger, Lavelle, Umphress, & Gee, 2002). Hence, indignation is not readily explained by purely functional perspectives such as evolutionary theory (although conceptions may be stretched to account for these types of emotions).

6. *Jealousy*. Jealousy is aroused when one fears being supplanted by another as the recipient of affection from a beloved person. An important determinant of jealousy is why the jealous person believes he or she no longer is the target of affection. "Jealousy [is] more often experienced when a romantic partner was believed to have full control over a transgression, as opposed to being powerless to prevent it" (Bauerle, Amirkhan, & Hupka, 2002, p. 316). Thus, jealousy is more likely when the cause of an indiscretion is traced to the partner rather than to overpowering surrounding circumstances and when that partner intended to act as he or she did (Mikulincer, Bizman, & Aizenberg, 1989). Jealousy is associated with other-blame and judgments of responsibility, revealing that it also has moral components.

7. *Regret*. Regret is experienced when it is realized that an outcome could have been more positive had better choices been made. It has been contrasted with disappointment, which is felt when a decision turns out badly, regardless of the reason for this negative outcome (see van Dijk & Zeelenberg, 2002; van Dijk, Zeelenberg, & van der Pligt, 1999). That is, of these two emotions, only regret has self-agency and personal responsibility among its cognitive antecedents, or appraisals (see Frijda, Kuipers, & Ter Schure, 1989). Regret, in a manner similar to guilt, also evokes desires to "kick oneself and to correct one's mistake, and wanting to undo the event and get a second chance" (van Dijk & Zeelenberg, 2002, p. 324). However, unlike guilt, regret results from intrapersonal harm, whereas guilt is more associated with interpersonal harm (see Berndsen, van der Pligt, Doosje, & Manstead, 2004).

8. *Schadenfreude*. The suffering and misfortune of others at times results in an observer feeling pleasure. This emotional reaction is termed *Schadenfreude*, a word literally denoting joy with the shame of another (see Ben-Ze'ev, 1992). Schadenfreude requires a sequence of successes or positive outcomes followed by failures or negative outcomes. Among the antecedents of this emotion are envy, social comparison, and a deserved misfortune. For example, if a student attains a comparatively high rank in class (eliciting social comparison envy) because of cheating (undeserved success), and then fails an exam, fellow students could experience Schadenfreude. Often Schadenfreude experiences require the negative event to not be too extreme, so if the student is sentenced to a lengthy prison term for cheating on a test, then joy may not be felt (see Hareli & Weiner, 2002).

In support of this line of reasoning, Feather (1999) conducted a number of investigations documenting reactions to the fall of "tall poppies," that is, those who stand above others (often politicians, athletes, and persons in the pubic eye). The more underserved their success (e.g., due to luck, inheritance, help) and the more the individual is disliked, the more likely the feeling of Schadenfreude given a subsequent failure. Schadenfreude thus also has moral components (see Hareli & Weiner, 2002).

A Taxonomy of Moral Emotions

A taxonomy can be created by combining the two properties of the moral emotions suggested thus far: direction or target of the feeling (toward self or other), and causal antecedent (ability and uncontrollability versus effort and controllability). Table 3.1 presents a factorial crossing of these two dimensions. A third characteristic of these emotions also is shown in the table: whether they are positive or negative. Subdivision of the table to include three properties would deplete the number of emotions within each cell (representing a third dimension in Table 3.1 would result in eight cells or differentiations for only 12 emotions). Hence, emotional valence is not visually represented as a third dimension in the table.

Inspection of Table 3.1 reveals some interesting features of these moral emotions:

1. They are more likely to be other- than self-directed (in the table, respectively 9 versus 3).
2. They are more likely to be effort- rather than ability-linked (in the table, respectively 8 versus 4).
3. They are more likely to be negative rather than positive (in the table, respectively 9 versus 3).

TABLE 3.1

Classification of the Moral Emotions

		Emotional Target	
		Self	*Other*
Causal Link	Ability	Shame (–)	Envy (–) Scorn (contempt) (–) Sympathy (+)
	Effort	Guilt (–) Regret (–)	Admiration (+) Anger (–) Gratitude (+) Indignation (–) Jealousy (–) Schadenfreude (–)

It then logically follows that the majority of moral emotions (4) are directed toward others, effort linked, and negative. That is, the instigating action was controllable and the transgressor is regarded as responsible for the negative event or outcome.

Why should a disproportionate number of emotions be in the negative, other-effort cell? Emotions function to regulate social behavior. Anger, indignation, jealousy and Schadenfreude direct others to desist from what they are doing or face punishment. That is, moral emotions primarily communicate that the person is doing or has done something wrong or bad, and this is not acceptable. Moral emotions are regulators of moral actions directed toward vice-ridden persons.

Attribution–Affect–Action Theory

I argue throughout this book that sin is differentiated from sickness, and that sequences of controllable-responsible-anger-antisocial behavior and uncontrollable-not responsible-sympathy-prosocial behavior capture the two main types of motivational episodes. But now I introduced the possibility that, for example, nonresponsibility for a negative act is followed by scorn from some rather than sympathy. Does this invalidate prior arguments or diminish the generality of the theory?

I do not believe this is the case. Just as moderators, including political ideology, affect the perceived cause of an event, moderators also intervene between a cause and the emotional reaction to that appraisal. For the most part, persons react to uncontrollable failure with sympathy. But, in certain situations, some respond with scorn. It is unknown what individual difference characteristic or situational determinant produces this disparity. However, the behavior that follows is guided by the emotional experience (as illustrated in Box 3.1). Again, therefore, there is an attribution–affect–action ordering, the so-called deep structure of motivation, but the specifics of the sequence are not invariant between individuals or situations (although one particular set of reactions is likely to be dominant). Thus, the following two temporal sequences are theoretically compatible because they adhere to the same motivational ordering. That is, although they are phenotypically dissimilar, they are genotypically identical.

1. Failure—Caused by lack of ability—Uncontrollable—Not responsible—Sympathy—Help
2. Failure—Caused by lack of ability—Uncontrollable—Not responsible—Scorn and contempt—Neglect

These sequences may be represented as follows:

Failure—Caused by lack of ability—Uncontrollable—Not responsible
Sympathy—Help
Scorn—Neglect

What is needed is specification of the moderator intervening between the appraisal of nonresponsibility and the disparate emotional reactions to the shared appraisal.

Similarly, other sequences follow from the prior discussion, such as:

1. Success of the other because of hard work—admiration—social acceptance
2. Personal success because of help from friends—gratitude—reciprocation
3. Failure of the other following undeserved success—Schadenfreude—refusal to help

In all these instances, a motivated action is preceded by a causal appraisal and its linked emotion.

ON CREATING POSITIVE MORAL IMPRESSIONS

The world of moral emotions often is difficult to navigate. For example, it has been contended that failure ascribed to lack of ability usually elicits sympathy and help. Yet it also might evoke scorn and rejection. Should, then, a failing person attempt to create an image of low ability? In a similar manner, failure ascribed by involved observers to lack of effort tends to arouse anger. However, among teen-age peers this causal belief may evoke positive feelings because of defiance toward adult-generated principles and school-based norms. Juvonen (2000) and Juvonen and Murdock (1993) report that when teen-age children fail in school, they communicate lack of ability to teachers but lack of effort to peers. These "tailor-made" impression management strategies maximize positive affective reactions from their target audiences.

Even sending positive moral messages to others is not without conflict and complex cost–benefit analyses. For example, as already indicated, intentional help from others often elicits gratitude. But within the context of achievement, gratitude conveys that the cause of success lies outside the self. This belief conflicts with hedonic biases reflected in ascriptions of success to the self and failure to external causes, which maximize self-esteem and pride in accomplishment. Indeed, there is evidence that public expressions of gratitude and overt ascriptions of success to others exceed private beliefs that another caused the success (Baumeister & Ilko, 1995). In this manner, one again enhances personal benefits by endorsing alternative causal beliefs as a function of the target (self or other) of these attributions.

Even greater complexity is added to this emotional mix in light of evidence that gratefulness enhances personal well-being and health (Emmons & McCullough, 2003; Watkins, Woodward, Stone, & Kolts, 2003). Should one, then, maximize pride in accomplishment (self-attribution for success), or positive reactions from others (public and/or private other-ascription for success and expression of gratitude)? It is evident, then, that the experience and expression of moral emotions can be accompanied by conflict; attempts to maximize personal gain and minimize loss are likely to be difficult struggles.

ARROGANCE AND ENVY; MODESTY AND ADMIRATION

Given the interpersonal context of most achievement striving, there are many social consequences that accompany success or failure in achievement settings. As already discussed, a high grade in a course could elicit envy and/or admiration and the person may be the object of dislike or praise. And failure could elicit sympathy, anger, scorn, or Schadenfreude. At times, these reactions from others override the achievement itself in psychological significance and in determining future behavior. Indeed, feedback from my peers regarding this book may be more important to my future motivation than are my private feelings about its worth.

Observers of an achievement not only react to the achiever with a variety of emotions and behaviors, they also reach inferences about the aptitudes, character, and personality of the achiever. The achiever may be regarded as smart or dumb, lazy or industrious, and so on. Many inferences are possible, and there are numerous antecedents of these judgments. The determinant I consider here is what the achiever communicates to others regarding the cause of success or failure, and the inferences I examine concern the perceived arrogance or modesty of the achiever, which have moral associations.

Inferring Arrogance and Modesty

Arrogance or arrogant communications emphasize that one has qualities superior to others (Ben-Ze'ev, 1993). Arrogance, therefore, is linked with causes perceived as internal and stable, for these denote properties, traits, or qualities that describe the person. In addition, communicating uncontrollable causes that are internal and stable especially is perceived as arrogant because they refer to qualities relatively unique to the person. For example, describing success as attained because of high aptitude, intelligence, or great beauty is considered arrogant. These causes or attributes are "given" to the individual and are neither volitionally attainable nor descriptive of many others. Recall it also was argued that such causes elicit envy. Thus, arrogant communications and envy are linked to the same attribution or attribute.

It follows that modesty and modest communications for success highlight that one has characteristics not different from those of others. Hence, if persons downplay their role in bringing about success, then they are perceived as modest. In support of this position, Carlston and Shovar (1983) found that accounts for success are modest (not arrogant) if they ascribe the outcome to an external cause, such as help from others, good luck, or task ease, rather than to an internal one. In addition, an effort attribution is a self-described cause of success perceived as relatively modest, even though internal to the individual. Effort is a rather modest account because others also can try hard; that is, effort expenditure is not a unique aspect of a person. Admiration, which is linked to effort attributions and "deserved" success, also is associated with modesty. The connections between causes (ability and effort), emotions (envy and admiration), and personality inferences (arrogance and modesty) are summarized in Table 3.2

Based in part on Table 3.2, the following sequences are proposed in situations of success:

1. Internal, stable, uncontrollable causes are communicated (e.g., ability) —arrogance is inferred; envy and dislike are elicited—antisocial reactions follow.
2. Internal, controllable causes are communicated (e.g., effort)—modesty is inferred; admiration and liking are elicited—prosocial reactions follow.

Again we see attribution–affect–action sequences, but now trait inferences about the person also are included that drive and/or accompany the emotional reactions.

TABLE 3.2
Attribution-Related Affects and Personality Inferences

	Success	
Cause	High Ability	High Effort
Affect reaction	Envy	Admiration
Personality inference if communicated	Arrogance	Modesty

In an initial study testing these ideas, we (Hareli & Weiner, 2000) presented research participants with a description of another person's account for personal success. Readers are invited to complete a variant of this experiment, given in Box 3.2. Eight accounts (rather than the four given in Box 3.2) were provided by Hareli and Weiner (2000). These accounts varied according to the three causal properties of locus, controllability, and stability, resulting in a 2 × 2 × 2 factorial design. Furthermore, the accounts were paired with either a mundane achievement (receiving the grade of A- in a class), or with a substantial accomplishment (setting the class curve and being invited by the professor to be a teaching assistant).

BOX 3.2   Reaction to Accounts of Others Regarding the Causes of Success

Imagine a situation in which a person did rather well in a class (grade of A–) and you asked him or her the reason for the success. In the following you are given what the person said to you. Evaluate two characteristics of the person (arrogance and modesty) and your affective reactions (envy, admiration, and liking about this person). Ratings are made on 7-point scales ranging from 1 (high arrogance, modesty, envy, admiration, and liking) to 7 (low arrogance, modesty, envy, admiration, and liking).

Communicated Cause	Arrogance	Modesty	Envy	Admiration	Liking
I am smart					
I tried hard					
I was lucky					
I had help from friends					

Now imagine this same situation except the person not only did rather well in class, but set the curve and was asked by the professor to be a paid teaching assistant in that class the next quarter.

Communicated Cause	Arrogance	Modesty	Envy	Admiration	Liking
I am smart					
I tried hard					
I was lucky					
I had help from friends					

Specifically, participants were asked to imagine overhearing the following conversation between two students:

Jim: So, David, how was your last quarter? I heard that you received an A– (or, the highest grade in class …) in the introductory psychology course. How did you manage to do it?

David: Well, I succeeded because I have very high ability (or, I always try very hard; I had a sudden insight; This time I tried very hard; The course is easy for everyone; I always get help from others; I had good luck; Just that time I received help from others).

Participants rated how arrogant or modest they consider David, whether David believes he is better than others, and if he thinks he has a quality others lack. In addition, participants indicated the degree to which they would like to achieve success due to the same cause.

The data from this study are shown in Tables 3.3 and 3.4. Table 3.3 reveals that stating high ability as the cause of success is rated significantly more arrogant than any other communicated cause. Or, phrased in the reverse direction, all accounts with the exception of high ability are perceived as relatively modest. The arrogance and modesty ratings surely will be replicated in the readers' personal data, given in Box 3.2.

To test other predictions regarding the consequences or associations of arrogant and modest communications, correlations were computed between these inferences and other dependent variables. Table 3.4 shows, as anticipated, that arrogance is positively associated with observers' believing the account conveys that the person is better than others ($r = .63$), has a quality that others lack ($r = .50$), and others desire to succeed because of the same cause ($r = .22$). The correlations for modesty are in the reverse direction.

Level of achievement did not influence these results. One is judged equally arrogant when attributing an A– or the best grade in the class to high ability.

TABLE 3.3

Means of Arrogance and Modesty Ratings by Type of Account

	Type of Account							
	Ability	Constant effort	Constant help	Easy course	Insight	Occasional effort	Occasional help	Luck
Arrogance	5.33	3.43	2.27	4.09	3.27	2.57	1.91	2.85
Modesty	2.50	4.57	5.00	5.00	4.80	4.71	5.36	4.77

Note. Data from Hareli and Weiner (2000), p. 223.

TABLE 3.4

Correlations Among Modesty, Arrogance, Desirability of the Cause,
the Degree to Which the Person Thinks He Is better Than Others
and That He Has a Quality That Others Lack

Variable	1	2	3	4	5
1. Arrogance					
2. Modesty	−.56**				
3. Thinks he is better than others	.63**	−.37**			
4. Thinks he has quality that others lack	.50**	−.31**	.66**		
5. Desirable cause	.22**	−.23**	.41**	.42**	

Note. *p < .05. ** p < .01. Data from Hareli and Weiner (2000), p. 224.

Other research (Hareli & Weiner, 2000) revealed that even when winning a gold medal in a world championship race and setting a world record, a public attribution to high ability is regarded as arrogant. This intimates that even truthful communications can be arrogant, an issue I now turn to in greater detail inasmuch as truth is closely tied to morality.

What About the Truth?

In the prior investigation I reported that public communications affect inferences about the person. But are evaluations of these communications also influenced by their truth value? It is known, for example, that understatements of performance enhance perceptions of modesty, whereas exaggerations of accomplishments increase perceptions of arrogance (Schlenker & Leary, 1982). Thus, judgments of modesty and arrogance are sensitive to the extent that communications of the presenter match reality.

One might also ask, are personal statements of ability regarded as arrogant when it also is the case that ability is the real cause of success? Individuals prefer honest communications (Schlenker, 1975), just as do judges in a courtroom. Hence, perhaps a true claim of high ability is not regarded as arrogant and actually increases liking of the other. In a similar manner, perhaps a true claim that success was due to an external, unstable, and uncontrollable cause (e.g., good luck) will not be regarded as modest. These examples suggest that accurate or honest communications mitigate impressions of arrogance and modesty. On the other hand, honesty of communications may be irrelevant to perceptions of arrogance or modesty.

To examine this issue, we (Hareli, Weiner, & Yee, 2004) conducted an investigation manipulating real as well as communicated causes of success. Participants read a story about a person succeeding in school. This was followed by 16 combinations of information, composed of four real causes times four communicated causes. The four real and communicated causes of the outcome were ability, effort, help from others, and luck. For example, participants read that a student succeeded because of ability and said so, or succeeded because of ability but said he tried hard, or succeeded because of effort but communicated that success was because of high ability, and so on. One group of participants rated the arrogance and honesty of the communicator, while another rated modesty and honesty. In addition to personality inferences, ratings of two moral emotions, envy and admiration, were made.

First consider the emotional reactions of envy and admiration. Envy was only influenced by the real cause of success (see Fig. 3.1). Participants (college students) envied those succeeding because of internal (self-related) reasons, and particularly those succeeding because of high ability. Thus, as previously reasoned, others having unique qualities that are not attainable are most envied. However, envy is not confined to unattainable personal qualities inasmuch as successful effort also elicits this emotion.

Admiration also is heightened when the real causes of success are internal to the person. Figure 3.2 shows that ability and effort are equally admired. Hence, admiration may not be tied to causal controllability (although it is linked to causal locus). In addition, communicated causes to some extent influence ad-

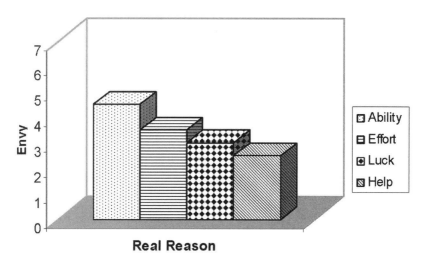

FIG. 3.1. Envy as a function of the real reason for success (adapted from Hareli, Weiner, & Yee, 2004).

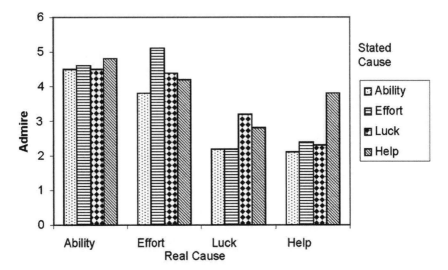

FIG. 3.2. Admiration as a function of stated and real causes of success (adapted from Hareli, Weiner, & Yee, 2004).

miration—the person most admired succeeded because of hard work and communicated this cause.

But what about arrogance and modesty and their relations to honesty? Here the associations are more complex. Figure 3.3 depicts the arrogance ratings as a function of real and stated causes. It is evident from the figure that one primarily is regarded as arrogant for stating ability as the cause of success. Furthermore, this inference is not affected by real causes. That is, stating ability when it was the actual cause of success does not mitigate perceptions of arrogance. Einstein is arrogant if he states, "I am an Einstein." On the other hand, an interaction between real and communicated causes influences other judgments of arrogance. For example, if one succeeded because of effort and communicated this, then arrogance is not elicited. However, it is arrogant to state that one succeeded because of effort when external causes (help from others or luck) were the real causes. That is, the truth value of the communication regarding effort, but not ability, influences perceived arrogance. The only other combination of causes generating a high degree of arrogance is success because of effort while stating that luck is the cause. In this case, luck apparently is viewed as a characteristic of the person, akin to ability in being internal, stable, and uncontrollable.

One might think modesty is the mirror opposite of arrogance and findings regarding modesty merely reverse what has already been reported. However,

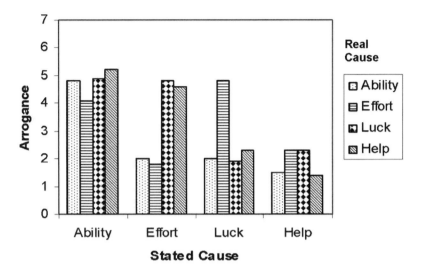

FIG. 3.3.   Arrogance as a function of stated and real causes of success (adapted from Hareli, Weiner, & Yee, 2004).

that is not the case, as shown in Fig. 3.4. Statements of external causes are regarded as modest (just as statements of internal causality are considered arrogant). However, this is particularly true when the real causes are internal to the person. For example, stating that success was because of luck when ability was the true cause is rated very modest. Hence, modesty is, in part, a lie. Persons who have ability and try hard, therefore, have a greater potential to be regarded as fully modest, whereas those who are unable or have not put forth effort cannot mask real internal causes of success and are limited in the extent they can be perceived as modest. On the other hand, all persons have the potential to be regarded as arrogant; arrogance is a claim that one has ability, regardless of the truth value of this statement.

Finally, not all lies are equal. A person succeeding because of ability, for example, but communicating luck or help as the true cause is considered more honest than the person succeeding because of luck or help and stating ability was the real cause of success. Thus, impressions of honesty take into account inferences of arrogance and modesty and the inferred reason for lying.

In sum, causal perceptions traced back to ability and effort relate not only to emotions, but also to personality inferences that have moral connotations. There are moral and immoral communications, with these labels attached to particular causal statements.

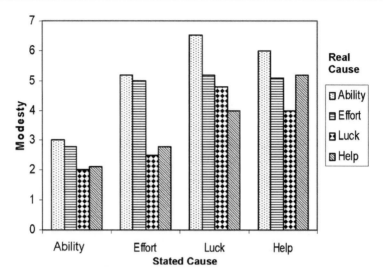

FIG. 3.4. Modesty as a function of stated and real causes of success (adapted from Hareli, Weiner, & Yee, 2004).

IMPRESSION FORMATION AND EXCUSES

It has been shown that impression formation is alive and well in situations of success, and this can be accomplished by manipulating causal communications. It is particularly functional in regard to social goals to convey that success was not because of high ability but rather was accomplished by means of hard work and hence is especially deserved.

But the context of achievement success may not be the richest arena to study impression formation and moral emotions, as opposed to situations in which there has been a social and/or moral transgression (failure). This is because achievement strivings take place within a reward-oriented system—one is especially rewarded for distinctive actions (products) or behavioral consequences at variance with social norms. On the other hand, moral transgressions are evaluated within a punishment-oriented system—one is particularly punished for behaviors that differ from social norms (see Weiner & Peter, 1973). Persons are particularly prone to search for strategies to repair social damage in the context of immoral actions and seek to limit punishment by creating a more favorable self-impression. This follows from the principle that attributional search especially is elicited by negative events (see Weiner, 1985b).

What strategies are available to transgressing individuals to decrease negative reactions of others? These others may be judges in a courtroom following a criminal act or victims left waiting in front of the movie theater because the friend is late (a "social predicament"). It has been contended throughout this book that reducing perceptions of personal responsibility for a negative event, state, behavior, and the like reduce punishment. Therefore, alteration in beliefs about responsibility is one goal sought by transgressors and may be reached by providing appropriate accounts.

An account can be described with the language (metaphor) of commercial exchange. It is said we "owe," "give," or "offer" an account, whereas the other "receives," "accepts," or "refuses" this explanation. Thus, there is a transaction between two individuals, the harm doer and the harmed. The account often attempts to "neutralize" anticipated negative evaluations (Scott & Lyman, 1968). That is, an account is a "conversational move" to prevent reprimand and punishment; it serves social as well as personal needs and goals.

In my prior book, *Judgments of Responsibility* (Weiner, 1995), a taxonomic scheme for the classification of accounts was proposed that I still find useful (see Table 3.5). The left side of Table 3.5 shows the stages in the process of finding the other fully responsible. The initial stage requires a negative outcome (state, behavior, event, etc.), such as being left waiting at the movie theater. Then the outcome is ascribed by the harmed person to personal causes within the harm doer ("It is because of Jane."). In the next stage, that personal cause is considered controllable by her ("She makes no effort to come on time."). Finally, there are no mitigating circumstances such as, "She always has to help her mother to bed before she can leave the house." Given an action ascribed to internal controllable causes without mitigation, the other is held fully responsible.

The right half of Table 3.5 reveals strategies that decrease responsibility and blame of the account provider. These stop the responsibility process. First, it may be contended the negative outcome did not occur (denial). This is a primitive strategy, used most likely by the very young ("Cookies are not missing"; or "I did not take the cookies."). However, denial is not confined to any age group (e.g., one may state to the accusing other at the movie theater: "I am not late; we agreed to meet at this time."). Nonetheless, denial is elemental—it often can be disproved and does not require sophisticated understanding of the responsibility process. Denial has been labeled an aggravating/assertive account and often augments interpersonal conflict. This contrasts with other accounts, labeled mitigating/nonassertive, which seek to decrease conflict between involved parties (see McLaughlin, Cody, & O'Hair, 1983; Takaku, 2000).

TABLE 3.5

The Responsibility Process Related to Strategies That Promote Nonresponsibility

Stage in the responsibility process	Strategy
Negative outcome occurs	Disavow outcome (denial)
Outcome is ascribed by others to causes within the harm doer	Ascribe to external factors (excuse)
Outcome is ascribed by others to causes controllable by the harm doer	Ascribe to uncontrollable causes (excuse)
No mitigating circumstances are perceived	Indicate mitigating circumstances (excuse and justification)
Responsibility inference is made	Apologize and confess

Note. From Weiner (1995), p. 218. Reprinted with permission from The Guilford Press.

Excuses

In the next two steps in Table 3.5, the responsibility process is disengaged by agreeing that the negative event occurred but the ascription either is not to the self or is to the self but the cause was not controllable. These attributional manipulations or impression management techniques are labeled *excuses* (ex = from, cuse = cause; hence, from one cause to another). As Schlenker, Pontari, and Christopher (2001) state:

> Excuses are self-serving explanations, or accounts, that aim to reduce personal responsibility for questionable events, thereby disengaging core components of the self from the incident (Schlenker, 1980, 1982, 1997; Scott & Lyman, 1968; Snyder, Higgins, & Stucky, 1983; Tedeschi & Riess, 1981). Their goal is to convince audiences, often the actor included, that a questionable event is not as much the actor's fault as it might otherwise appear to be…. By so doing, the actor may minimize the negative repercussions of the event, … and punishment for failures and transgressions. (p. 15)

Excuses have been regarded as intermediate between aggravating/assertive and mitigating/nonassertive accounts. They have qualities that decrease interpersonal conflict by reducing responsibility, yet conflict may be augmented because the harmed person regards the transgressor as neither accepting responsibility nor engaging in appropriate actions that promote forgiveness.

Of course, there may not be agreement between individuals on the acceptability of an excuse. Dillon (1998) gave college students and faculty 48 reasons for a student missing class and asked them to evaluate if "this is a reasonable cause." Some are included in Box 3.3 for readers to evaluate.

For 21 of the excuses, the students and faculty agreed they either were reasonable ("I had the flu." "I had an appointment with the doctor." "I had jury duty." "I went on a field trip for another class"; see 1–4 in Box 3.3) or unreasonable ("I ran out of groceries." "I needed to work out." "I had to be home to have the phone installed." "My roommate had a problem with her boyfriend"; see 7–8 in Box 3.3). It is evident from these examples that acceptable excuses are either external to the student (jury duty) or internal but not subject to volitional control (the flu), whereas poor excuses are controllable by the excuse giver and personally changeable. Given the former excuses, the faculty member should not be angry or reprimand the student, whereas for the unacceptable reasons, anger and reprimand are expected to follow. The readers can determine from Box 3.3 whether they agree with these assessments.

There was a significant difference between students and faculty members regarding the acceptability of 27 excuses (see 9–12 in Box 3.3). The greatest difference of opinion was on the cause "The alarm did not go off," which students but not faculty consider acceptable. Students apparently construe this cause external and uncontrollable, conceptually similar to jury duty, whereas faculty regard this as internal and controllable, or negligence (the student had

---

BOX 3.3   Acceptability of Excuses

Rate the following on their acceptability as excuses (Yes or No)

1. I had the flu.   _____

2. I had jury duty.   _____

3. I went on a field trip for another class.   _____

4. The bus was late.   _____

5. My allergies were bothering me.   _____

6. I had a sore throat.   _____

7. I had to be home to have the phone installed.   _____

8. I needed to work out.   _____

9. The alarm did not go off.   _____

10. I had a test to study for.   _____

11. My plane reservation was scheduled on the same day.   _____

12. I had to register for next semester classes.   _____

power to control the cause and is responsible, even though the outcome was not intended). Among other reasons on which ratings differed were: "My plane reservation was scheduled on the same day." "I got held up at a meeting." and "I was feeling stressed." Given these excuses, conflict is anticipated between faculty, who feel the student engaged in a moral transgression that justifies punishment, and students, who believe negative reactions from the faculty are undeserved and unfair.

These classification disagreements pose no theoretical threat inasmuch as attribution theory is guided by an acceptance of phenomenology. Whether a cause is regarded as controllable or uncontrollable is determined by "how it seems to me." What seems controllable and negligent to a faculty member may be regarded uncontrollable by the student. But once the cause is classified, a specified emotion typically follows (e.g., anger from the faculty member), although moderators are possible that alter the dominant sequences.

Pursuing the issue of excuse giving further, in a methodology involving an experimental manipulation rather than recollections or mere judgments, Weiner, Amirkhan, Folkes, and Verette (1987) had pairs of participants come for an experiment. The participants reported to different rooms. One of the participants was then delayed for 15 minutes, while the second was led to believe his or her partner was late.

The delayed participant was then told to join the partner and deliver a "bad excuse," a "good" excuse, or just any excuse. Table 3.6 shows the reports of the delayed persons. In the "bad excuse" condition, controllable causes including negligence ("I forgot") or coming late by free choice ("I saw some friends and stopped to talk") were communicated. On the other hand, in the good excuse condition participants conveyed moral justifications involving a sudden obligation ("I had to take my mother to the hospital"), or uncontrollable causes such as transportation/arrival problems ("I could not find the experimental room") or school demands ("My midterm took longer than expected"). The reports in the "any excuse" condition were similar to those in the "good excuse" condition, so participants normally state causes absolving them of personal responsibility.

To also provide evidence regarding the goals and effectiveness of excuses, the partners were asked their impressions of the tardy participants after hearing the manipulated communications. This was indexed by ratings of emotional reactions (positive and negative affects), traits (favorable and unfavorable) and future social behaviors. These data, shown in Table 3.7, reveal that positivity of feelings, perceived character, and favorable interpersonal behaviors are lower following a bad as opposed to a good excuse or any excuse (which was, in fact, good). Thus, excuses are functional, shifting the

TABLE 3.6

Categories of Explanations and Frequencies as a Function of the Experimental Condition

	Experimental Condition		
Categories of Explanation	Bad (n = 17)	Good (n = 18)	Any (n = 19)
Sudden obligation	1	6	3
Transportation, distance, space	1	5	3
School demand	0	4	5
Negligence	7	0	2
Free choice	6	0	0
Something missing	1	2	2
Miscellaneous/multiple categories	1	1	4

Note. Data from Weiner, Amirkhan, Folkes, and Verette (1987), p. 321.

TABLE 3.7

Mean Judgments as a Function of the Experimental Condition Among Excuse Receivers

	Experimental Condition		
	Good	Any	Bad
Positive Emotions	6.15	5.92	5.32
Favorable Traits	5.37	5.29	4.71
Social Behaviors	5.76	5.84	5.18

Note. Data from Weiner, Amirkhan, Folkes, and Verette (1987), p. 322.

conceptual location of the giver from the top half of Fig. 1.4 (responsible) to the bottom half of that figure (not responsible). Attributions to external and uncontrollable causes have been documented in children experiencing academic difficulty (Tollefson, Hsia, & Townsend, 1991), spouse abusers (Overholser & Moll, 1990), rapists (Kleinke, Wallis, & Stadler, 1992; Scully & Marolla, 1984), and violent offenders (Henderson & Hewstone, 1984), which attest to the pervasiveness and extensity of excuses in situations of failure and transgression.

Given the use and effectiveness of accounts in individual and legal settings, it should not come as a surprise to find them also employed in organizational contexts. To again quote Schlenker et al. (2001):

In organizational settings, excuses can be used by employees to repair a damaged image, by management to appease workers, and by the organization itself to rectify its image to unhappy customers or even the public at large (Rosenfeld et al., 1995). Excuses have even been labeled a *legitimatization strategy* in organizations because evidence shows they are highly effective in maintaining employee morale when used during difficult times, such as budget cuts, underpayment, layoffs, and poor performance evaluations (Bies & Sitkin, 1992). The recent "spin doctor" position in most large companies illustrates the importance of being able to provide creative, image-repairing, excuses to the public. (p. 16)

Of course, there is much more to excuse giving than reducing responsibility, anger, and punishment from others. Excuses can be used by individuals to protect themselves from low self-esteem that accompanies personal attributions for failure (see Crocker & Major, 1989; Major, Kaiser, & McCoy, 2003). Excuses also vary as a function of many factors, including age of the transgressor, social status of both the transgressor and the target of the communication, cultural context of the transgression, and on and on. In addition, excuses are not always effective (see Lee & Robinson, 2000), particularly when construed by the listener as devices to be freed from responsibility. As Schlenker et al. (2001) point out, excuses often damage the integrity of the excuse giver and may not be in the best interests of all parties.

What has been presented, therefore, is not a detailed examination of the complexity of excuses, but rather incontrovertible findings that excuses are part of naïve or everyday psychology, commonly used, and effective strategic devices to alter responsibility judgments, anger, and punishment. Two sequences appear to be involved in the excuse process. They include one order anticipated by the transgressor and another that, if all goes as planned, is substituted. These are respectively:

1. Social transgression—perceived as internal to the transgressor, controllable, and without mitigation—perpetrator is responsible—others are angry—anticipated rejection, punishment, or retaliation.

2. Social transgression—perceived as external to the transgressor, uncontrollable, and/or with mitigation—perpetrator is not responsible —others are not angry—no rejection, punishment, or retaliation anticipated.

That is, the transgressor conceptually is attempting to retreat from the top half of Fig. 1.4 to the bottom half, or from "sin" to "sickness" (although this is not likely to be his or her self-description).

Justification

This conceptual relocation from the top to the bottom half of Fig. 1.4 also is in evidence when individuals justify transgressions by maintaining that their behavior was guided by higher moral goals. For example, late arrival to the movies brought about by aiding a blind person in need would be regarded as justified; that is, justice was served, thereby decreasing responsibility for the lateness and defusing anger. Although the tardiness was brought about by free choice, an antecedent of perceived responsibility, the transgressor nonetheless is free from blame and the penalties of sin. However, similar to excuse giving, justification often is classified as a more aggravating than mitigating account, for the offered justification may not be accepted. For instance, the plea "I had to take my mother shopping," may arouse reactance because one perhaps could have gone shopping at a different time, or some other day.

Although worthy of more attention, I do not pursue justification strategies further in this context. Rather, I turn attention to confession and forgiveness, in part because these have been the subject of more thought and experimental research.

CONFESSION

Confession is the most nonassertive account following a transgression. Indeed, confession may not even be an account, which has the goal of altering the meaning of an event from sin to something more acceptable. Abel (1998) considers confession a means for the offender to express "moral inferiority," leaving the victim the decision to accept the confession, which then equalizes the status of the transgressor and the victim, or to reject it, in which case the imbalance remains.

In addition, a confession may not be a conscious ploy to alter the meaning of an event, but can spring from overriding guilt. Jung (1933) stated, "Every personal secret has the effect of sin or guilt" (p. 34), which goads the individual to admit fault. A compulsion to confess has been acknowledged in psychoanalytic literature (see Belgum, 1963), bolstered by the occasional surprise admission of a crime committed years earlier by an uncaught yet tormented criminal.

Whether or not one regards confession as an account, it is a "conversational move," with improved interpersonal relations often its goal. Foremost among the aims of confession is to have the victim forgive the transgressor. There is an accepted association between confession and forgiveness. This relation is found in aphorisms, as in the saying "A fault confessed is half forgiven," and the scriptures state confession is the sine qua non for divine pardon. In the Saint John affirmation of the divine, it is written: "If we confess our sins, He is faithful and righteous to forgive us" (1 John l: 9). Prayers are based in this belief: Witness the supplication, "I have sinned, O Lord, forgive me." The linkage of forgiveness to confession is consistent with the approach to motivation advocated here, which is guided by theological principles.

Experts agree a confession has a number of components. These include (a) acceptance of responsibility for the action; (b) expression of an associated emotion, such as shame and sadness; (c) indication of remorse or regret; (d) an offer of compensation or reparation that "evens the scales of justice"; and (e) a promise not to engage in such actions in the future. The elements of confession all contribute to its realization; the more included in a public statement, the greater the completeness of the confession (see Holtgraves, 1989; Petrucci, 2002; Scher & Darley, 1997).

There is a reasonable amount of experimental and observational evidence that confessions "work," that is, they are effective in reducing negative trait perceptions, undesirable emotional reactions, retaliatory punishment, and the like, while increasing forgiveness and restoring interpersonal relationships to their prior level of trust and acceptance. In one set of studies I conducted with colleagues (Weiner, Graham, Peter, & Zmuidinas, 1991), we gave participants a vignette in which an elected public official (a senator) was correctly accused of misusing funds. The readers also may take part in this experiment, which is partially reproduced in Box 3.4.

In these scenarios, the accused senator confessed, denied the accusation, or said nothing. Participants rated the honesty and trustworthiness of the senator, emotional reactions of sympathy and anger, and behaviors toward that individual including forgiveness, punishment, and voting preference. The results, shown in Table 3.8, reveal positive affects of confession on all these variables. Confession increases perceptions of honesty and trustworthiness, augments sympathy while lowering anger, and so on. These findings are consistent with many other investigations (e.g., Cody & McLaughlin, 1990; Ohbuchi, Agarie, & Kameda, 1989; see review in Gold & Weiner, 2000).

In a subsequent study (Gold & Weiner, 2000), we were particularly interested in the role played by remorse in determining the effectiveness of confession. Scenarios were created depicting a person working in the State Department caught passing secret documents to Russia. In one condition there was no confession, a second condition included a confession without remorse, while a third condition incorporated overriding remorse into the confession ("She cried and cried and said how sorry she was for what she had done—sobbing, she said that she felt absolutely terrible about her behavior. It was clear

BOX 3.4

1. Senator James Dunn has been accused of misusing his senatorial expense account. When informed of this charge, Senator Dunn refused to comment. The charge was subsequently substantiated.

Please answer the following questions about Senator Dunn.

1. How honest is Senator Dunn?

1	2	3	4	5	6	7	8	9	10

Totally honest   Totally dishonest

2. How trustworthy is Senator Dunn?

1	2	3	4	5	6	7	8	9	10

Totally trustworthy   Totally untrustworthy

3. How much sympathy do you feel toward Senator Dunn?

1	2	3	4	5	6	7	8	9	10

A great deal   None at all

4. How angry would you be at Senator Dunn?

1	2	3	4	5	6	7	8	9	10

Very   Not at all

5. Would you forgive Senator Dunn?

1	2	3	4	5	6	7	8	9	10

Definitely yes   Definitely not

6. What kind of punishment should be given to Senator Dunn?

1	2	3	4	5	6	7	8	9	10

None at all   The maximum possible

7. Would you vote for Senator Dunn?

1	2	3	4	5	6	7	8	9	10

Definitely no   Definitely Yes

2. Senator Thomas has been accused of misusing his senatorial expense account. This charge was subsequently substantiated. When informed of this charge, Senator Case said: "I apologize; I'm terribly sorry for what has happened, I feel terribly guilty. It's my fault; I am responsible for this. I have gone through all the entries to my expense account and have paid back all the expenses that even have a remote possibility of having been used to fund my campaign."

(continued)

BOX 3.4 *(continued)*

Please answer the following questions about Senator Case.

1. How honest is Senator Case?

1	2	3	4	5	6	7	8	9	10

Totally honest   Totally dishonest

2. How trustworthy is Senator Case?

1	2	3	4	5	6	7	8	9	10

Totally trustworthy   Totally untrustworthy

3. How much sympathy do you feel toward Senator Case?

1	2	3	4	5	6	7	8	9	10

A great deal   None at all

4. How angry would you be at Senator Case?

1	2	3	4	5	6	7	8	9	10

Very   Not at all

5. Would you forgive Senator Case?

1	2	3	4	5	6	7	8	9	10

Definitely yes   Definitely not

6. What kind of punishment should be given to Senator Case?

1	2	3	4	5	6	7	8	9	10

None at all   The maximum possible

7. Would you vote for Senator Case?

1	2	3	4	5	6	7	8	9	10

Definitely no   Definitely yes

that she truly felt tremendously remorseful for what she had done" Gold & Weiner, 2000, p. 293). Subsequently, participants reported their perceptions of the transgressor (how moral), affective reactions (anger and sympathy), likelihood that she might commit another such crime in the future, recommended punishment, and forgiveness.

As shown in Table 3.9, the confessor showing no remorse does not fare much better than the person not confessing; both are viewed unfavorably. On the other hand, confession accompanied by remorse results in positive moral impressions, reduced anger, increased sympathy, decreased beliefs the person would commit another such crime, and forgiveness.

TABLE 3.8

Mean Judgments in Three Experimental Conditions

| | Experimental Conditions | | |
	Control	Confess	Deny
Honesty	1.71	4.13	2.71
Trustworthiness	1.75	3.16	2.62
Sympathy	2.75	3.20	2.58
Anger	6.13	4.25	4.37
Forgiveness	1.96	4.08	2.66
Punishment	6.33	4.38	5.38
Vote	1.75	3.29	3.29

Note. Data from Weiner, Graham, Peter, and Zmuidinas (1991), p. 297.

TABLE 3.9

Rating as a Function of Confession With and Without Remorse, and No Confession

| | Experimental Condition | | |
	Remorse	No remorse	No confess
Morality	3.65	3.09	2.62
Anger	4.29	4.69	4.56
Sympathy	3.55	2.28	2.42
Crime again	3.29	5.72	4.83
Punishment	4.66	4.69	4.56
Forgive	4.47	2.91	3.49

Note. Data from Gold and Weiner (2000), p. 295.

These findings relate to a situation widely discussed in the media. Pete Rose, a famous former baseball star, was accused of betting on baseball games, which is illegal and could compromise the outcome of a game in which Rose was a participant. For many years Rose denied guilt but nonetheless, because of strong evidence, was not permitted to fulfill his desires to coach baseball and be considered for admission into the Hall of Fame (which would be certain if not for the gambling charge). In an autobiography and in media interviews he now confessed, admitting wrongdoing. Based on the experimental evidence just reviewed, one might anticipate that this confession would result in forgiveness and removal of obstacles to his participation in baseball. However, his confession has not been positively accepted. A major problem is that Rose has exhibited little, if any, remorse. Recognizing this shortcoming, Rose said he is not the type of person easily expressing emotions. This explanation has been met with skepticism and the belief he confessed as an impression management ploy for personal benefits. That is, he is not genuinely remorseful. Thus far, the forgiveness sought by Rose has not been attained.

The case of Pete Rose is the converse of more typical instances in which well-known individuals are forgiven following a confession or are judged harshly in part because they failed to confess. Richard Nixon refused to confess for a burglary of the Democratic headquarters, in which he obviously played a role. Many scholars believe had he confessed, impeachment would not have occurred (see review in Weiner, 1995).

Why do individuals not confess when this is known to be an effective strategy for forgiveness and other gains? It may be these wrongdoers fail to recognize the damage their transgression has caused. Alternately, perhaps denial and other ego-enhancing mechanisms interfere with rational judgments. Whatever the reason, it is usually dysfunctional for an individual not to admit involvement in a transgression; denial when known to be guilty invariably has adverse consequences, particularly in comparison to a confession (see Weiner et al., 1991). On the other hand, if guilt is uncertain, then indeed denial may be a more effective personal strategy than confession. Confession to a police officer that you went through a red light probably will result in a ticket!

Why Confession Is Effective

An issue in need of understanding is why confession works. From an attribution perspective, confession should have adverse consequences. The transgressor accepts full responsibility, which theoretically increases anger and subsequent punishment, retaliation, and so forth. Yet the converse holds true. Does this mean the theory does not extend into this domain, or might it be possible to incorporate these apparently contradictory findings within the scope of the theory?

Numerous explanations have been offered for why confession is an effective strategy, although there is insufficient empirical evidence to accept any as definitive. It is likely a number of mechanisms contribute to the positive consequences of confession. Some of these explanations can be traced to two purposes of punishment addressed in detail in the following chapter: utility (instrumental change of the person) and retribution (getting "back at" the transgressor). Among the specific utilitarian reasons for the effectiveness of confession, it has been suggested that confession with remorse signals recognition by the transgressor that a moral rule has been violated and the value of that rule is accepted. Blumstein et al. (1974) express this as follows:

> An offender may also return to a proper moral position by a display of penitence. By showing respect for the rule he broke, the offender lays claim to the right to re-enter the moral graces of the offended party.... Showing penitence, like claiming reduced responsibility, splits the identity of the offender. He asserts his own guilt for the act and accepts the momentary blows to his moral character, while at the same time reaffirms his overriding righteousness (awareness of the rules). (p. 552)

An alternate statement of this position is that confession repairs one's social identity. A confession acknowledges that a bad act has been done, but not by a bad person. That is, there is a "human side" to the offender. In attribution terms, the confession severs the act-to-disposition link. As stated by Goffman (1971), "An apology (a term often used synonymously with confession) is a gesture through which the individual splits himself into two parts, the part that is guilty of an offense and the part that dissociates itself from the deed and affirms a belief in the offended rule" (p. 113).

To capture this position within the current theoretical framework, an additional concept and relation may be needed. As currently postulated, the theory proceeds from the act to a cause, then to inferences of personal control and act responsibility, emotions of anger and sympathy, and behavior. The additional step needed is from act responsibility to the character of the person, which then also provokes emotion and action. A confession breaks the act–character connection, with the transgressor no longer regarded as a bad person. That is, as previously indicated, the confessor asserts guilt but remains a moral person. This can be theoretically represented as follow:

Transgression—Cause—Controllability—Act Responsibility
                                    Confession   Emotions—Action
                                        Character (Trait)

In most situations, generalization from the act to the person is not necessary for predictions. However, in some instances it does appear reasonable and perhaps necessary to incorporate this addition. A "good" person engaging in a bad act is likely to be punished less than a "bad" person committing the same transgression, although being judged equally responsible. This may dictate the need for an additional theoretical linkage to the person. This link was added as well when discussing arrogance and modesty.

There is an alternative conceptualization of the "good person-bad act" explanation that relies on mechanisms other than perceptions of morality. Recall that, in addition to causal controllability, another property distinguishing causes is stability. Some causes are perceived as relatively enduring (e.g., aptitude), whereas others are regarded as transient (e.g., luck). A confession may influence thoughts about the stability of the underlying cause of a misdeed, which affects expectations about the likelihood of future transgressions. A transgression without a confession or confession without remorse signals that the crime was due to a "bad seed," or some other enduring personality trait. On the other hand, if confession breaks the link between the act and the attribution to enduring characteristics of the person, then the transgression is likely to be ascribed to a less stable cause (such as a momentary error in judgment). That is, rather than (or in addition to) affecting anger, the attribution change brought about by confession influences causal stability and the expectancy of future immoral behavior. If expectancy is lowered, then the utilitarian purpose of punishment is not invoked and punishment is reduced.

In support of this position, recall that in the study by Gold and Weiner (2000), a crime was described in which secrets were passed to Russia and the treasonous person confessed with or without remorse or said nothing. Confession with remorse, as shown in Table 3.9, was effective in lowering a variety of negative judgments. The most significant effect related to perceptions of causal stability and the expectancy of future transgressions ("crime again"), which were significantly reduced following a remorseful confession. Furthermore, using complex statistical procedures, we documented that if the effect of remorse on stability was accounted for (controlled), then the effects of remorse on the other measured variables was greatly reduced, with the exception of moral judgments. This supports the belief that the effectiveness of confession primarily is determined by perceptions of causal and behavioral stability and, to a lesser degree, by the perceived morality of the transgressor.

Whereas this discussion centered primarily on a confession–utilitarian punishment connection, there also are speculative explanations regarding confession effectiveness related to confession–retribution associations. It may be that a confession with high remorse signals the transgressor feels guilty and has suffered. Hence, some of the sentence to be imposed, which has retributive or "get even" goals, already has been served. This results in lowered punishment.

Forgiveness.   It appears from this discussion that following a confession (or even an excuse), one is or is not forgiven. But forgiveness takes place over time and is not a sudden, all-or-none process. Forgiving is determined by numerous variables including empathy and perspective taking, rumination over the harm done, relational satisfaction and commitment, and so forth (see

McCullough, 2000). It is an adaptive response in that lack of forgiveness for a transgression produces high motivation to avoid the other, along with a desire for revenge or some other harm. These antisocial responses dissipate with forgiveness. Hence, forgiveness is a prosocial act reestablishing relatedness (see Fincham, 2000).

According to Fincham (2000), "The construct of responsibility has much to offer an analysis of forgiveness" (p. 3). This is in part because if the other is not responsible for a transgression, then there is nothing to forgive. Hence, "forgiveness occurs in full knowledge that the transgressor is responsible for the injury, that he or she thereby forfeits any right to the victim's sympathy, affection or trust, and that the victim has a right to feel resentful" (Fincham, 2000, p. 4). Furthermore, the process influencing responsibility judgments also influences forgiveness; that is, concepts including cause and intent and emotions including sympathy and anger play a role in forgiveness. I will not delve further into the process of forgiveness, which takes me too far from the goals of this book. However, it is important to recognize that the confession–forgiveness link is of great complexity.

FINAL THOUGHTS ON ACCOUNT GIVING

In the discussion of denial, excuses, justification, and confession, I have again been guilty of the search for simplicity and parsimony (which I do not regard as a crime). In so doing, I have been remiss in not recognizing the myriad of factors that influence the choice of, or preference for, an account, the content of the account, its effectiveness, and so on. There are great disparities concerning accounts as a function of gender, developmental level, status of both the giver of the account and the recipient, and on and on (see Takaku, 2000). To give one straightforward example, women are more likely to apologize and express regret, and they have more positive reactions to a confession than men.

In addition, culture impacts many aspects of account giving. Consider data from Takaku (2000) regarding the appropriateness of accounts when judged by participants from Japan and the United States. In his research, in addition to culture, the status of the victim of a transgression was experimentally varied. He reports that apology (confession) is regarded as more appropriate by Japanese participants, whereas Americans consider excuse, justification, and avoidance (denial) more acceptable than the Japanese. That is, Japanese approve of nonassertive accounts, whereas Americans prefer assertive/aggravating communications. It is known that Japanese, more than Americans, desire to maintain positive interpersonal relationships and the social order, which would account for this pattern of data. In addition, an apology in Japan is particularly appropriate when the victim is of high social status. Thus, two variables I ignored in my discussion, culture and status, affect account giving.

However, as Takaku (2000) notes:

> The attributional analyses conducted on responsibility, anger, and sympathy ratings as a function of account types strongly support ... that the Japanese and the Americans' attributional patterns were very similar.... Regardless of cultural background, all participants anticipated similar patterns of emotional responses to the various accounts, and these emotions were directly related to the effectiveness of the account in manipulating perceptions of the transgressor's responsibility. (pp. 385–386)

In sum, as argued throughout this book, cultural and individual differences can be incorporated into the general conception without modifying the "deep structure" of motivation. Even though there are differences in what account may be chosen in different cultures, or between genders, the same underlying process is in evidence: events—attributional beliefs—responsibility judgments —emotions—actions.

SUMMARY

The most basic principle espoused in this book is that motivation is a direct result of feelings, which are guided by thoughts or, more specifically, cognitive appraisals regarding causal attributions and perceptions of responsibility. These causes have moral implications and are associated with words such as should could, ought, and blame. Emotions associated with these descriptors also have moral connotations.

Twelve moral emotions were identified in this chapter. Two of these, anger and sympathy, were extensively explored in prior chapters and mediate behaviors including achievement evaluation, reactions to the stigmatized, help giving, responses to a coercive transgression, and aggression. Additional moral emotions are admiration, envy, gratitude, guilt, indignation, jealousy, regret, Schadenfreude, scorn, and shame. These emotions can be described according to three properties: target of expression (self versus other); causal linkage (ability versus effort); and valence (positive or negative). Most moral emotions (e.g., anger and gratitude) are directed toward others and are effort-linked, which is consistent with their regulatory function. Furthermore, three emotions are labeled "immoral" (envy, scorn, shame) inasmuch as punishment (a negative emotion) is inflicted given a cause (lack of ability) beyond volitional control of the target.

The identification of moral emotions other than anger and sympathy provided the opportunity to examine additional cause–emotion–behavior linkages. The "deep structure" of motivation is not confined to anger/sympathy emotions and their linked behaviors but transcends any particular emotion–behavior response pattern. Hence, the sequence lack of ability–scorn–neglect is consistent with the theme of this book, although these reactions to low ability do not include sympathy and prosocial behavior. To develop general laws, the underlying structure, or the genotype, rather than the external specifics, or the phenotype, must be examined.

If one is a target of moral emotions, then it benefits this individual to communicate causes portraying himself or herself in a positive moral light. Effort as the cause of success and lack of ability as the cause of failure are among the antecedent causes promoting positive moral reactions from others. One is admired when succeeding because of hard work, while failure due to low ability evokes sympathy. Knowledge of these relations results in individuals selecting causal communications that have positive personal benefits, such as publicly stating that effort or luck were causes of success. This promotes inferences of modesty. Conversely, communication of high ability as the cause of personal success generates inferences of arrogance, regardless of the true cause.

The communication of causes occurs in a variety of contexts and finds expression in excuses, justifications, and confession. In an excuse, the excuse giver attempts to shift from internal and controllable to external and/or uncontrollable causality. This defuses anger and antisocial behaviors aroused by that emotion. Excuses are adaptive responses, although they are somewhat assertive accounts having possible negative repercussions. In a similar manner, a justification is somewhat assertive in that the person justifies a transgression by appealing to a higher moral goal rather than accepting responsibility.

On the other hand, confession is a nonassertive account, for the transgressor fully accepts responsibility. Confession with remorse is an especially effective tactic—the transgressor is perceived to be a better (more moral) person and the perceived likelihood that the transgression will take place again is reduced. Confession often (but not always) leads to forgiveness, which itself is a complex psychological process with many determinants.

It is contended throughout this book that social life is guided by principles from theology and rules of the law. It is therefore necessary to show that emotions have moral underpinnings and can be embraced within this theological umbrella. Emotions, just as responsibility judgments, are regarded as good or bad, or right or wrong. They are considered "just" or "deserved" in the same manner as punishment and reprimand. Emotions therefore are moral or immoral, and the metaphors of the person as a judge and life as a courtroom embrace feeling states.

4

Reward and Punishment

The important role of reward and punishment in the motivation process has been evident throughout the book, although it typically has been implicit rather than explicit. For example, achievement evaluation can be regarded as rewarding or punishing; helping another is a reward, whereas aggression can be considered a form of punishment; and transgression was discussed in the context of reward and punishment as sources of power. Even emotions directed at self (pride, guilt) and others (gratitude, anger) have reward and punishment value. Thus, I now turn to this topic and explicitly address the antecedents and consequences of reward and punishment from an attribution perspective.

One of the most studied topics in psychology falls under the joint rubric of reward and punishment. This prevalence can be traced in part to (a) everyday observations that reward and punishment have evident effects on motivation and performance, and (b) the influence of behaviorism in psychology. It was logically reasoned from the behaviorist point of view and experimentally documented that reward increases the likelihood of a response, whereas punishment reduces the probability of a response from reoccurring. These principles or laws found their earliest expression in the writings of Thorndike (1911), who was a student of William James. Based on his observations of animal learning, Thorndike (1911) postulated his influential Law of Effect. The law states that when a stimulus–response sequence is followed by a "satisfying state of affairs," the strength of that bond increases. On the other hand, when this association is followed by an "annoying state of affairs," the strength of that bond or linkage is weakened. Thorndike's Law of Effect captured a "hedonism of the past" in that positive and negative outcomes alter the likelihood of the preceding response, rather than pulling the organism to a desired state or a "hedonism of the future," as expressed in Expectancy $\times$ Value theory.

Thorndike's conclusions are in accord with everyday beliefs and part of "naïve psychology." If our child engages in a behavior we approve, then he or she is rewarded in the hope that the same behavior will take place in the future. On the other hand, if that child puts his hand in the cookie jar, then a verbal reprimand is expected to inhibit the current transgression and such future actions as well. Later in his career, Thorndike was less certain about the effects of punishment on learning and performance. However, his original statement remained highly cited, particularly among Skinner and his followers and others in the behaviorist camp.

It subsequently became apparent, however, that the effects of reward and punishment on learning and motivation are far more complex than recognized by behaviorists. Attribution theory has been among the conceptions illuminating subtleties regarding the consequences of reward and punishment. In this context, I examine three research directions applying the attribution theory of social motivation and social justice to the effects of reward and punishment. These three pursuits include:

1. Investigations documenting reward may decrease, and punishment increase, motivation to engage in achievement-related tasks, with the augmentation not due to the goal of avoiding further punishment. This contradicts the position stated by Thorndike. Reward and punishment following success and failure have unexpected implications for perceived causality that mediate the reversed effects.

2. Studies that focus on the aims of punishment, guided by a long-standing distinction in philosophy between retributive and utilitarian goals. These goals of punishment are overlooked when focus is on the simple desire to change the behavior of the organism. The perceived cause of a transgression in part determines when retribution, as opposed to utility, is sought.

3. Research on person perception regarding judgments by others following compliance to engage in a transgression when compliance is to gain reward as opposed to avoiding punishment (as already introduced in chap. 1). It will be seen that positive versus aversive incentives to induce compliance produce disparate beliefs about the person being a cause of the transgression. Social inferences go far beyond the scope addressed by Thorndike.

In sum, these areas of study document the narrowness and constraints of behaviorist conceptions regarding reward and punishment and point out new avenues for empirical and theoretical advances generated by an attribution analysis.

REWARD AS AN INHIBITOR OF MOTIVATION AND PUNISHMENT AS A POSITIVE MOTIVATOR

The effects of reward and punishment on motivation from the perspective advanced here are best understood by returning to Fig. 1.4 (for another attributional approach to this issue see, for example, Deci, 1975). This scaffold, which links thinking, feeling, and action, suggests the conditions that result in reward inhibiting and punishment facilitating motivation. To understand this logic, readers must proceed backward (right-to-left) rather than forward (left-to-right) through the proposed sequence in Fig. 1.4. This reversal has been neglected in the book, although bi-directionality was acknowledged earlier as a theoretical possibility. In addition, the current analysis regarding the effects of reward and punishment requires some understanding of an intrapersonal theory of motivation not examined in this book but the subject of prior attention (see Weiner, 1986). Nonetheless, readers will be able to follow the logic of the present analysis.

To document negative effects of reward and positive effects of punishment on motivation, consider an achievement failure. The general argument is as follows: If failure is reacted to with anger, criticism, or some other form of negative feedback and punishment, then this indicates that the individual is personally responsible for the poor outcome. Given personal responsibility, the cause of failure must have been controllable by the actor. The dominant controllable cause of failure is lack of effort. Inasmuch as the perceived cause is the absence of "trying," the individual can do something about it, such as studying longer and harder in a school context. Hence, punishment and other types of negative feedback for nonattainment of a goal communicate to recipients of this feedback that they "can," but need to try harder. This, in turn, may result in increased motivation (see Bandura, 1986), not to avoid the punishment but because the punishment provides information that enhances output.

On the other hand, if anger, blame, punishment, and other antisocial responses are absent given failure, and/or if sympathy, praise, help, or other prosocial responses are offered instead, then according to the theory (again moving right-to-left), the actor is perceived to be not responsible for failure. If the person is not responsible (not able to respond), then it is likely that the cause of the poor outcome is uncontrollable by the actor (student). Among the main uncontrollable causes of achievement failure is lack of ability (aptitude). Hence, in certain contexts such as failure at an easy task, an absence of punishment for failure and the presence of sympathy or other prosocial responses communicate to the student he or she "cannot." This inhibits positive motivation (see Bandura, 1986), although it is recognized that prosocial reactions from others also may give comfort that could enhance performance.

These analyses assume that attribution-linked emotions, behaviors, and other feedback from the observer are not only communicated to the failing pupil but also that the pupil uses this information to infer personal causation and responsibility. It further assumes that the observer in fact is angry at a lack of trying (there can be exceptions to this linkage) and that the positive effects of sympathy as an expression of acceptance and unconditional regard do not override its negative effects as a low-ability cue. Self-directed causal beliefs guided by this attributional information (along with self-directed emotions not discussed) then would influence subsequent motivation in the manner already indicated.

These hypothesized sequences are summarized as follows:

1. Failure—communication of anger, blame, and/or criticism—inference by the actor that the observer believes the actor is responsible for failure—inference by the actor that the observer believes the actor can control the cause (e.g., lack of effort)—actor accepts this responsibility judgment, causal categorization, and causal belief and uses this information to infer the presence of ability and lack of effort—motivational enhancement.

2. Failure—communication of sympathy and/or lack of criticism—inference by the actor that the observer believes the actor is not responsible for failure—inference by the actor that the observer believes the actor has no control over the cause (e.g., lack of aptitude)—actor accepts this responsibility judgment, causal characterization, and causal belief and uses this information to infer personal lack of aptitude—motivation inhibition.

There is a scarcity of empirical evidence addressing these lengthy and complex sequences. A reasonably large, quite systematic and supportive set of data is available concerning the more simple right-to-left relation between communicated pro- or anti-social emotional reactions of others and inferences about their causal beliefs. I now turn to this body of work. Once again, it is not my goal to present a complete literature search, in this case concerning linkages between emotion and/or behavior and an inferred cause. Rather, I introduce readers to exemplar studies illustrating the phenomena under consideration.

From Communicated Emotions and Behaviors to Causal Inferences

Studies documenting that communicated emotions and behaviors can serve as antecedents of (cues for) causal inferences have been conducted primarily in developmental contexts (see Graham, 1990), although this research was initially guided by investigations using adult participants (Meyer, Bachmann, Biermann, Hempelmann, Ploeger, & Spiller, 1979). Let us first consider the research of Meyer et al. (1979). Readers are invited to complete a variant of their procedure, given in Box 4.1, before reading further.

Meyer et al. (1979) had adult participants respond to a questionnaire containing information about two students who either solved an easy math problem or failed in this attempt (see Box 4.l for the failure condition only). In the success outcome condition, one of the two students was praised by the teacher, whereas the other was simply told the answer was correct. In the failure outcome condition, one of the two students was the target of displeasure and anger from the teacher, whereas the other was not. Then in both conditions research participants indicated the teacher's beliefs regarding the relative ability and effort of the two students.

The findings in the success outcome condition revealed that the student receiving praise was regarded as lower in ability and higher in effort than the student not praised. The logic of this conclusion is as follows: One is most praised when success is due to high effort (see chap. 1 and Fig. 1.1). But success due to high effort implies that the person has relatively low ability (see Kun & Weiner, 1973). Hence, the person praised is regarded as putting forth more effort but having less ability than the neglected other.

In the failure condition, the student receiving criticism was judged more able but trying less hard than the student not the recipient of such feedback (also see your responses in Box 4.1). One is blamed when failure is due to an absence of effort (see again Fig. 1.1). Failure perceived to be due to low effort suggests that the person is relatively high in ability. In sum, praise (reward) is a cue for low ability, which inhibits motivation, whereas displeasure and anger (punishment) provide information that the person has high ability but put forth insufficient effort, which enhances motivation.

In one derivative study from Meyer et al. (1979), Weiner, Graham, Stern, and Lawson (1982) tested individuals ranging in age from 9 years old to adults and broadened the communicated emotions. We gave participants the following scenarios: "A student failed a test and the teacher got (or felt): angry, pity, guilty, surprised, or sad. Why did the teacher think the student failed?" Six causal attributions (combined here into four categories) were offered as re-

BOX 4.1   From Punishment to Cause

Imagine that there are two students taking a test in a classroom. Both receive the identical grade of C. As feedback to one of the students (call her Jane), the teacher merely says, "You received the grade of C." To the other student (call her Mary), the teacher says, "You received the grade of C. I am very displeased and angry." Answer the following questions about the students.

Jane

How able or smart do you think the teacher regards Jane?
   2. Very smart
   3. Smart
   4. Average
   5. Below Average
   6. Dumb.

How hard do you think the teacher feels that Jane prepared for the exam?
   1. Very hard
   2. Hard
   3. Average
   4. Below Average
   5. Hardly at all.

Mary

How able or smart do you think the teacher regards Mary?
   1. Very smart
   2. Smart
   3. Average
   4. Below Average
   5. Dumb.

How hard do you think the teacher feels that Mary prepared for the exam?
   1. Very hard
   2. Hard
   3. Average
   4. Below Average
   5. Hardly at all.

Both students

Circle the name of the student whom the teacher regards as smarter, Jane or Mary.

Circle the name of the student whom the teacher regards as having worked harder, Jane or Mary.

sponses: did not study hard enough/never studies; low ability; the test was too hard/ the teacher was unclear; and the student was unlucky. There was no reward condition or praise feedback in this investigation.

For the present purposes, I report only data regarding the communication of anger and pity, for it is known that these are elicited respectively by ascriptions of failure to lack of effort and to low ability, which form the basis for Fig. l.4. Table 4.1 shows that, given communication of anger, participants infer that the teacher attributed the cause of student failure to lack of effort ($x = 7.7$) rather than to low ability ($x = 3.9$) or to the other causes (teacher and luck). On the other hand, given expression of pity, participants believe the teacher ascribed the failure to a lack of student ability ($x = 6.1$) rather than to the absence of effort ($x = 3.3$) or the other causes. This pattern of inferences is true across all age groups of participants.

In a follow-up study by Weiner et al. (1982), participants were as young as 5 years of age. A similar (although not identical) procedure was used in which participants had a choice between only ability and effort as causal alternatives given expressed anger and pity. Table 4.2 shows the percentage choice of the "correct" alternative as a function of expressed emotion and participant age. It is evident from Table 4.2 that even 5-year-olds (77%) infer lack of effort as the cause of failure given an expression of anger. But this youngest age group exhibits less cognitive development when pity is the communicated cause. Pity does function as a causal antecedent at age 7, when 62% of the children use this cue to infer that lack of ability is the cause of failure. A study conducted in Italy by Caprara, Pastorelli, and Weiner (1994) replicated this pattern of findings with participants 7 years of age and older, even among children classified at-risk because of emotional instability and aggressiveness.

In sum, given an expression of anger, a third party "observer" (the subject) infers that the failing individual is regarded as responsible and that the angry

TABLE 4.1

Causal Ratings as a Function of Reported Affect

	Affect Communicated	
Cause	Anger	Pity
Effort	7.7	3.3
Ability	3.9	6.1
Teacher/ task	2.5	5.3
Luck	2.5	5.0

Note. Data from Weiner, Graham, Stern, and Lawson (1982), p. 281.

TABLE 4.2

Percentage Choice of Effort Given the Anger Cue and Ability
Given the Pity Cue as a Function of Age

	Age		
Linkage	5	7	9
Anger–effort	77	89	100
Pity–ability	50	62	72

Note. Data from Weiner, Graham, Stern, and Lawson (1982), p. 283.

person is ascribing failure to a controllable cause (an absence of effort). In a similar manner, given an expression of sympathy or pity, persons infer that the other regards the failing individual as not responsible and is ascribing the negative plight to an uncontrollable cause (lack of ability).

Graham and Barker (1990) then advanced this research to include inferences when students are helped versus neglected. Using a video methodology, they filmed a simulated classroom sequence in which two students were solving math problems in the presence of their teacher. The teacher gave unsolicited help to one of the students, whereas the other was left alone. After viewing the video, the 5- to 12-year-old participants rated the effort and ability of the students. Among all age groups, the student receiving help was rated lower in ability than the neglected student (see Table 4.3). For children up to the age of 10, effort also was perceived as less among those being helped. However, there was a developmental reversal such that among the oldest group of children, the student being helped was regarded as putting forth more effort than the neglected student (or, to phrase this in the opposite direction, the student being neglected was perceived to be trying less hard than the student receiving help).

These studies illustrate that among older children and adults, not only do expressed emotions communicate information in a direction consistent with attribution theory, but so does helping behavior. That is, praise and blame (Meyer et al., 1979), pity and anger (Weiner, Graham, Stern, & Lawson, 1982) and giving versus withholding help (Graham & Barker, 1990) produce the same pattern of attribution inferences. If confronted with failure, then an absence of blame, the presence of pity, and unsolicited help elicit inferences of lack of responsibility, uncontrollable causality, and low ability. On the other hand, blame, anger, and neglect arouse responsibility beliefs, controllable causality, and lack of effort judgments.

In sum, there is ample evidence that individuals use emotional and behavioral information to infer causality. However, in the studies just reviewed, judg-

TABLE 4.3

Ability and Effort Ratings as a Function of Age Groups and Help Condition

Condition	Age Group			
	5–6	7–8	9–10	11–12
	Perceived Student Ability			
Helped	3.1	2.3	3.3	4.3
Not Helped	5.7	6.9	6.4	6.0
	Perceived Student Effort			
Helped	3.6	3.6	5.2	6.1
Not Helped	5.7	6.8	6.4	4.3

Note. Data from Graham and Barker (1990), p. 10.

ments of other responsibility and causal controllability were not assessed, nor was evidence presented regarding the effects of these communications on self-related beliefs, personal motivation, and performance. I now turn to one study that expanded the number of dependent variables and was conducted in a "real" (albeit experimental) context as opposed to a "pretend" or simulation setting. It shows that the findings (only) partially support the theory.

From Communicated Emotions and/or Inferred Causes to Self-Attributions

Graham (1984) had sixth-grade children experience failure at an achievement task. She then varied the feedback given to participants. To some, both verbal and nonverbal cues (e.g., facial features, posture) communicated anger; to others, the feedback was sympathy; and still other participants received no attribution-relevant cues from the "teacher." The children then indicated, among a number of dependent variables, why the teacher thought they failed, self-beliefs regarding the causes of their own failure, and their expectancy of future success.

Consider first whether the teacher feedback contained causal information. Figure 4.1 shows that following sympathy, the children inferred that the teacher believed they failed because of low ability. On the other hand, given anger feedback, the children inferred that teachers thought they failed because of insufficient effort. These findings confirm that communicated affects provide cues to understand causal thoughts of others, with the direction of inferences in accord with attribution-generated hypotheses.

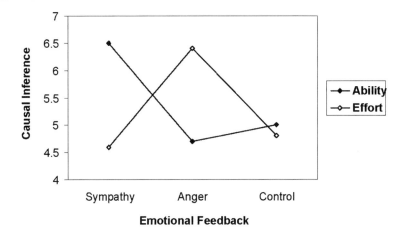

FIG. 4.1.   Inferred experimenter attributions as a function of communicated affect (data from Graham, 1984, p. 45).

But do teachers' expressed emotions and their inferred causal beliefs influence what one thinks about oneself? Figure 4.2 depicts self-stated causal statements as a function of the affective feedback. The figure shows that if the teacher expresses sympathy, then students' reason they failed because of low ability rather than lack of effort. That is, students accept the apparent causal conclusion of their teacher. However, given anger from the teacher, predictions are not supported because children do not differ in self-endorsements of

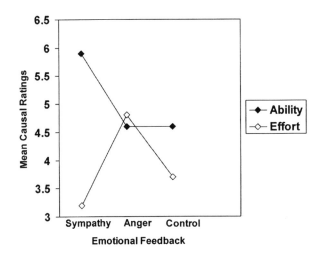

FIG. 4.2.   Self-ascription for failure as a function of communicated affect (data from Graham, 1984).

lack of effort versus low ability as causes of personal failure. A display of anger is insufficient for them to conclude that they have not tried hard enough.

Graham (1984) also found expectancy of success related to affective cues in the predicted manner: Personal expectancies were highest given anger feedback and lowest following expressions of sympathy. This ranking follows because low effort is regarded as subject to volitional change to a greater extent than low ability, so expectancy of the future should be higher given an ascription to the absence of trying. That is, effort expenditure, in contrast to ability level, is more readily altered and "improved" (see the later discussion in this chapter regarding causal stability).

In sum, the research by Graham in a "real" setting supports findings in simulation studies that communicated affects provide information regarding what the other is thinking (a right-to-left relation). She added to this by documenting that inferences about what the other is thinking influence personal causal beliefs, although only when the affective cue is sympathy and not when it is anger. In addition, personal expectancy of success is altered by displays of sympathy and presumably by inferred and then self-generated causal beliefs. Hence, findings by Graham (1984) present a cup that may be considered half full or half empty, depending on what side of the theoretical fence one falls. In my role as champion of the theory, I fall within the half full perception; in my declaration not to hide contradictory findings, I fall within the half empty description. But the general message of this body of research is that reward and other positive feedback can dampen motivation, whereas punishment and other negative feedback can augment motivation to undertake a task (for reasons other than to avoid further punishment), which is in direct opposition to the behaviorist position.

THE GOALS OF PUNISHMENT

The purpose of punishment, given the behaviorist position, is to decrease the likelihood of an unwanted response. However, in human social contexts, goals of punishment are far more complex than what is considered when investigating the consequences of an aversive stimulus on the operant behavior of an organism. Foremost among the goals of punishment are two that philosophers have long identified, namely, retribution and utilitarianism (see, for example, Gert, 1988; Moore, 1987; Rawls, 1955; Vidmar, 2000; Vidmar & Miller, 1980; for further discussion by psychologists, see Carlsmith, Darley, & Robinson, 2002; Orth, 2003). These two general purposes of punishment embrace various subcategories that are important to differentiate as well.

Retribution

Retribution pertains to retaliation for a past wrong; the goal is to avenge a prior evil deed. This aim is based on a theory of justice proposing that we should "do unto others as they have done unto us"; that is, "the punishment should fit the crime." The principle of matched retribution is vividly portrayed in a phrase quoted previously: "An eye for an eye, tooth for tooth, and hand for hand" (Exodus 21:24). The offender then gets "what is deserved," or "just deserts." Hence, the transgressor "pays a debt" owed to the victim (which is ultimately society itself). In so doing, social balance or equilibrium in the distribution of positive and negative experiences is attained (see Darley & Pittman, 2003).

Just deserts may be guided by the rule of "strict liability," where only severity of wrongdoing determines punishment. However, subjective factors typically are included among the determinants of retribution. In criminal justice as practiced in most countries and in social justice as practiced by most individuals, agents of punishment take into account not only magnitude of harm (*actus reas*) but also inferences of personal responsibility, intent, and presence or absence of a "guilty mind" (*mens rea*; Hart & Honoré, 1959; Katz, 1987; also see chap. 1 regarding outcome and effort as determinants of achievement evaluation). This is because factors comprising "a guilty mind" also "affect the moral outrage felt by citizens and, therefore, the magnitude of punishment that is called for" (Carlsmith et al., 2002, p. 285). Moral justification may serve as a mitigating factor in determining retributive justice in the same manner as caring for a sick parent is a mitigating factor for lack of effort and failure in achievement contexts. Thus, "a person who embezzles to maintain a lavish and lascivious lifestyle is judged more harshly than one who embezzles the same amount for the relatively noble purpose of subsidizing the company's underpaid and exploited overseas workers" (see Carlsmith et al., 2002, p. 284 and the discussion of justification in chap. 3).

The majority of individuals in the United States base punishment sentences on retributive justice (see Carlsmith et al., 2002; Gerber & Engelhardt-Greer, 1996). There is a very high correlation between ratings of the seriousness of various crimes and the length of prison sentences recommended (see, for example, Klein, Newman, Weis, & Bobner, 1982). In addition, the death penalty as a response to murder is endorsed by most citizens of most countries. Nonetheless, retribution as practiced often includes the goals of revenge and expiation, or making the victim suffer, which are not elements of retribution. Retribution is distinct from revenge in that revenge need not be for a criminal act (e.g., social rejection), and in revenge, as opposed to retribution, the harmed person desires to witness the other suffering. The law is clear regarding retribution rather than revenge as its goal: If the harmed other also has the job of executioner, he is not allowed to perform the execution of the harm-doer (see Nozick, 1981, for a fuller discussion of the retribution/revenge distinction). The blurring of retribution with revenge is one reason some in the lay public consider retribution a primitive system of justice (although Batson, Bowers, Leonard, & Smith, 2000, note it represents a cultural advance over an earlier principle of escalated retribution demanding greater cost than the evil done, such as "two eyes for an eye"). Another shortcoming of a retributive system of justice is that the punishment to be imposed often is unclear. For example, if my neighbor kills my wife and is unmarried, then what retribution balances the scales of justice? And if he had a wife should she be killed?

Utilitarianism

In contrast to retributive goals, which focus on past wrongs, utilitarian goals are future-oriented, with aims reached through reduction in the likelihood of the misdeed by the perpetrator and/or by others in society (Murphy & Coleman, 1990). This also is known as the *consequentialist position* and is grouped under the general rubric of deterrence theory. It also provides the basis for the behaviorist position for it focuses on behavior control.

As noted by Carlsmith et al. (2002), deterrence theory assumes potential transgressors are rational. Thus, to prevent transgressions, the costs and benefits of a situation need to be at the least equivalent so potential immoral acts do not "pay off." Bentham (1962), the philosopher most identified with the principle of hedonism, stated, "If the apparent magnitude or rather the value of the pain be greater than the apparent magnitude or value of the pleasure or good he expects to be the consequences of the act, he will be absolutely prevented from performing it." (p. 396).

This position results in some rather startling conclusions regarding punishment. For example, from a deterrence perspective, private punishment serves only the limited function of dissuading the specific person who committed the crime but not others in society. Punishment given a deterrence philosophy, therefore, should be publicly administered so others realize the negative consequences of any transgression. Furthermore, the more public the punishment, the greater should be its severity (and vice versa) inasmuch as it then has maximum impact. In addition, guided by the Expectancy × Value framework of decision theory, if an immoral act has a small likelihood of detection (low expectancy of being caught), then according to deterrence theory, its punishment should be very severe to minimize the expected value of the transgression. Given the utilitarian perspective, punishment severity is not necessarily related to the magnitude of the crime but is determined by its function as a reducer of future transgressions.

Guided by a utilitarian point of view, there are numerous ways to reap the benefits of punishment. They include:

1. Isolate offenders from society, thereby insuring the safety of the public and/or the particular person victimized by the prior transgression. This can be for a temporary or a more permanent period. Thus, a jail sentence is appropriate from a utilitarian perspective.

2. Rehabilitate offenders. This can be achieved when an intervention "opens the eyes" of violators so they recognize past errors. That is, the perpetrators of misdeeds are changed so their desires, values, and behaviors become consistent with the larger society. Rehabilitation may take place during a period of isolation, although this is not a precondition for such punishment, and isolation need not (and often does not) presume the possibility of rehabilitation. Rather, a person may be removed from society without any belief by punishing agents in the efficacy of techniques designed to make offenders more moral.

3. Create fear in offenders. Retaliatory responses toward immoral conduct may reduce the likelihood that transgressors will repeat unwanted behavior because transgressions are now associated with aversive outcomes. This is consistent with the behaviorist view as well as with hedonic principles of action. Individuals holding this position may want to make prison more aversive by, for example, eliminating conjugal visits, removing athletic facilities, and the like. Note that in isolation there is no opportunity for the undesired conduct; given rehabilitation, the violator eliminates the "evil" desire; and with the creation of fear generated by anticipated punishment, the transgressor may suppress further wrongdoings.

4. Promote general deterrence. Utilitarian-guided punishment relates not only to offenders. Punishment can also warn others in society, as previously noted when discussing the need for punishment to be public. That is, the public must be educated about the consequences of a transgression so it understands what behaviors are unacceptable.

As was the case for retributive justice, there are those who argue against the utilitarian position on moral grounds. For example, it is sometimes contended that a utilitarian position supports "punishment of the innocent" if this brings about greater good for society. It addition, some philosophers believe any decision regarding a personal sentence must be divorced from its effects on others who were not part of the transgression. Furthermore, by often neglecting crime severity and mitigating circumstances as determinants of justice, the consequentialist position ignores many moral aspects of punishment. And finally, as already intimated, it is likely that trivial crimes will be punished more harshly given a utilitarian than a retributive perspective. Hence, the belief that utilitarianism is "more moral" and more indicative of advanced civilization than is a retributive philosophy is not universally accepted.

PUNISHMENT GOALS FROM AN ATTRIBUTIONAL PERSPECTIVE

Quite often, retributive and utilitarian goals of punishment are simultaneously achieved by a punitive act (e.g., a death sentence ensures that a murderer will not kill again and also may be a "payment in kind"). In a similar manner, a retributionist may give a long prison sentence to mete out justice, whereas the rehabilitationist adopts the same sentence to allow time for correction of the perpetrator. Nonetheless, it is reasonable to ask what determines the goal of punishment and which means to that goal will be dominant at a given time. A myriad of factors bear on answers to these questions, including norms of the culture, gender of the person rendering judgment, amount of crime and fear in the society, political benefits gained by publicly endorsing certain beliefs, and on and on (see Bailey & Peterson, 1994; Ellsworth & Gross, 1994; Roberts & Stalans, 1997). Causal attributions for the transgression are among the determinants of punishment goals, so attributions are relevant to this issue.

Returning again to the guiding motivation process, the following temporal order captures a sequence including causal attributions and the goals of punishment following a transgression:

Transgression—perceived cause—controllability of that cause—inferences of responsibility—emotional reaction—punishment goal.

To examine this sequence more closely, consider first a transgression controllable by the person, as shown in the top half of Fig. 1.4. Given a controllable cause as well as a linked judgment of responsibility and anger, it is proposed that the judge will seek retributive justice. That is, retribution requires the perception of free will and a judgment of sin. On the other hand, transgressions also occur given uncontrollable causality, as depicted in the bottom half of Fig. 1.4. Uncontrollable causality is expected to elicit a judgment of no responsibility and sympathy. If imposed, punishment in this case is hypothesized to be guided by utilitarian rather than retributive goals. The prior sequence incorporating punishment goals, therefore, can be subdivided into two more specific motivation chains:

1. Transgression—perceived cause—cause is controllable—person is responsible—anger, no sympathy—retributive goal is primary.

2. Transgression—perceived cause—cause is uncontrollable—person is not responsible—no anger, sympathy—utilitarian goal is primary.

Causal Stability

The principles outlined earlier are not independent of another key property of phenomenal causality introduced in chapter 1, that of causal stability. Recall causes have three basic characteristics (locus, controllability, and stability), although thus far I have focused on the former two. But stability also is an essential causal property and is crucial when considering punishment goals and decisions.

The basic idea of causal stability is easily conveyed. If a cause is considered stable, such as an aptitude, a genetic predisposition, or an unchanging environment, then effects brought about by that cause are anticipated to occur again on future occasions (see review in Weiner, 1986). After all, if the cause will reappear then, according to Western logic, so will the effect. One therefore expects that someone who lost at basketball because of being too short, failed at math because of little math aptitude, or committed a crime because of an "evil personality" would again fail or transgress (see Carroll, 1979; Carroll & Burke, 1990). This is important in the present context because if a cause is considered enduring, then certain utilitarian goals (e.g., rehabilitation) are perceived unreachable and this effects punishment decisions and means. It may be considered fruitless to attempt altering a "bad seed."

On the other hand, other causes are construed as unstable. Performing poorly at basketball because of a sprained ankle, failing math because of temporary lack of effort or severe flu, and transgressing due to a desire to buy a special gift for a friend may lead to beliefs that these negative acts will not be repeated because the cause will be absent. Given unstable causality, the future is seen as possibly different from the present. A full range of options and interventions are then available to punishing agents, who believe they can exert a positive effect on the transgressor.

Empirical Research Relating Perceived Causality to Punishment Goals and Decisions

A first issue needing attention is whether the ideas introduced earlier are applicable in transgression contexts ranging from achievement failure to criminal activities, for these have been discussed as amenable to the same laws. To explore the issue of the generality of rules regarding punishment, we (Weiner,

Graham, & Reyna, 1997) had adults respond to scenarios created by varying the controllability and stability of causes of three types of "misdeeds": achievement failure, burglary, and murder. Participants were asked to recommend punishment severity and indicate to what extent this punishment was for utilitarian purposes and to what extent the aim was retributive. Readers can give their responses to some of these scenarios, which are provided in Box 4.2.

In Box 4.2 it can be seen that in the controllable, stable achievement scenario a pupil is described as failing an exam because of never trying. Corresponding causal scenarios for burglary (not in Box 4.2) and murder conveyed that the defendant repeatedly chose to steal or had a long history of intentional violence, including murder. Regarding uncontrollable and unstable vignettes, in the achievement setting the failing student was required to transfer late into a class, while in criminal scenarios an auto accident involving the violator was caused by a brain injury that temporarily interfered with rational judgment, resulting in a subsequent death. Hence, controllability was varied by indications of intent and the presence or absence of responsibility mitigators, while stability was conveyed by the anticipated presence or absence of the apparent cause over time or by consistency of behavior over time.

Among the questions asked of respondents was agreement with the following statements (with somewhat different wording for achievement failure): (a) I gave this sentence because it was deserved [retribution]. (b) I gave this sentence to reduce the likelihood of the person engaging in this behavior again [utility].

Figure 4.3 shows endorsement of retributive versus utilitarian goals as a function of the type of transgression. The figure reveals that punishment goals are influenced by the event being considered, with murder most likely to evoke retributive desires (see Ellsworth & Gross, 1994) and achievement failure most likely to elicit utilitarian concerns. Of greater importance in this context, Fig. 4.3 reveals that causes of the event also influence endorsement of punishment goals.

If the causes of these outcomes are uncontrollable, that is, the person is not responsible (the left half of each so-called misdeed), then punishment goals are less retributive than when the causes are controllable and the transgressor is responsible (the right half of each misdeed). Given controllable and stable causality (the last point within each transgression), the goal of punishment is particularly retributive in all three contexts. Thus, one punishes repeated intentional criminal offenders, as well as lazy students, to "get back" at them. I presume the responses of readers will reveal a similar pattern. In sum, there is differential endorsement of punishment goals as a function of the causes of the transgression.

In the research just reviewed, the link between the cause of the act and purpose of the punishment was examined, but the proposed motivation sequence was not considered. In other studies we also tested the intervening, mediational process. In the next investigations (Graham, Weiner, & Zucker, 1997),

---

BOX 4.2   Goals of Punishment

Below are given three types of "misdeeds": achievement failure, burglary, and murder. In addition, the cause of this outcome is indicated. You are asked what severity of punishment should be given to the individual and to what extent that recommendation is for the following two goals:

a. Retribution. This punishment is recommended because it is deserved.
b. Utility. This punishment is recommended to reduce the likelihood of the person engaging in this behavior again.

Achievement Failure

1. A pupil failed an exam because of never trying.

1	2	3	4	5	6	7

Minimum   Maximum
punishment   punishment

a. I gave this punishment because it was deserved (retribution).

1	2	3	4	5	6	7

No, not at all   Yes, definitely

b. I gave this punishment to reduce the likelihood of this happening again.

1	2	3	4	5	6	7

No, not at all   Yes, definitely

2. A pupil failed an exam because of having to transfer late into the class.

1	2	3	4	5	6	7

Minimum   Maximum
punishment   punishment

a. I gave this punishment because it was deserved (retribution).

1	2	3	4	5	6	7

No, not at all   Yes, definitely

b. I gave this punishment to reduce the likelihood of this happening again.

1	2	3	4	5	6	7

No, not at all   Yes, definitely

(continued)

BOX 4.2   (*continued*)

3. A person was involved in an auto accident that killed another individual. Because of a recent brain injury that is now healing, the individual made an irrational judgment regarding which direction to turn, which resulted in a subsequent accidental death.

| 1 | 2 | 3 | 4 | 5 | 6 | 7 |

Minimum   Maximum
punishment   punishment

a. I gave this punishment because it was deserved (retribution).

| 1 | 2 | 3 | 4 | 5 | 6 | 7 |

No, not at all   Yes, definitely

b. I gave this punishment to reduce the likelihood of this happening again.

| 1 | 2 | 3 | 4 | 5 | 6 | 7 |

No, not at all   Yes, definitely

4. A person intentionally killed another individual. The accused individual has a long history of intentional violence.

| 1 | 2 | 3 | 4 | 5 | 6 | 7 |

Minimum   Maximum
punishment   punishment

a. I gave this punishment because it was deserved (retribution).

| 1 | 2 | 3 | 4 | 5 | 6 | 7 |

No, not at all   Yes, definitely

b. I gave this punishment to reduce the likelihood of this happening again.

| 1 | 2 | 3 | 4 | 5 | 6 | 7 |

No, not at all   Yes, definitely

only a criminal theme was given to participants. After examining this research, the punishment process in achievement contexts is considered (Reyna & Weiner, 2001).

The Punishment Process in Criminal Contexts.   In the study reported next (Graham et al., 1997), the controllability and stability of causes of a murder were varied. Scenarios depicted a murder by a harm doer who had: (a) a long criminal record with intent to kill (controllable and stable causal condition); (b) no prior record but intent on this occasion (controllable, unstable); (c) a genetic panic disorder that frequently resulted in violent behavior (un-

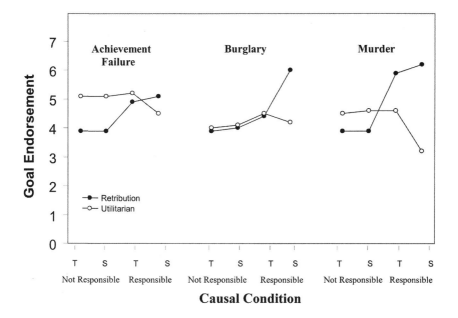

FIG. 4.3.   The endorsement of retributive versus utilitarian punishment goals as a function of responsibility of the person and stability of the causes of achievement failure, burglary, and murder (T = temporary; S = stable; data from Weiner, Graham, & Reyna, 1997, p. 441).

controllable, stable); and (d) a panic disorder leading to violence only under unique circumstances that resulted in this killing (uncontrollable, unstable).

Respondents were asked several questions related to punishment for the crime. Among their responses, they indicated the controllability and stability of the cause of the crime, responsibility judgments, affects of anger and sympathy, expectancy of future criminal activity, and the goal (retributive or utilitarian) of their recommended punishment. In addition, some philosophers have proposed that individuals have trait-like beliefs about the goals of punishment. Some individuals are labeled retributionists, whereas others are utilitarians. Assessment of this general tendency was undertaken prior to the reading of the specific scenarios. Research participants were asked their agreement with two items: "Punishment should be for the purpose of making the offender pay for his or her wrongdoing" [retribution] and "Punishment is only justifiable if it contributes to the greater good of society" [utilitarianism].

Table 4.4 shows the most pertinent responses in the four experimental conditions. The table reveals that responsibility and anger are higher given con-

TABLE 4.4

Means on Attributional Variables as a Function of Causal Condition

Variable	Causal Condition			
	Controllable		Uncontrollable	
	Stable	Unstable	Stable	Unstable
Responsibility	6.1	6.2	4.8	5.5
Anger	5.5	5.6	4.3	3.9
Sympathy	2.3	2.9	3.8	3.8
Expectancy	5.1	3.6	5.4	4.3

Note. Data from Graham, Weiner, and Zucker (1997), p. 341.

trollable than uncontrollable causes of crime, whereas sympathy is augmented given uncontrollable rather than controllable causality. In addition, expectancy of future crimes is enhanced given stable causality. These findings confirm predictions.

Figure 4.4 depicts the relation of these variables to chosen goals of punishment. Considering first retribution, the figure reveals that a general retributive position (Retribution 1) predicts retributive desires in the current situation (Retribution 2, $\beta = .16$). In addition, responsibility ($\beta = .17$) and anger ($\beta = .15$) positively relate to retributive goals, whereas sympathy ($\beta = -.22$) negatively predicts retributive desires. Utilitarian goals represented in the bottom portion of Fig. 4.4, are unrelated to perceptions of responsibility and emotions but are associated with general utilitarian beliefs ($\beta = .25$) and expectancy of future transgressions ($\beta = .19$).

In sum, retributive and utilitarian functions of punishment are driven by different properties of causality. Retributive goals are rooted in moral judgments and the emotions these generate, whereas utilitarian goals are more divorced from moral concerns and focus on the future rather than the past. These findings are consistent with philosophical discussions of the purposes of punishment.

It is apparent that research presented thus far regarding punishment purpose has a "pretend" character. When presenting the meta-analysis of help giving and aggression, I noted that attribution theorists have been criticized because their research often is hypothetical and involves role-playing. These meta-analyses therefore included research setting (hypothetical versus real) as a moderator variable. Recall the results indicated the theory was equally valid in simulation and real research settings. To again address this "reality" issue, we

(Graham et al, 1997) also examined a real life event, the alleged murders by O. J. Simpson, which received a great deal of public attention, to determine if the ideas presented about punishment goals also hold in actual life contexts.

I will not delve into the case in detail but remind readers that O. J. Simpson, a famous football hero and movie star, was accused of killing his wife and another man out of apparent jealousy. Soon after the crime, we had respondents report their perceived cause of the murders and make judgments of control, responsibility, anger, sympathy, stability, and the expectancy of future crimes by Mr. Simpson. We also described the goals of punishment, including retribution and three utilitarian goals: rehabilitation, protection of harmed others, and more general deterrence. Participants were asked to what extent they would punish Mr. Simpson and the reason this sentence was recommended.

Table 4.5 displays the determinants of retributive and utilitarian goals. In this table, the variables are regressed on four punishment goals to determine their relative influence (the beta sign indicates strength of the relations or the

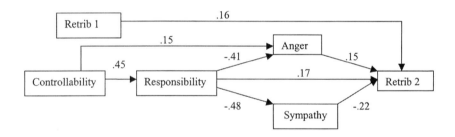

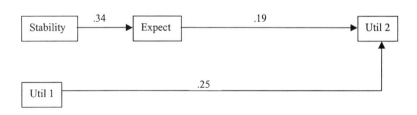

FIG. 4.4.   Best fitting model relating controllability, stability, and general punishment goals (Retrib 1 and Util 1) to cognitive and affective mediators and specific punishment goals (Retrib 2 and Util 2) for this crime (data from Graham, Weiner, & Zucker, 1997, p. 343).

TABLE 4.5

Multiple Regressions Predicting Punishment Goals From the Attribution Variables

| | | | | | Punishment Goal | | | | |
| | Retribution | | Rehabilitation | | Protection | | Deterrence | |
Predictors	β	t	β	t	β	t	β	t
Control	–.05	< 1	–.05	< 1	–.03	< 1	.15	1.90
Responsibility	.17	2.07*	.00	< 1	.04	< 1	.19	2.15*
Anger	.30	4.04***	.11	1.54	–.03	< 1	–.04	< 1
Sympathy	–.30	–3.68***	.39	5.18***	–.07	< 1	–.13	–1.54
Stability	–.01	< 1	–.34	–4.85***	.19	2.33***	.04	< 1
Expectancy	–.10	–1.33	–.06	< 1	.27	3.36***	.08	1.04

Note. Data from Graham, Weiner, and Zucker (1997), p. 337.

variance accounted for holding all else constant). Table 4.5 reveals that desires for retribution are primarily determined by anger and sympathy, followed in importance by perceptions of responsibility. This is consistent with data in the simulation study depicted in Fig. 4.4. Findings regarding utilitarian goals are more complex and not the same between the utilitarian distinctions. The clearest result is one of absence: only one of the utilitarian goals is associated with an emotional reaction (rehabilitation with sympathy), and responsibility only relates to deterrence goals (but see Feather, Boeckmann, & McKee, 2001, who find that sympathy plays a role in sentencing decisions). On the other hand, causal stability, which is associated with future expectations, predicts two utilitarian goals (rehabilitation and protection). In general, then, the pattern of data closely (but not perfectly) replicates those reported in simulation studies. Retribution is a reaction to moral injustice (perceived responsibility and the affects this generates), whereas utilitarian goals reflect a preoccupation with the future, which is determined by perceptions of causal stability.

The Punishment Process in Achievement Contexts.   I now turn from criminal contexts to achievement settings. The same general research paradigms in the criminal contexts were repeated given achievement settings, again using both simulation and real life settings (Reyna & Weiner, 2001). In the simulation research, controllability and stability were manipulated as in prior experiments. Specifically, failure was described as due to permanent (the student is lazy) or temporary lack of effort, or permanent (low intelligence) or temporary lack of ability. In addition to assessing endorsement of retributive and utilitarian goals, there was measurement of perceived controllability, responsibility, anger, and sympathy in the four conditions. Thus, all variables in the proposed motivation sequence were included.

Table 4.6 shows endorsement of the punishment goals as a function of the controllability and stability of the causes. Retribution is more often chosen as the goal of punishment given controllable rather than uncontrollable causality, whereas this is not the case given utilitarian goals. Furthermore, if the cause is controllable and stable (laziness), then endorsement of retributive goals exceeds utilitarian ratings, whereas given uncontrollability, goals of punishment are more utilitarian than retributive.

Figure 4.5 depicts the path diagram relating retributive goals to causal beliefs and emotions. The figure reveals controllable causality elicits responsibility judgments. Responsibility, in turn, augments anger, which increases retributive desires, and reduces sympathy, which decreases retributive goals. In sum, the model for retribution perfectly supports the theoretical analysis. Utilitarian goals, not shown here, relate only to causal stability.

TABLE 4.6

Mean Endorsement of Retributive and Utilitarian Goals for Feedback, Across
the Attribution Dimensions of Controllability and Stability

	Retribution		Utility	
	Stable	Not Stable	Stable	Not Stable
Controllable	5.48	4.68	4.63	5.56
Not Controllable	3.77	3.90	5.31	5.16

Note. Data from Reyna and Weiner (2001), p. 311.

In a final study in achievement contexts, we examined teachers' judgments about punishment in classroom contexts. In the public education system, teachers have considerable freedom to operate their classrooms as they see fit, as long as their system conforms to guidelines of conduct mandated by their school district and the law. This leaves teachers with a number of possible interventions for motivating and/or reprimanding students who commit classroom transgressions.

To determine what intervention decisions teachers use in the classroom, we conducted a focus group with teachers, which generated 18 common disciplinary actions. These ranged in severity from sending the student to the principal and removing privileges to ignoring the student, giving extra work assignments, and even praise. The teachers also rated whether these interventions served retributive or utilitarian goals. Endorsement of these 18 items and their ratings on punishment goals revealed they could be classified into distinct categories. Two of these categories were labeled *punitive intervention* and *retribution*. The interventions described by these factors included scolding the student in front of the classroom and giving detention. Two other scales were labeled *positive reinforcement* and *favors*. The behaviors on these scales included praising and rewarding the student, using different grading criteria than for other class members, and giving the student the opportunity to make up for a bad grade. These strategies were rated by teachers as more utilitarian than retributive.

Then another group of teachers was given the four achievement scenarios already described and shown in Box 4.2. These teachers rated their likelihood of using the 18 disciplinary actions, which had been classified as retributive or utilitarian, as well as indicating their responsibility beliefs and anger and sympathy. Figure 4.6 depicts the findings. The figure shows that controllability relates to responsibility, which promotes anger and a lack of sympathy. Only (lack of) sympathy predicts retributive desires. Hence, at times anger, at times sympathy, and on

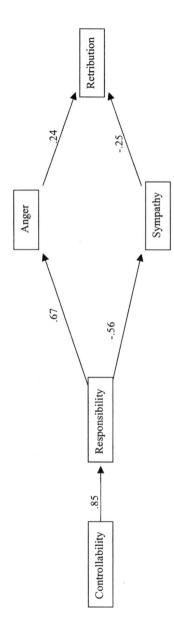

FIG. 4.5.   Mediational model between attributions, responsibility inferences, emotions, and retributive goals (data from Reyna & Weiner, 2001, p. 313).

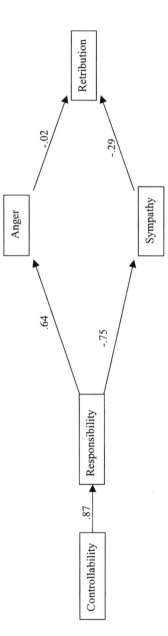

FIG. 4.6.   Mediational model between attributions, responsibility inferences, emotions, and retributive goals (data from Reyna & Weiner, 2001, p. 314).

other occasions both these emotions, along with perceptions of responsibility, directly relate to retribution. The reason for this inconsistency is unknown and is one indication of the complexity of this process. In addition, utilitarian desires, again not shown in the figure, relate primarily to causal stability.

Hence, although the same actions have retributive and utilitarian functions, teacher disciplinary actions differentially capture these goals in a manner consistent with attribution theorizing. Even classroom teachers, who generally consider the future and behavior change, use retributive punishment and select punishment strategies based on beliefs about causes of classroom shortcomings.

Summary

It has been documented that there is more to punishment life than desiring to change responses of the acting organism. Some of the reasons for punishment, neglected from an operant perspective, include retribution, which might or might not include revenge and expiation; rehabilitation; and altering the likelihood of transgressions of noninvolved or third-party others.

These socially oriented goals of punishment are closely linked to causal beliefs. Controllable causality is associated with retributive rather than utilitarian functions, whereas causal stability is more linked with utilitarian than retributive goals. These rules transcend criminal contexts, being applicable as well to the classroom and achievement settings. Principles derived from law, theology, and philosophy thus again display their importance in the study of motivated behavior.

Two areas of punishment addressed by attribution theory—the reversed motivation effects of reward and punishment and the varied purposes of punishment—have been examined. I now turn to a third avenue of attribution research, namely, how compliance for anticipated reward as opposed to compliance because of threatened punishment influence responsibility judgments and the consequences of that compliance.

CONSEQUENCES OF ANTICIPATED REWARD AND THREAT OF PUNISHMENT ON JUDGMENTS OF RESPONSIBILITY

Early in the study of attribution theory, it was postulated that inferences about dispositions of others are most certain when the observed behavior is inconsistent with social norms in that context. For example, one is likely to attribute an aggressive disposition to a job applicant acting in a hostile manner (inconsistent with norms), whereas it is unclear whether this person is generally "submissive" based on evidence of acting in an overly polite manner during a job interview, which is consistent with normative behavior (Jones, Davis, & Gergen, 1961). In a similar manner, a person talking in the library is regarded as more extroverted than another who engages in the same behavior while at a party.

The determinants of dispositional attributions also have been studied by attribution theorists in contexts of surveillance and potential punishment. For example, Strickland (1958) assigned a subject to act as supervisor over two other (fictitious) students supposedly performing a dull task. The supervisor had the power to observe and punish one of the workers more than the other. The subject (supervisor) was given feedback that the two workers exhibited identical satisfactory performance and punishment was never administered. Nevertheless, compared to the unsupervised worker, participants ascribed performance of the monitored worker more to external threat of punishment, verbalized less trust of him, and monitored him more when later tasks were given. In sum, power over another, even if not used, results in attributions for successful outcomes to the power source.

There are many types of power used to induce compliance, including reward and punishment (see discussion in chap. 1), which I focus on here. Research initiated by Rodrigues (1995) and Rodrigues and Lloyd (1998) documents that if a person complies with a request to transgress, then consequences differ when compliance is induced by potential reward as opposed to threatened punishment. The asymmetry reported by Rodrigues (1995) and Rodrigues and Lloyd (1998) was compliance to transgress given the promise of reward is more attributed to the person, and that individual is considered more responsible for the transgression, than given behavior compliance when threatened with punishment (see Reeder & Spores, 1983; Wells, 1980). Specifically, for example, as indicated in chapter 1, if a nurse carries out the request of a doctor to administer a drug not officially approved, then the nurse is more responsible for this transgression when the compliance follows the promise of a pay raise, as opposed to a threat that wages will be lowered if the drug is not administered. Accepting reward for a transgression marks the person a sinner and places him or her in the top half of Fig. 1.4, whereas undertaking the transgression to avoid punishment results in the complier being placed conceptually at the bottom half of Fig. 1.4. The potential punishment mitigates a judgment of responsibility.

Here I address three questions raised by these findings:

1. Are these effects observed across a variety of transgressions and incentives? That is, how general and reliable are these findings?

2. Are these effects due to differences in perceived rates of compliance, that is, to unequal social norms associated with the behavior, as illustrated in the talking in the library versus at a party example given earlier? If more individuals are believed to perform a transgression to avoid punishment than to receive a reward, then differences in attribution judgments could be due to disparate social norms associated with the behavior rather than to the incentive valence per se. Stated somewhat differently, if many individuals transgress to avoid punishment, then the cause of the action is considered the negative incentive rather than the person. Conversely, if few individuals transgress to gain reward, then the cause of the transgression is ascribed to the person rather than the incentive. Controlling social norms associated with the behavior is in some sense equivalent to holding the subjective magnitude of the incentives constant.

3. What are some possible theoretical explanations of these phenomena and how do they relate to the theory of social motivation and social justice advocated here?

Further Empirical Evidence and the Role of Social Norms

Consider the following vignette, used in a series of studies conducted by Greitemeyer and Weiner (2003):

> A faculty member is teaching a large class. This person approaches the teaching assistant (TA) and says that the ratings have not been high enough and asks if the TA would insert about 20 false ratings [faked class evaluations] into the packet, even though that is illegal. What the faculty member says to the TA is given below. The TA complies and inserts 20 false ratings into the packet. (p. 1373)

Some of the incentives offered the TA are shown in Box 4.3, which readers are invited to complete. They are, for example, "I will make sure you do [or, in the case of punishment, do not] get the fellowship you applied for next year." The readers, just as the participants, are asked to report to what extent the TA is responsible for compliance and what percentage of TAs would comply with the request.

The data for this study are given in Table 4.7, which shows the paired incentives, ratings of personal responsibility (R) for the transgression and perceived compliance (C) rates (that is, what percent of TAs would engage in the behavior) in three different experiments. It first should be noted that the perceived compliance rates do not differ as a function of incentive valence (reward or positive valence versus punishment or negative valence). Thus, any differ-

BOX 4.3   Responsibility for a Transgression

A faculty member is teaching a large class. This person approaches the teaching assistant (TA) and says that the ratings have not been high enough and asks if the TA would insert about 20 false ratings in the packet, even though that is illegal. What the faculty member says to the TA is given below. The TA complies and inserts 20 false ratings into the packet. You are asked to indicate how responsible the TA is for the compliance and what percentage of the TAs do you think would comply with the request. Responsibility ratings are from 9 (very responsible) to 1 (not responsible at all). Compliance ratings are from 0% to 100%.

	Responsibility 1 = not responsible at all 9 = very responsible	Compliance 0% to 100%
1. I will make sure that you get the fellowship you applied for next year.		
2. I will make sure that you don't get the fellowship you applied for next year.		
3. I will write a strong letter of recommondation for the job you applied for next year.		
4. I will write a weak letter of recommendation for the job you applied for next year.		
5. I will do you a favor.		
6. I won't do you a favor.		

ences in perceived responsibility as a function of incentive valence are not due to inequalities in perceived social norms.

The table also reveals that perceived responsibility is greater in the reward than punishment incentive condition. Thus, for example, if the TA complies to receive a strong letter of recommendation, then he or she is more responsible ($x = 7.15$ across three experiments) than when complying to prevent a weak letter of recommendation ($x = 6.35$). But this finding does interact with perceived social norms (see Fig. 4.7). Figure 4.7 shows the judgments of responsibility as a function of the valence of the incentive and perceived com-

TABLE 4.7

Mean Ratings for Rates of Compliance and Perceived Responsibility as a Function of Kinds of Positive and Negative Incentives in Three Experiments

Positive and Negative Incentives	Experiment 1		Experiment 2		Experiment 3	
	C	R	C	R	C	R
I will make sure you get the fellowship you applied for next year.	74.1	6.83	54.3	7.24	55.7	6.68
I will make sure that you don't get the fellowship you applied for next year.	66.2	5.91	51.0	6.35	57.6	4.45
I will give you a very high grade on your final thesis.	66.8	7.28	50.4	7.32	57.6	7.32
I will give you a poor grade on your final thesis.	70.1	5.60	50.1	6.41	62.2	4.77
I will see to it that you get the job you applied for next year.	69.2	6.93	51.9	7.49	58.0	7.15
I will see to it that you won't get the job you applied for next year.	66.8	5.48	52.9	6.81	59.3	4.87
I will write a strong letter of recommendation for the job you applied for next year.	62.9	7.13	45.6	7.35	45.7	6.96
I will write a weak letter of recommendation for the job you applied for next year.	49.5	6.37	45.1	6.81	40.0	5.87
I will see to it that you will get some extra TA-money.	46.4	7.50	39.7	7.81	37.0	7.26
I will see to it that you get less TA-money.	55.8	6.21	37.4	7.16	46.9	5.89
I will make sure you get an easy TA-ship next year.	45.1	7.11	36.2	7.92	35.6	7.15
I will make sure you get a difficult TA-ship next year.	34.1	5.95	40.7	7.30	30.4	5.60
I won't ask you to help with the grading and other work during the final exam.	33.3	7.26	30.5	8.16	34.6	7.04
I will give you a great deal of work with the grading and other tasks regarding the final exam.	38.9	6.49	36.4	7.54	31.8	6.04
I will give you a great deal of work with the grading and other tasks regarding the final exam.	38.9	6.49	36.4	7.54	31.8	6.04
I will do you a favor.	42.0	7.27	40.5	8.22	33.0	7.38
I won't do you a favor.	22.6	7.10	40.8	8.22	20.2	7.09
I will be very grateful.	30.5	6.95	27.1	8.05	28.5	7.00
I will be very angry.	33.6	6.67	28.4	8.05	29.6	6.00

Note. The positive incentive followed the words: "If you do this"; the negative incentive followed the words: "If you don't do this."
C = Compliance; R = Responsibility. Data from Greitemeyer and Weiner (2003), p. 1374.

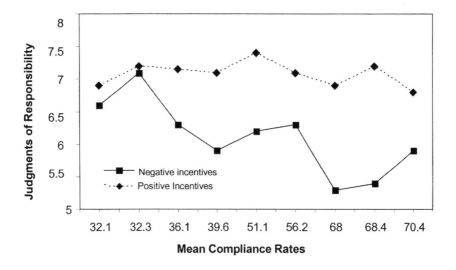

FIG. 4.7.   Judgments of responsibility for a transgression as a function of mean compliance rates and the valence of the incentive given for the transgression (data from Greitemeyer & Weiner, 2003, p. 1374).

pliance rates in nine incentive conditions. The figure reveals that when compliance rates are low (e.g., 32%), then incentive valence has relatively little effect on responsibility judgments. On the other hand, when there is high compliance (e.g., 70%), then the difference between reward and punishment on perception of responsibility is augmented. Even though many people are presumed to comply with a transgression request when the incentive is very attractive, the compliers nonetheless are held responsible. That is, social norms do not mitigate the responsibility judgment. Another way of stating these relations is that low social norms result in judgments of high responsibility for transgressions given either reward and punishment. On the other hand, high norms lower judged responsibility when the incentive valence is negative but not when it is positive. For example, if everyone agrees to commit a minor crime for a million dollars, this reveals not only that the reward is a highly valued incentive but also that compliers are greedy (immoral). However, if all agree to commit a small crime to avoid something of great value being taken away, then this primarily shows the loss is major and not that compliers are to be faulted. We have found this pattern of results using a variety of transgression settings and incentives, so it is a "fact" (see Greitemeyer & Weiner, 2003). I believe the responses of the readers in Box 4.3 also support this conclusion.

Theoretical Interpretations

Theoretical explanations of these findings are available, although none has been subject to direct testing or is able to account for all the data. Possible interpretations are derived from legal theory, Lewinian theory, and prospect theory. These are examined in turn.

Legal Theory. In the law, duress mitigates responsibility (see LaFave & Scott, 1986, chap. 5). If someone is illegally forced to do (or to forbear) some act by threat of violence or fear of serious injury, then that person is not responsible for a subsequent misdeed. For example, if a bank robber forces a customer in the bank to assist in the collection of money by pointing a gun at him or her, then that bank customer is not held responsible for the act. In the law, duress can be inferred only given the possibility of physical violence, and typically only extreme violence. Thus, if the robber says: "Help me pick up the money or I will hit you on the arm," then duress is not presumed and the person is fully responsible if assistance was given. In the compliance vignettes described here, threats by the professor did not include physical violence. Nonetheless, to the layperson, many threats of hardship are regarded as duress and reduce perceptions of responsibility (see Robinson & Darley, 1995, for other legal–layperson discrepancies). Reward, on the other hand, does not have the same status as a mitigator of duress; responsibility is not lessened given positive incentives to commit a transgression.

Although this explanation seems quite reasonable and "correct," it also has characteristics of circularity in merely stating, albeit in a more general language, what actually occurred. That is, given duress (a negative incentive), responsibility in some conditions is lessened, whereas this is not the case given a reward. Hence, one can question its value as providing an "explanation." Two other theoretical approaches do not have this shortcoming and are grounded in psychological concepts and theories rather than the law.

Lewinian Theory. Kurt Lewin (1935) has been mentioned frequently in this book, not only for positing one of the now defunct "grand theories," but also as one of the earliest Expectancy × Value theorists. His ideas had great impact on Fritz Heider, the "founder" of attribution theory (see Weiner, 1990).

In Lewinian theory, a need, desire, or want creates (imbues an object with) a positive incentive (valence) that fulfills the need state. Food, for example, becomes a positive incentive if and only if one is hungry. And a special raise is an incentive only to a person desirous of money. Positive incentives and person inferences are joined, or linked, in Lewinian theory in that incentives do not psychologically exist without a corresponding need in the person.

But Lewin could not readily apply this analysis to situations of negative va-lence. Aversive incentives are less dependent on and intertwined with the needs of the person. For example, the desire to avoid shock exists even when one is not being shocked. It therefore would be anticipated, given this theoreti-cal perspective, that there are greater person inferences given compliance for reward rather than for fear of anticipated punishment.

Prospect Theory. Prospect theory, as formulated by Kahneman and Tversky (1979; see Tversky & Kahneman, 1992) is a theory of choice behavior but nonetheless is applicable in the present context. This theory points out there are different evaluations for gains and losses such that losses loom larger than gains. Kahneman and Tversky (1979) state, "The aggravation that one experiences in losing a sum of money appears to be greater than the pleasure as-sociated with gaining the same amount" (p. 279). If losses are weighted more than gains in choice, then perhaps this also is reflected in the importance of in-centive valence in determining, and mitigating, responsibility judgments. The greater importance of an aversive relative to a positive incentive in inducing behavior implies that the person is less causal given a negative than a positive incentive.

Although this theory captures the findings regarding responsibility judg-ments, there were no compliance differences between the positive and nega-tive valence situations we examined, as prospect theory anticipates. Hence, the applicability of this theory to the present findings is unclear, although it cer-tainly provides food for thought.

In sum, as already indicated, observations regarding the asymmetrical ef-fects of reward and punishment on attribution judgments are quite consistent. This finding is beyond the range of Thorndike and Skinner, given their concern with behavior and behavior change. However, the theoretical explanation of the phenomenon remains uncertain. What is certain is that accepting rewards for a transgression is regarded as immoral, no matter how enticing the reward, whereas transgressing to avoid punishment relatively frees one from the "sin-ner" label.

SUMMARY

The theme of reward/punishment remains very central in psychological study. These behavioral consequences are believed to cement or weaken what hap-pened in the past and to pull the organisms to behaviors in the future because of their linkage to hedonic pursuits that characterize living things. In this chapter, I have shown how causal attributions and judgments of responsibility call into question some previous principles regarding reward and punishment and provide new research directions.

1. It has been documented that reward for behavior might decrease motivation, whereas punishment can increase motivation. These observations, which contradict simple behaviorist notions, arise because reward and punishment provide information about ability and effort to the person undertaking a task. Reward for success may indicate that the outcome was due to high effort, implying that the rewarded individual has relatively low ability. This self-perception can impact negatively on future motivation. Conversely, punishment for failure implies that the negative outcome was due to lack of effort and that the person has high ability. High ability as a personal construal positively contributes to motivation. These theoretical derivations are supported in empirical studies where causal ascriptions are assessed following reward and punishment, praise and criticism, and help as opposed to neglect.

2. Punishment is not administered merely to change the behavior of the actor, which is the position of behaviorism. Rather, punishment is given for retributive and/or utilitarian purposes. Retributive goals are elicited when the cause of a negative outcome is controllable by the person. Hence, the individual is considered responsible and is the target of anger rather than sympathy. On the other hand, utilitarian goals are guided by perceptions of causal stability, which impact future expectancies. These theoretical analyses were upheld empirically in criminal as well as achievement contexts and in simulation and "real" settings.

3. Anticipated reward and threat of punishment for compliance to commit a transgression result in unequal inferences about causes of the compliance. Given a promised reward, the person undertaking an immoral act is regarded as responsible, even though many others engage in the behavior. That is, high social norms do not mitigate responsibility judgments. On the other hand, given a transgression to avoid punishment, the person engaging in the misdeed is relatively absolved from responsibility, particularly when others also commit the transgression. That is, given behavior to avoid punishment, high compliance norms mitigate responsibility judgments. Explanations derived from legal theory, Lewinian theory, and prospect theory may account for these findings, although this remains to be proven.

I have shown that attribution theory expands our understanding of some issues associated with reward/punishment in a manner not addressed by other conceptions. These empirical and theoretical extensions are important in that punishment is at the core of social motivation and social justice. The applicability of the theory to topics related to punishment again illustrates the potential richness and relational fertility of this approach.

✿ 5 ✿

A Visit to the Courtroom Settings: Is the Theory Useful?

I hold Kurt Lewin personally responsible for spreading the rumor that "there is nothing as practical as a good theory." In my experience, there is nothing as practical as a simple, atheoretical rule! The principle that reward increases the probability of the prior response whereas punishment decreases that likelihood has been used in millions of homes and schools to change behavior by individuals who never heard the name "Skinner" or know the meaning of "theory." This rule does not invariably hold, as indicated in chapter 3 when discussing reward as a cue for low ability and punishment as a cue for lack of effort. However, it is sufficiently accurate to be used in thousands of pharmaceutical trials to assess the incentive value of various substances.

It is difficult to find any practical value in theories of motivation or social psychology. The proposed conceptual systems do add knowledge and understanding; if mastery is one of the goals of humans, then the theories certainly serve that function. But if someone severely depressed is seeking relief, surely drugs will prove more helpful than a theory of human motivation. And if we wish a rat to turn right at a choice point, then placing food there will be effective without a conceptual analysis of incentive. When social psychologists are asked about the practical value of their ideas, they often search their memories back to the 30-year old studies of obedience by Milgram or the prison research by Zimbardo or the "group-think" of Janis, or even earlier to the research on group dynamics by Lewin (see Zimbardo, 2004). Yet even these demonstrations have been rarely applied to change human conduct (assuming they in fact would be successful), and they are derived from social psychology rather than from the study of motivation. Perhaps Lewin should have said, "There is nothing practical in a good theory," or "Practicality needs no theory," and found contentment in his conceptual representation of the so-called "life space," leaving applications to others with less theoretical desires.

Alas, however, it is difficult to prevent seeking personal validation by applying one's theory to everyday concerns. I share this frailty and in this chapter the usefulness of the proposed attribution theory of social motivation and justice is considered. Inasmuch as this theory often captures naïve beliefs, a difficult challenge is faced in that a number of practical suggestions already are in use. For example, one derivation from the theory is that reprimand for a transgression might be escaped with a good excuse (see chap. 4). Theoretically, this alters attributions from controllable to uncontrollable, decreases anger, and increases prosocial responses. I have never had a student say to me, "Would you consider raising my grade on the final? I did poorly because I did not bother to study." But the proverbial excuses "my grandmother died" or "I had the flu" are given. These students have not had (formal) training in attribution theory, yet they give the "correct" excuse; that is, they make use of attribution principles in daily interactions. Is the theory therefore "useful" and "applicable," or will it prove irrelevant to everyday concerns inasmuch as the theory is being applied without knowledge of the formal conception?

In this chapter the practical application issue is addressed. The focus is not on what is an outgrowth of naïve attribution analyses, although these observations are not completely neglected. Rather, I consider logical deductions from the theory that can be of future use. I address six topics: the classroom, mental illness and other stigmas including lung cancer, marital satisfaction, consumer behavior, and aggression. Impression management also is considered within these settings.

THE CLASSROOM AS A COURTROOM

One can identify a variety of metaphors pertinent to education and classroom behavior. Among these, educational institutions have been described as "temples of learning" and one hears of the "hallowed halls" of academia, which capture the metaphor of school and the classroom as religious or sacred sites. Conversely, schools may be regarded as commercial settings, under whose roofs there is a "marketplace of ideas" where "free exchange" and "give and take" are fostered. It is not unreasonable to speculate that these respective metaphors of the spiritual and the material are associated with (give rise to?) disparate types of instructional activity, classroom behavior, and school norms. Indeed, even the architecture linked with these contrasting metaphors is likely to be distinct (Gothic structures versus open walls).

"The classroom is a courtroom" (a variant of the book theme that life is a courtroom) is another metaphor pertinent to learning institutions and classroom settings. Consider the following findings consistent with this metaphor, which were introduced in prior chapters of the book:

1. Evaluative exam feedback, just as criminal sentencing, is determined by (at least) two components: objective exam outcome (given failure, the seriousness of the crime, or *actus reas*), and the degree to which the failing student is blameworthy or responsible for the poor performance (effort expenditure, or *mens rea*; see chap. 1). In more primitive settings and at levels of lesser moral development, criminal punishment may be based solely on crime seriousness (strict liability). Similarly, in many school settings, performance score is the only principle of evaluation.

2. It is regarded as fair or just to use beliefs about responsibility and inferences of a "guilty mind" as one determinant of achievement appraisal (see chap. 1). This may not be as taken for granted in achievement as in criminal contexts, but nonetheless the rule is consistent with an accepted code of conduct. Individuals low in ability are held to a different standard of accountability than are the highly able.

3. Retributive versus utilitarian goals underlie punishment of a failing student as well as a criminal offender. In both educational and criminal settings, responsibility for a transgression (exam failure or a crime) affects which goal is pursued, with inferences of responsibility evoking retributive goals whereas nonresponsibility promotes utilitarian ends. Although classroom teachers focus on the future and behavior change, they nonetheless also make use of retributive punishment (see chap. 4).

4. There is a similarity in the impression management techniques, or devices used to "look good," in achievement and criminal contexts. In both settings the accused seeks to decrease attributions of controllability and inferences of personal responsibility (see chap. 3). The achievement literature has maintained that students wish to convey they have high ability (see Covington, 1992). But the metaphor of the classroom as a courtroom aids in understanding why this is not always the case—low ability/high effort communications are functional for they reduce punishment given failure. The impression management strategies of students, as well as criminals, therefore include communicating lack of capacity, which reduces responsibility and antisocial reactions.

In sum, there is a great deal of evidence that the classroom is guided by the same rules and beliefs evident in the courtroom.

Practical Considerations

Unlike most metaphors, which are relatively benign, the metaphor of the classroom as a courtroom seems especially pernicious. One reason for this is that a metaphor is not merely imposed as an aid to understanding but also guides behavior. A student considering the classroom as a courtroom is apt to be motivated by the avoidance of punishment. Hence, acceptable classroom strategies include deceit and excuse giving (hoping one will not "get caught"), while the construal of a teacher is not as an ally or helper, but rather as a judge or prison guard who administers "just deserts." A school, just like the courtroom, is therefore a place to be avoided—an aversive setting with in-group and out-group divisions (accusers and the accused, teachers and students).

This description contrasts with students directed by the metaphors of the classroom as a "temple of learning" or "marketplace of ideas," which promote the goals of understanding and mastery rather than deceit and escape from punishment. Temples and marketplaces are associated with respect and excitement, locations to be sought rather than avoided.

A setting fostering a courtroom metaphor also will disappoint teachers, for it is unlikely they want to be considered "judges of crimes" as opposed to facilitators of learning. Additionally, those who have been sentenced seek to impose their own retributive justice and revenge to "get back" at the judges. This is increasingly apparent in schools, where violence toward teachers has increased dramatically.

What, then, can be done by teachers and educational administrators to combat this metaphor? Unfortunately, this question is more readily formulated than answered. One might eliminate grading systems and other forms of evaluation (one of the most repeated sentences imposed by teachers), but this comes with great costs, and universities attempting to do this have not met with success. In one variant of this strategy, when Maynard Hutchins was chancellor of the University of Chicago, in the 1940s, course exams were neither created nor graded by the classroom teacher, but rather were under the control of an external Board of Examiners. This facilitated a student–teacher relationship less linked to evaluation, and therefore the perception of the teacher as a judge should have weakened.

Classroom seating arrangements (e.g., circular rather than hierarchical), accessibility and demeanor of the teacher (democratic rather than authoritarian), and the type of feedback given to students (informative rather than evaluative) are just a few strategic interventions that could decrease activation of the classroom as courtroom metaphor. As already admitted, and to no one's surprise, changing the perception of the teacher from a judge to a helper, facilitator, and promoter is not readily solvable by this writer and surely falls beyond the range of this book and my expertise. But the courtroom metaphor is useful when considering classroom interventions to augment student motivation.

A Teacher-Training Course

A number of additional principles voiced throughout the book can prove helpful to teachers as they go about their difficult tasks. These include the following:

1. Certain communications to students function as low-ability cues, although this was not the intent of the teacher. The good intention–bad outcome practices include praise and/or other rewards for success at an easy task; lack of punishment, the absence of anger, and sympathy given failure at an easy task; and help extended when it is not needed (see chap. 4). These conclusions follow because of the bidirectional linkages in the theory (e.g., just as lack of ability begets sympathy, expressions of sympathy indicate to the student he or she "cannot"). It is important that teachers in and out of the classroom be aware of the presence and dangers of low-ability communications. For example, on the baseball field I recently heard a coach say: "The team picking Jimmy gets to bat first"; followed by: "Jimmy, you play right field; Johnny, you play second base and play deep to help Jimmy." This coach did not intend to undermine Jimmy's esteem, but surely that was one outcome of these messages. The potential to transfer increased awareness into practice is a central component of the value of attribution theory.

2. It was documented in chapter 4 that the use of punishment to alter behavior results in an attribution for behavior change to that aversive incentive, whereas behavioral improvement in the presence of reward also produces an attribution for change to the person. Hence, from the perspective advanced here, reward is a more effective motivator than punishment in that it promotes positive attributions. This, in turn, will elicit reduced monitoring of the "criminal" and more opportunities for his or her self-enhancement.

The applications of attribution theory to the classroom are more salient when considering intrapersonal rather than interpersonal behavior. Changing personal attributions for success and failure has significant effects on subsequent performance. For example, altering attributions for failure from low aptitude to lack of effort enhances expectancy of success, reduces shame, promotes guilt, and fosters motivation. The applications of the interpersonal theory may be less evident and dramatic, requiring the effects to be initiated from the perspective of observers. Nevertheless, as indicated in the prior pages, the interpersonal theory certainly is applicable to ameliorate classroom problems.

THE MENTALLY ILL AND OTHERS STIGMATIZED IN THE COURTROOM OF LIFE

In the courtroom, the mentally ill are not treated as severely for a crime as the sane. Mental illness mitigates responsibility—to be held fully responsible or accountable for an untoward action, the transgressor must be able to discriminate right from wrong, or good from evil. In addition, the perpetrator of the crime must be perceived as having volitional control over his or her actions. Committing a crime because inner voices "command" that deed indicates that one is not fully responsible for a transgression. The sentence, therefore, is less retributive and severe than would be the case without this mitigator of responsibility.

But how do the mentally ill fare in the courtroom of life as opposed to the legal courtroom, and particularly within the context of the family? Are ordinary people as responsive to the plight of the mentally ill as courtroom judges? Are the mentally ill judged "sick" and forgiven, or perceived as "sinners," to be dealt with harshly?

At one time in American history, mental illness was viewed moralistically, with demonic possession considered a product of sin because of intentional cavorting with the devil. In a relatively recent study still supporting some aspects of this view, Neff and Husaini (1985) report that in a survey of about 700 rural respondents, more than 40% of the sample considered mentally ill others morally weak and responsible for their behaviors.

However, perceptions of the cause of illness and stigmas can dramatically shift over time. For example, homosexuality increasingly is being viewed as caused by biological givens rather than weak morals, and the cause of AIDS no longer is considered by many to be God's desire for vengeance. In a similar manner, the perceived causes of mental illness are undergoing change and currently there are great disparities in people's beliefs. These differences, and their consequences, are captured in an area of research known as expressed emotion, or EE.

Expressed Emotion

In the current climate of the growth of neuropsychology and medical models of mental illness, genetic (biological) explanations for the major mental disorders of schizophrenia and depression (particularly bipolar depression) predominate, along with drug treatments rather than extensive psychotherapy. Correspondingly, attention given to psychosocial influences on severe mental illness has declined. Among the psychosocial concerns and constructs exhibiting staying power and vitality is expressed emotion, or what is known as EE, which calls attention to the moral aspects of mental illness (but not devil worship).

EE reflects critical and hostile attitudes on the part of a family member toward a relative with a disorder or impairment. EE is not just general emotional expressiveness; it concerns the extent to which an individual family member talks about another family member in a negative manner. EE has assumed a central place in the psychosocial mental health literature because "EE is now a well-validated predictor of poor clinical outcome for this disorder [schizophrenia] as well as for other psychiatric conditions" (Barrowclough & Hooley, 2003, p. 849). Supporting this conclusion, in a meta-analysis of 26 studies (Butzlaff & Hooley, 1998), it was concluded that "living in a high-EE home environment more than doubled the baseline relapse rate for schizophrenia patients 9 to 12 months after hospitalization" (Barrowclough & Hooley, 2003, p. 849).

Throughout this book, it has been reasoned that verbal and behavioral aggression often follow anger, and anger is a product of attributions of control and inferences of responsibility for a negative act. Hence, the conceptual analysis of EE from an attribution perspective is:

Schizophrenic behaviors—perceived under personal control—mentally ill
    person is responsible for these actions—anger and hostile response
    toward that person (EE)—poor clinical outcome (recidivism)

What is the empirical evidence supporting the assertion that the EE literature is amenable to an attribution perspective, which adds notions of free will and responsibility into the analysis? How are the research studies conducted and what are the findings? Typically, in this research a semistructured interview is given to the main caretaker of the mentally ill person. This audiotaped interview is then rated for indicators of hostility and criticism, and the respondents are classified as high or low on EE (as well as a category of total overinvolvement not discussed here). In addition, the tapes can be scored for attributions of personal control (in some research, rating scales of attributions also are administered). This attributional direction, primarily originated by Hooley (1985, 1987), examines whether the respondent believes undesirable behaviors can be volitionally changed by the patient (e.g., "Just because he has schizophrenia doesn't mean he can't wash once in a while"). Finally, the relapse rates for the schizophrenic patients also are determined.

In their review of the pertinent research, Barrowclough and Hooley (2003) found 13 published studies with different samples that examined the relation between attributions for the negative behavior of the mentally ill person and EE. They conclude:

> There is one clear and consistent finding that stands out in any review of the EE and attribution literature. Stated simply, relatives who are high-EE by virtue of being critical or hostile make attributions that are different from relatives who are low-EE.... Across all studies, relatives who are rated as high-EE because they are critical consistently attribute more control to patients for their symptoms and problems than do relatives who are low in criticism. This is even true of relatives of high-EE patients in China. (Yang et al., 2003)

> There is also a positive correlation between numbers of criticisms relatives make and the size of the controllability attribution bias that they hold. (Barrowclough & Hooley, 2003, p. 863)

Given the strength and consistency of the research findings, one might think most issues surrounding EE and attribution have been laid to rest. This is not the case. For example, according to the theory espoused here, EE (affect) should be a better and more proximate predictor of relapse than are attributions, whereas Barrowclough, Tarrier, and Johnston (1994) make a contrasting argument for the prime importance of attributions. Thus, even theoretically derived hypotheses are at issue. In addition, some researchers (e.g., Lopez et al., 1999) find that attributions and criticisms together are the best predictors of relapse, thereby again posing the question of the direct rather than (or, in addition to) indirect influence of thoughts on action. Furthermore, an argument might be made that uncontrollable attributions lead to positive affects and these, in turn, should decrease relapse rate. Although there is some support for this line of reasoning (see Weisman, Lopez, Karno, & Jenkins, 1993), the evidence is sparse. In sum (and as usual), much further research is needed. However, it is evident that the theoretical and empirical foundations for this research have been established.

Practical Implications

If EE harms the patient by promoting relapse, psychoeducational interventions with caregivers are called for to alter perceptions of the controllability of the illness symptoms and the linked negative affects and hostile responding that promote relapse. That is, attribution training should be instituted to change the home environment. Although family-based interventions with schizophrenic patients are prevalent, the focus on attributions and their consequences is in the beginning stage. On a positive note, relapse rates for patients in high-EE families are reduced when hostility and criticism by family members lessen (see Pitschel-Waltz, Leucht, Bauml, Kissling, & Engel, 2001). Clearly needed is research guided by the full theory, gathering empirical data for all postulated constructs.

There also are some difficult issues related to the implications of the theory. Reductions in attributions of control are anticipated to improve the affective climate of the home by decreasing anger. But does this imply caretakers should communicate to patients that they are not responsible for their negative actions? This would be equivalent to telling low ability, failing students that they do not have to expend effort and that extra effort cannot compensate for ability limitations. In addressing the issue of the double-edged sword accompanying communications of nonresponsibility, Weisman et al. (1993) state: "Families who cope well with their disturbed relatives may be those who maintain a delicate balance between perceiving some control while recognizing that some of the odd or disruptive behavior is an inevitable side effect of a genuine illness" (p. 604). That is, the psychoeducational interventions must walk a careful line between the positive and negative consequences of taking away responsibility for unwanted behaviors. Perhaps emphasis on nonresponsibility for illness onset (with sympathy) but some responsibility for its offset (with motivational expectations) is one useful distinction to decrease blame while still imposing demands.

The well-known and oft-quoted prayer offered by theologian Reinhold Niebuhr, which now is associated with Alcoholics Anonymous, is pertinent in this context. Niebuhr wrote:

> God, give us Grace to accept with Serenity the things that cannot be changed,
> Courage to change the things that should be changed,
> And Wisdom to distinguish the one from the other.

In the context of perceptions and reactions to the mentally ill, this might be altered to read:

> God, give us Grace to accept with Serenity the things that others cannot change,
> Courage to ask for change by others when things are changeable,
> And Wisdom to distinguish the one from the other.

In light of the associations between high perceived responsibility/anger/demands versus no perceived responsibility/sympathy/no demands, it may prove insightful to turn to observations in other cultures to find how families of ill individuals act toward their schizophrenic family members. Support for the mentally ill does vary across national and ethnic groups, and it is generally the case that:

> High-EE attitudes tend to be less prevalent in developing or more traditional cultures than they are in more industrialized or developed parts of the world ...

patients with schizophrenia who live in less industrialized or more traditional societies have a generally better prognosis than do patients who live in more industrialized societies.... Quite possibly, the better clinical outcome of patients in more traditional societies is related to differences in attribution patterns or causal beliefs about the illness that are linked to culture. (Barrowclough & Hooley, 2003, p. 886)

In sum, schizophrenics face different judgments in their life courtrooms. Some individuals regard them as sick. These judges tend to reside in less developed countries and respond with warmth rather than hostility, a home environment conducive to recovery. On the other hand, many judges perceive the schizophrenic a sinner; they tend to reside in better developed countries. These individuals respond with anger and create a home environment fostering relapse. Heightened general level of education does not necessarily augment uncontrollable attributions and warmth. To the contrary, those in industrialized nations believe more in independence, free will, and personal responsibility, which increase anger and recidivism.

For the applied attribution theorist, psychoeducational interventions for the family are based on increasing awareness of the uncontrollability of some actions of the patient. When symptoms are "active," such as hallucinations, persons generally regard those as uncontrollable. But more passive symptoms, including apathy and failure at self-care, tend to be perceived as controllable and amenable to volitional alteration. These attitudes may be changeable and the patient made more understandable in the eyes of the everyday judge. This cognitive shift should have positive affective consequences and long-term results related to relapse prevention. The development of appropriate interventions guided by attribution theory already is taking place and is a promising future direction for theoretical application.

Lung Cancer and Other Stigmas

Studies of other psychiatric conditions, particularly depression (see Butzlaff & Hooley, 1998), also find relations between EE and the course of the illness, so researchers are now examining the role of causal beliefs as antecedents of EE for these conditions. The identical theoretical analysis presented in the discussion of schizophrenia is applicable to these mental illnesses as well. And there is no reason to limit generalizability to psychiatric illness while excluding other medical conditions (see Thompson, Medvene, & Freedman, 1995; Wearden, Tarrier, Barrowclough, Zastowny, & Rahill, 2000).

What may be of special interest in this regard is an examination of illnesses (and stigmas) ordinarily perceived to be under onset and/or offset volitional control. For example, as discussed earlier in the book, obesity often is believed due to lack of willpower or moral weakness. The obese person has eaten too much and/or exercised too little. Given these beliefs, overweight individuals will be the target of anger and negative reactions. This type of home climate is likely to exacerbate personal anxiety and, in turn, promote more eating. Hence, psychoeducational family interventions could also prove beneficial in this context, with the difficult issue again the distinction between what behaviors and outcomes are subject to change and what is uncontrollable. This will be known here as "The Niebuhr Conflict."

In general, there is increasing belief that illness is caused by "lifestyle" (although, as previously indicated, this is not true for all conditions, such as the stigma of homosexuality). Lifestyle includes a broad array of controllable behaviors related to diet, exercise, risk taking, choices of activities, and on and on. That is, both the onset and offset of illnesses are increasingly perceived as amenable to personal control. This is certainly true for obesity and drug use (just say "no") and also is applicable to two of the most prevalent diseases in our society—cancer and heart ailments. Here I address cancer, but the analysis applies to heart disease and other medical conditions as well.

There are many forms of cancer, with lung cancer among the most prevalent. It is well known by the public that a main contributor to lung cancer is smoking. There are increasingly negative public reactions to smoking (see Kim & Shanahan, 2003), and lung cancer victims as well as their families blame the smoker for having brought about this painful disease (Cooper, 1984). This causal finger pointing produces family strain and difficulties in communication (see Zhang & Siminoff, 2003). Hence, both the victim and his or her spouse and other family members do not share fears, concerns, and thoughts and feelings about the disease and related life factors. These consequences are of special importance because family environment exerts great impact on the course of chronic illness, as documented in the social support literature. Blame and withdrawal of social support may be less evident given other forms of cancer (e.g., pancreatic, prostate) not readily amenable to controllable causal ascriptions. Data are needed regarding this speculation.

What interventions might be recommended for family members of those with lung cancer? As already indicated, smoking is perceived to be a volitional choice, so there is likely to be blame and anger for the onset of the illness. As is discussed soon concerning marital conflict, perhaps family interventions emphasizing forgiveness with or without confession may prove beneficial for improving the home climate and fostering social support. And again the Niebuhr Conflict will be evident, particularly when there is continuation of smoking behavior in spite of the illness. Attribution theory does not offer specific recommendations for intervention programs, as opposed to providing an understanding of the attributional conflict and consequences of particular causal beliefs.

SPOUSES IN THE COURTROOM

Most moral judgments are likely to occur in spousal and parent–child relationships. Here the stakes are highest in terms of personal well-being, so it is of prime importance that the social (moral) order is upheld. The role of judge and moral vigilante is assumed by both members of the dyad. This can have dire consequences, as spouses blame one another for alleged transgressions and parents hold children responsible for supposed misdeeds, while children perceive parents as unfair and unjust.

Causal beliefs, responsibility judgments, and blame as determinants of marital satisfaction have been subject to extensive study (see reviews in Bradbury, Beach, Fincham, & Nelson, 1996; Bradbury & Fincham, 1990). The conclusions are complex and, as is true for the EE literature, many issues remain unresolved. Contributing to the research difficulties is that marital satisfaction—just as, for example, reactions to the stigmatized, help giving, and aggression—has multiple antecedents. Unfortunately for the attribution theorist, there is much more to life than causal beliefs. For example, marital satisfaction is influenced by economic conditions, job stress, adjustment to children, and even in-laws. Inferences of responsibility are unlikely to be the major cause of marital success and failure. Hence, demonstrating the significance of responsibility beliefs for marital distress is difficult. But this does not mean they do not have a significant impact on relationship satisfaction. Indeed, the context of marriage has provided an important direction for the application of attribution theory.

Research Goals and Findings

The basic goal of the pertinent empirical studies is relatively straightforward—ascertaining if there is an association between attributions for the causes of positive and negative marital events and marital satisfaction. It has been suggested that in a distressed marriage, the negative behavior of one spouse (e.g., not being pleasant to one's in-laws) is more attributed to a controllable cause and perceived as intended (e.g., "You want to stop their visits so your own family can come more often") than it is in a positive marriage (where an attribution might be, "My father certainly has been acting strange lately. No wonder you were bugged.").

The attributions made in marriage often are examined by presenting spouses with real or hypothetical marital events and then ascertaining beliefs about the causes of those events. Properties or dimensions of causes are assessed, including characteristics other than locus and stability such as generality over time, and responsibility inferences and blame are determined. In some studies, data are gathered at multiple time periods.

The general conclusions from this research, as summarized by Bradbury et al. (1996), are: "Distressed spouses ... are more likely than nondistressed spouses to blame the partner for marital difficulties and to see the partner's negative actions as intentional and selfishly motivated. These findings appear to be robust" (p. 569).

Although these results suggest the importance of attributions in marital distress, the conclusions have been weakened by recent findings that pursue with greater methodological sophistication a number of pertinent issues, including:

1. Do attributions reflect an enduring, relatively traitlike tendency? If attributions in marriage are unstable, or change as a result of marital satisfaction, then their causal role may be questioned (see Karney & Bradbury, 2000).

2. Do attributions cause marital satisfaction, or does marital satisfaction alter attributions? That is, what is the temporal sequence regarding the attribution–marital satisfaction association? Do attributions predict level of subsequent satisfaction more than satisfaction predicts future attributions? These questions clearly are not independent of the stability issue raised in the first question. Such queries promote testing on multiple occasions so sequence issues may be better resolved.

3. Do external circumstances and conditions, the "many other determinants of marital satisfaction," influence the attribution–satisfaction association (see Neff and Karney, 2004)? That is, are there moderators of the attribution–satisfaction linkage?

At this point in time, it appears the answers to these questions are:

1. There is no support for the assumption that attributions remain constant over time and situations, that is, they are not akin to traits having temporal and situational generality (see Karney & Bradbury, 2000). Rather, attributions change as conditions within the marriage change. In addition, attributions tend to be specific for particular circumstances—blaming a spouse for being late to an appointment can be accompanied by an absence of spousal blame for purchasing a defective

appliance. This is not entirely surprising, as there is evidence of attribution specificity in other research areas.

2. Given the lack of temporal and situational consistency in attributions, it is difficult to support the assertion that attributions precede marital distress rather than marital distress preceding attributions. There nonetheless is suggestive evidence that attributions predict change in marital satisfaction to a greater extent than marital satisfaction predicts changes in attribution (see Karney & Bradbury, 2000).

3. Among the factors that alter the attribution–marital satisfaction relation is the general level of marital stress (see Neff & Karney, 2004). "Stressful circumstances frequently create a lowered relationship evaluation, which is known as 'stress spillover'" (Tesser & Beach, 1998). It appears that "for wives, increases in stress were associated with an increased tendency to blame partners for their behavioral transgressions.... That is, stress was associated with the nature of wives' responsibility attributions" (Neff & Karney, 2004, p. 145). This lends credulence to the argument that attributions are not stable and there are moderators to attribution–distress relations.

Thus, the influence of attributions on marital satisfaction is complex. However, this does not minimize the importance of causal beliefs within a marriage (or, for that matter, in any interpersonal relationship).

Theoretical Applications

Whether attribution theory can be used to alleviate marital conflict remains to be documented. If it is the case that cognitive inferences in regard to causality and other-responsibility determine relationship satisfaction (and this appears to have some truth), then interventions may be possible that improve marriage satisfaction by altering attribution inferences. This is conceptually identical to arguments made regarding EE and schizophrenic relapse. Some findings supporting the efficacy of such interventions have been reported. For example, Margolin and Weiss (1978) gave marital counseling to help spouses "abandon blaming attributions, accept greater personal responsibility for relationship failure, and to be more accepting of their partners' positive efforts" (p. 1485). Following the training period, marital satisfaction increased. However, intervention studies to date have yielded mixed results and few have been undertaken (see Bradbury & Fincham, 1990).

Given this uncertainty and the ever-presence of the Niebuhr conflict (decreasing responsibility of the other reduces blame but also other-effort), different interventions related to attribution theory have been suggested. On one hand, it has been suggested that partners make less demands on their spouses, accept their flaws, and not try to change the other (Christensen & Jacobson, 2000). That is, the blaming spouse is asked to give up the role of judge and abandon the "life is a courtroom" metaphor as a guide to interpersonal action. This might be considered akin to telling the accuser to move (cognitively) to another culture and adopt a new way of construing others, one less judgmental, with corresponding decreasing beliefs in controllability and, in turn, negative affect.

Is this possible? Some religions ask us not to seek revenge but rather to "turn the other cheek." It is likely that for some people on some occasions this goal is attainable. But whether it can prove an efficacious intervention technique remains to be seen.

A variant of this position, which also focuses on the accuser rather than the transgressor, asks the victim to forgive the other (see Fincham, 2002). As discussed previously in this book, forgiveness is facilitated by a confession (which indicates the transgressor is a good person who engaged in a bad act). In addition, beliefs in nonresponsibility also promote forgiveness (in fact, if the other is perceived not responsible, forgiveness is not required). Forgiving the other when perceived responsible is similar to "turning the other cheek" and acting in a saintly manner. Again, if this will prove possible for an angry spouse, and whether this will decrease marital stress, remains to be demonstrated. Note that these more recent intervention suggestions focus on actions of the victim (accept, forgive) rather than on the consequences of what the victim believes about the transgressor. Thus, they more embrace an intrapersonal model in this interpersonal context.

BUSINESSES IN THE COURTROOM

Lawsuits abound related to unfair business practices. Secret deals to fix prices, knowingly selling a defective product, and cheating others out of money are just the tip of this iceberg of fraud and deceit. But not all fraud is criminal. The person selling meat to another chooses the oldest meat to sell first; the car dealer wants to unload the model that is least popular; the salesperson says the color of the suit is perfect when that is not the case.

For consumers, if there is outcome dissatisfaction, the cause might be self-ascribed ("I am just no good with computers") or be attributed to the product ("This computer is not user-friendly"). Furthermore, the cause of consumer unhappiness could be attributed to external causes that are either uncontrollable ("The flight was delayed because of a blinding snowstorm") or controllable by the service or producing company ("The personnel are poorly trained so boarding took forever"). In the latter case, not only is there anger, but also a variety of anticompany reactions. Consumers may want to be reimbursed for the purchase, and there may be additional demands related to retributive punishment. A complaint may be initiated and some form of compensation sought (see Folkes, 1984; Weiner, 2000a).

This analysis leads to a number of unanswered and underresearched questions:

1. Some problems (just as some stigmas) lend themselves to controllable, or to uncontrollable, causal beliefs. Any service is subject to accusations of controllable error and personal responsibility, just as is any product (e.g., the automobile) that has a high degree of perceived human input. People frequently are angry at automobile mechanics, the airline, or their waiter for what are regarded as controllable (albeit not necessarily intentional) delays. Anger may give rise to active actions—going against rather than (in addition to) away from.

2. The accused company, or employee, or service, must then manage impressions. As indicated in chapter 3, excuses are among the adopted impression management strategies in organizations (e.g., "The airline delay was due to bad weather"). One wonders what excuses are in fact true or false, which are perceived as true when false, and vice versa. Humans are poor at detecting lies, which are often inferred when statements are in fact true (see review in Weiner, 1992a). For example, if an airline representative states the plane delay is due to poor weather, or if the auto mechanic says he cannot obtain the parts immediately, do consumers believe these statements are true? And how often are they true?

Furthermore, when there is a negative product-related outcome and there is blame, who is perceived responsible? For example, when there is an oil spill, is the perceived responsible party the captain of the ship or the CEO? In Japan, often the CEO takes responsibility for acts clearly beyond personal control, publicly admits guilt, and may even resign. Eventually the Navy (as a company) took responsibility for the Tailhook incidents (in which Navy personnel sexually harassed a number of females at a hotel), rather than placing blame only on the personnel who did the harassing. This higher-up acceptance of responsibility is not the case in the current Iraq prison abuse scandal. Senior authorities, such as generals or members of the government, have not accepted responsibility for these atrocities.

3. Thus far I have focused on negative outcomes for they are more likely to elicit attribution search than are positive experiences. However,

as noted earlier, there also are personal responsibility judgments for positive outcomes. These are associated with positive emotions and evoke behaviors that "balance" the moral system. For example, if a dentist stays late to treat a patient, or some other service provider "goes the extra mile" to accommodate a customer, then an attribution of controllability by the satisfied customer will give rise to gratitude. Gratitude, in turn, increases the likelihood that relations will be maintained with that individual or company. Other positive consequences could follow, such as a special Christmas gift. Perceptions of extra effort may instill product and/or person loyalty. For the applied attribution theorist, a number of very pertinent issues are raised by the prior discussion. If I were the CEO of a company (perish the thought), I would like to know under what conditions I should accept responsibility for the shortcomings of individuals in my company whom I do not even know. I would like to have some ideas about when to confess and apologize and when to deny personal responsibility. I would like to ensure that when there is a product failure, information is provided because people search for moral wrongdoing and impose sentences when information is insufficient to reach conclusions. For example, we are prone to blame airline companies for delay, even when there may be a snowstorm. But this is less likely when the storm conditions are clearly communicated to frustrated travelers.

These are only some issues that deserve investigation by an applied attribution theorist that have direct implications for business procedures and practices. The questions have their roots in the notion that individuals are judges, searching for an understanding of causality and determining who or what is responsible.

AGGRESSORS AND THEIR VICTIMS
IN THE COURTROOM OF LIFE

The determinants of aggression are voluminous. They range from personal attributes (e.g., prejudice) to environmental causes (e.g., hot weather); from enduring factors (e.g., genetic disposition for impulsivity) to transient causes (e.g., a frustrating event); and from uncontrollable sources (e.g., hormonal imbalance) to controllable roots (e.g., seeking financial benefits). As already indicated, given the vast number of sufficient causes of aggression, none of which appears to be necessary to instigate this type of activity, an all-encompassing theory of aggression is not possible (certainly not at this time, and perhaps not in the future as well).

In this book I have adhered to a social-cognitive approach to aggression, which presumes that perceptions of negative events, inferences about potential provocations, and other information-processing activities are pivotal to understanding how and why hostile behavior is enacted. Attributional analyses comprise one subtheme within this social-cognitive perspective. The causal construal most pertinent to understanding aggression is the perceived controllability of an act that may be interpreted as hostile. As already recognized, this tells only a small part of the aggression story; when guided by a particular theoretical path, there is an understanding that upper boundaries on understanding have been imposed because of the selection of only a subset of pertinent *variables*.

In this section of the chapter, I consider two aggressive populations: abusive mothers and adolescent violators. The theoretical interpretation of their behaviors is quite similar, although some of their nondiscussed sources of aggression do differ (e.g., child-rearing demands vs. peer pressure).

Abusive Mothers and Child Physical Abuse

Considering child physical abuse from the attribution perspective championed in the prior pages, the following exemplar sequences are anticipated:

1. Billy spills milk on the table and his new shirt. His mother thinks he did this on purpose to aggravate her. She feels enraged and hits him.

2. Billy spills milk on the table and his new shirt. His mother does not think this was done purposively or negligently because of his underdeveloped motor skills. She is upset about the incident and has to clean up, but she is not angry at her child (as opposed to frustrated because goals have been blocked). She may also feel sympathy because of his soiled shirt and gives help, rather than seeking harmful retaliation.

There are scattered sources of data supporting this attribution–affect–action interpretation of the causes of physical child abuse. At one time in the history of the study of child maltreatment, it was believed that a key antecedent of abuse was unrealistic parental expectations regarding the development of the child "and a corresponding disregard for the infant's or the child's own needs, limited abilities, and helplessness" (Spinetta & Rigler, 1972, p. 299). Physically abusive parents were characterized as lacking child-rearing knowledge; it was their false expectations and inferences of controllability that differentiated these individuals from others not abusing their children (Azar, Robinson, Hekimian & Twentyman, 1984; Bradley & Peters, 1991). This hypothesis is still regarded as plausible, although disconfirming data have been reported (see Rosenberg & Reppucci, 1983; Twentyman & Plotkin, 1982). One of the obstacles to confirming this hypothesis is the array of determinants of physical aggression, particularly alcohol and drug addiction among violent parents.

Related to this construal of abusive parents is that they tend to perceive adverse acts by the child as committed intentionally (see Golub, 1984) and believe the child is in control over expressed negative actions (Bugental, 1987; Bugental, Blue, & Cruzcosa, 1989). Other supporting research reports parents at-risk for physical child abuse are less likely than their nonrisk counterparts to alter inferences about child intent in the face of nonconfirming causal information (Milner & Foody, 1994).

From this attributional perspective, any distal factor increasing the perception of negative child behavior as intended should augment physical abuse. It is known, for example, that poverty increases incidents of child abuse. Given a causal approach, it can be argued that unemployment lowers one's threshold for viewing others' behavior as intentionally hostile (the "stress spillover" factor discussed as operative in distressed marriage). When stressed, abusive mothers are less aware of situational cues that allow them to judge the appropriateness of child behavior (Milner, 1993). This sequence can be summarized as follows:

> High parental stress—Child behavior perceived as negative—Inference of child
> responsibility—High anger—Hostile retaliation (high punishment)

In one experimental test of this analysis, Graham, Weiner, Cobb, and Henderson (2001) first identified abusive mothers, mothers at-risk for abuse as determined by addictions but no abusive history, and a control group of nonabusive, nonrisk mothers. The participants were shown videotapes in which children engaged in problematic behaviors, such as refusing to get dressed for school, arguing over food, avoiding bedtime, and the like. The mothers indicated how much they held the children responsible for the negative behaviors, their anger and sympathy ("feel sorry for"), and how much they thought the children should be punished. They also imagined their own child behaving like the protagonists in the film and repeated the ratings. In addition, a measure of parental stress was administered.

The findings, shown in Table 5.1, are averages of judgments regarding the children in the film and their own child, as these were so highly related. Table 5.1 shows that abusive parents were under more stress; rated the target children more responsible for the aversive behaviors; and were angrier, more sympathetic, and recommended more punishment, although the sympathy and punishment ratings did not significantly differ between the respondent

TABLE 5.1

Mean Differences on the Dependent Variables as a Function of Abuse Group

	Abuse Group		
	Abusive (N = 14)	At-risk (N = 28)	Nonabusive (N = 33)
Parent stress index	61.5	53.75	39.76
Attributional judgments			
Responsibility	4.61	4.06	3.83
Anger	4.50	3.91	3.59
Sympathy	3.92	3.63	3.42
Punishment	3.92	3.78	3.40

Note. Data from Graham, Weiner, Cobb, and Henderson (2001), p. 245.

groups. The sympathy findings were especially problematic in light of the hypotheses, but became clearer when interviews revealed that the abusive mothers were sorry for the children because of the severity of the punishment about to be delivered!

Regression analyses of these data showed that, once all the variables were taken into account, the most proximal determinant of endorsed punishment was how angry a mother felt toward the misbehaving children. This is in accord with theoretical expectations.

Interventions for Physical Abuse. Treatment programs for abusive parents often focus on enhancing caregivers' knowledge about child rearing and teaching parenting skills, particularly the effective use of discipline, and helping develop self-control strategies, including anger management (Azar, 1997; Fiendler & Becker, 1994; National Research Council, 1993). Because the focus is on changing overt behavior (the actual abuse), these multicomponent programs often pay little attention to the psychological processes and the thinking plus feeling antecedents that elicit action.

The prior discussion, and the findings shown in Table 5.1, have implications for interventions with abusive mothers and for preventive treatments with at-risk mothers. One reasonable starting point for intervention is to focus on attribution change, training abusive mothers to perceive their children as less responsible for their misbehavior. In addition, successful intervention may be achieved by moving back in the temporal sequence to the antecedents of responsibility inferences. For example, social norm information could be provided revealing that most children of a certain age engage in the target behavior, so it is not as "immoral" as it may appear, or that parental expectations for the child regarding this action are too high.

As already indicated, this discussion focused on one category of social cognition (causal beliefs), when surely numerous maladaptive behaviors and dysfunctional cognitive interpretations of social experience characterize abusive mothers. The multicomponent treatment programs for abusive parents tend to address a broad array of aggressive determinants. In such comprehensive programs, it is difficult to discern the essential intervention components. If one's goals are entirely applied and there is a desire for immediate payoff, then this lack of specificity may be of little concern. Whether the intervention was (or was not) effective is what counts. However, if one's goals also are theoretical, such as understanding what social cognitive processes map into (are causally related to) which specific kinds of behavior change, then the comprehensive intervention approach will not yield "good" (unambiguous) data. Clearly, there are trade-offs in intervention research between theoretical specificity and treatment breadth.

Adolescent Aggression

As was the case with abusive mothers, the determinants of adolescent aggression are voluminous. Aggression is particularly likely for an impulsivity-prone male who: "(a) is born prematurely to an unmarried mother who lacks adequate parenting skills, (b) scores poorly on IQ tests; and (c) prefers to stay home and watch TV rather than attend school" (Graham & Hudley, 1991, p. 77).

In addition, guided primarily by the work of Dodge and his colleagues (see review in Dodge & Crick, 1990), it has been reported that aggressive adolescents have an attribution bias to infer hostile intent following a peer-instigated negative event (see chap. 1). In one representative experiment supporting this conclusion, Graham, Hudley, and Williams (1992) first identified aggressive and nonaggressive adolescents based on peer nominations and teacher ratings. They gave these respondents hypothetical vignettes in which there was a negative outcome, such as damage to one's belongings. The cause of the damage was portrayed as accidental, intentional, or was ambiguous. Consistent with other research, these authors report that "aggressive subjects were more likely to believe that the hypothetical peer acted with malicious intent ... when the causal situation was portrayed as ambiguous" (Graham & Hudley, 1991, p. 84). Given a range of behavioral options, they also expressed a preference to "get even."

Why might aggressive and nonaggressive adolescents differ in the manner they represent or interpret social events? Graham and Hudley (1994) subsequently argued that these groups differ in the accessibility of constructs from their memory storage, with aggressive children inferring intentionality because their own life experiences are overly represented with instances of giving and receiving blame. To address this accessibility explanation, Graham and Hudley (1994) first had aggressive and nonaggressive adolescent subjects read vignettes that involved either intentional or unintentional peer provocation. These manipulations were devised to activate thoughts about intentionality. Then participants read a vignette ambiguous with regard to the cause of a negative action, reported the perceived cause of this action, their affect, and what they would do.

Graham and Hudley (1994) report that for aggressive children, ratings of intent, anger, and blame in the ambiguous story were not affected when the initial vignette depicted an intentional act. This was anticipated because intent was already believed to be activated in their construal of events. On the other hand, for nonaggressive children the ratings were significantly increased when the construct of intent was activated, presumably because this normally is not aroused to influence their construal of events. Thus, the data suggest "individual differences in the accessibility of causal beliefs capture a meaningful distinction between aggressive and nonaggressive early male adolescents" (Graham & Hudley, 1994, p. 370).

Interventions to Decrease Aggression. Guided by this basic research, Hudley (1991) developed a school-based cognitive intervention program designed to alter the intentionality inferences of aggressive-prone children. One component of this 6-week program was directed to improve the accuracy of inferences of intent among the participants. In addition, the cognitive availability of attributions of unintentionality in ambiguous causal situations was increased. This was accomplished through games, story telling, practice with peers, and the like (also see Hudley & Graham, 1993).

Pre- and post-measures to hypothetical social dilemmas were obtained to test the effectiveness of this intervention program. The aggressive social dilemmas were ambiguous with regard to causality. The results, depicted in Fig. 5.1, document the success of the intervention. Attributions of intent, anger, and the hostile responding decreased after the training program (experimental group) compared to a control group. Hence, this intervention technique appears to be a promising approach to reduce aggression among targeted adolescents.

Graham and Hudley (1991) suggest that those benefiting most from the intervention are reactively, rather than proactively, aggressive. That is, individu-

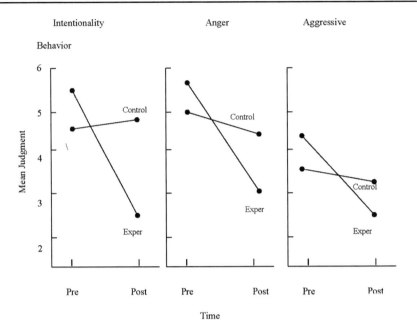

FIG. 5.1. Pre- and post- ratings by the experimental and control groups (from Graham & Hudley, 1991, p. 88).

als who respond with hostility following perceived threats from others are targets for this program, rather than adolescents who engage in aggression without provocation. Theoretically, among only the former group is the attribution process activated and an essential determinant of aggression.

Teaching Excuses. The intervention discussed for aggressive adolescents attempts to alter attributions regarding the actions of others from intentional to unintentional. In the hostile environments facing these individuals, this intervention may not be functional and accurate. A different approach is to have others interpret the aggressive child's own hostile behavior as less intentional, hence decreasing anger and potential retaliation. This might be accomplished by communicating something that is not true to the victim.

Although adherence to the truth and honesty are fundamental rules of conduct in most societies, social competence also entails realization that maintaining the social fabric often depends on miscommunications. Included in this discourse category are "white lies," withholding esteem-threatening knowledge, and excuse giving. In these instances, fidelity to the facts may give way to other goals. For example, a teenager might communicate that he missed a classmate's party because of illness, when in fact this absence was because of a pref-erence to be with other friends. In this example, adherence to the truth could have negative consequences.

Excuse giving and even insincere confession for a transgression often may have positive value when a transgression is committed. If the excuse or confession is accepted, the individual is either perceived as less responsible for the aversive action or is more likely to be forgiven. These consequences minimize anger from the other and help prevent a hostile encounter.

Research indicates that aggressive children are less likely than nonaggressives to pursue prosocial goals in their relations with others (see Crick & Ladd, 1990). Furthermore, aggressive children are relatively inaccurate in labeling emotions of others and express less concern about hurting peers' feelings (see Rabiner & Gordon, 1993). This suggests that aggressive children lack the necessary social skills to foster positive relationships and defuse hostility in conflict situations. Guided by these ideas, Graham, Weiner, and Benesh-Weiner (1995) hypothesized that aggressive children lack understanding of the function of excuse giving, which would increase the likelihood of overt conflict.

To investigate this hypothesis, Graham et al. (1995) provided aggressive vignettes to younger (Grades K–5) and older (Grades 6–8) aggressive and nonaggressive children. The participants were asked to imagine they had committed a transgression (e.g., not showing up at an agreed-upon time), with the target victim either their mother or a peer. Controllable causes were given for some vignettes and uncontrollable causes for others. The participants indicated how responsible they would be perceived in these situations, how angry the other person would be, and if they would reveal the true cause.

Table 5.2 shows the percentage of participants reporting they would reveal a controllable cause. The table indicates that among nonaggressive youths, the likelihood of communicating a controllable cause decreases with development. Stated another way, nonaggressive youths are more likely to lie (withhold controllable causes) as they become older and more socially sensitive. On the other hand, this trend is not displayed by aggressive children. The older aggressive youths are just as likely as younger ones to tell the truth and communicate a cause that arouses anger.

In addition, with increasing development, the perceived relations between causal controllability, anger, and response withholding grow for both age groups. That is, the intercorrelations of these ratings increase. However, as shown in Fig. 5.2, the magnitude of these relations, or indicators of social understanding, is much higher among the older nonaggressive than the older aggressive children.

TABLE 5.2

Percentage of Participants Revealing the Controllable Cause for Social Transgression
as a Function of Status Group, Age, and Target of Aggression

| | Status group | | | |
| | Aggressive | | Nonaggressive | |
Target	Younger (n=32)	Older (n=28)	Younger (n=22)	Older (n=24)
Mother	69	68	68	33
Peer	47	43	64	25

Note. Data from Graham, Weiner, and Benesh-Weiner (1995), p. 281.

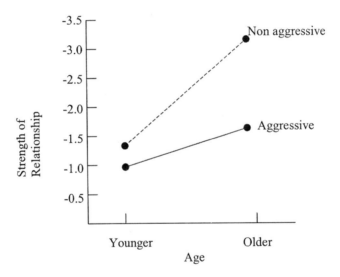

FIG. 5.2.   Mean on the social awareness index (correlations between the attribution
variables) as a function of status group and age (from Graham, Weiner, &
Benesh-Weiner, 1995, p. 281). Copyright © 1995 by the American Psychological Association. Reprinted with permission.

Given these findings, Graham et al. (1995) suggest that aggressive children
would benefit from intervention strategies that focus on changing how others
perceive them, rather than (in addition to) how they perceive others. Training
in the appropriate use of excuses, apologies, and other accounts to minimize
anger would provide the foundation of such intervention programs. In these
programs aggressive youths could also learn to honor the accounts of others, so

excuses and confession would be followed by forgiveness. This approach provides a different avenue for intervention, one nonetheless also derived from attribution theory.

SUMMARY

A stated goal among psychologists is to "give psychology away"; that is, communicate our knowledge to the public so it may be used in daily life. This
clearly has been achieved with, for example, mental testing and clinical diag-
noses and psychotherapy, where psychology has profound influence and impact on everyday life. On the other hand, giving away principles from the
study of social psychology and motivation has proven more difficult. It may be
that we do not know enough to give anything away, or what we know already
is known by others as they navigate through life, or we know a great deal that
is unknown to others but this knowledge primarily is theoretical and does not
have practical value.

   In this chapter I addressed the application issue in regard to the theory of social motivation and justice proposed in this book. The areas of potential application I addressed were the classroom, reactions among caregivers to others
with mental or physical health problems, distressed marriage, communications
to consumers, and aggression of abusive mothers and adolescents. In each of
these contexts, the metaphor of the person as a judge was of central importance: the teacher evaluating students, which elicits harmful construals of the
classroom as a courtroom; family caretakers critics of their schizophrenic and
cancer-infected family members, hence worsening the course of their illness;
marital partners blaming one another for problems, increasing the downward
spiral of marriage; manufacturers and service providers withholding information to the product-using public, hence increasing beliefs in responsibility and
desires to retaliate; and abusive mothers and aggressive adolescents perceiving
intent among others given an aversive event and not accepting offered accounts. Attribution theory is able to address these very disparate phenomena
because all involve perceptions of responsibility and anger.

   The specific interventions suggested are unlikely to make the reader (or the
writer) announce to the world that these social problems are ready for solution
by an attribution theorist. Will, for example, the elimination of grading improve the classroom climate? Will getting spouses not to blame one another improve their marriage? Will having airlines announce the weather conditions
improve consumer relations? Will getting abusive mothers and adolescents not
to blame others for negative events decrease aggression? Will teaching aggressive adolescents the value of excuses and the honoring of accounts decrease

aggression? I suspect the answers to all these questions are "yes," but with understanding that the magnitude of change will be small and there may be benefit for some but not for others. One must have modest (albeit positive) expectations and aspirations.

On the other hand, it also is the case that the attribution theory of social motivation and justice does have real-world applicability, and I am sure I have not touched on many of these opportunities. What is encouraging is that the principles of application originate directly from the theory, and successful application would contribute to one's confidence in the theory. Lewin would have been delighted if this indeed holds true.

Epilogue

The origin of attribution theory traces back to a long-standing philosophical interest in epistemology, or the study of knowledge. In an article providing a foundation for the theory, Heider (1944) asked why we see a building when it is only rays of sunlight hitting our eyes. This question later shifted to how we are able to infer intentions of others when inner thoughts are not directly observable. Heider believed that the laws of physical or object perception are similar to the laws of person or social perception (although the latter are more complex). In both, there must be transformation from "beyond the information given" to something inferred and not directly observable. That is, the observer moves sequentially in the perceptual sequence from the proximal or immediate stimulus, which is the sensory information, to the distal and inferred stimulus, which is a building or an intention. What has been presented here follows in this tradition. It has been contended that we observe someone who has not tried, and then infer that lack of effort is a controllable cause and the person is responsible or "immoral." The sequence is from proximal stimuli to "beyond the information given."

Guided by Heider's insights, attribution theory initially focused on the epistemological question of "how do we know," that is, what information and processes are involved when making causal inferences about the self and others? A few landmark publications addressed these issues, including Heider's (1958) book, *The Psychology of Interpersonal Relations*. This was followed with influential chapters by Jones and Davis (1965), concerned with dispositional or correspondent inferences, and by Kelley (1967), who specified the types of information (consistency, consensus, social norms) used in causal decision making. As indicated in the prologue of this book, special attention was given to whether causes of an event lay inside of (internal to) or outside of (external to) the person. Inferences about causal locus lay at the heart of attribution analyses and the search for why a particular event has occurred.

For motivation psychologists, the restriction to epistemology, or how one comes to know, renders the study of attribution of limited interest. On the other hand, bridging knowledge to action, linking "why" to "so what" or "therefore," elevates the study of causal beliefs to the heart of motivation psychology. This is because action tendencies are based on causal beliefs and on emotions generated by causal knowledge. It is of interest to understand how one comes to believe a child lacks ability or has not tried hard enough (a stimulus–cognition linkage). Proximal stimuli or information such as the number of others failing aids in this decision. And it is of interest that we classify lack of effort as subject to volitional control and regard the person as responsible. But, in addition, whether the failure of a child is ascribed to lack of ability as opposed to lack of effort is of fundamental importance in predicting the feelings and behaviors of his or her parents (cognition–emotion, cognition–action, and cognition–emotion–action connections). Will they experience sympathy and provide support or be angry and punish? For social and motivational psychologists, the richness of attribution analyses is found in consequences as opposed to (or, in addition to) antecedents of causal beliefs.

What situations might evoke conflicting causal beliefs, with consequences linked to these ascriptions? It certainly makes all the emotional and behavioral difference in the world whether a falling rock was caused by mountain erosion or someone throwing it at you. In a similar manner, as indicated earlier, how parents emotionally and behaviorally react to school failure of their child depends on whether they believe their child did not try as opposed to lacks capacity. And if a date fails to show up for an appointment, feelings and actions are not the same if later that evening you see him or her at the movie with another date as opposed to being called to visit that person in the hospital. These examples are endless. It does not add a great deal to the science of motivation or attribution theory to merely document such incidents, nor is this possible because of the infinite length of that list. A theory must be created to classify and combine specific instances, not on the basis of their phenotype or visible characteristics, but according to their genotype or underlying properties. The theory must have a structure with interconnected parts and the structure must be linked to the observational world. The theory also must address dynamics—forces and action tendencies producing emotional and/or behavioral change. In this book I have offered a theory of social motivation and justice having these qualities—a structure, interconnected parts, empirical anchoring, and prediction of feelings and behaviors. Because this theory is based on genotypic characteristics of causes and incidents, it has generality across many behavioral domains.

This theory was not created to account for all observations within any behavioral domain. Rather, it was devised to explain some observations within many, but not all, fields of motivation—there is a focus and range of theoretical applicability. The boundary conditions are in part determined by the concentration on morality, sin versus sickness, deservedness, justice, fairness, and the like. Thus, this is a conception for human rather than subhuman motivation, guided by precepts from theology and the law rather than from physical and biological sciences.

THE POSITIVES

What positive statements might be made about this approach and what has been accomplished?

The theory is able to address very broad categories and divisions within the study of human motivation, such as approach and avoidance tendencies; reward and punishment; going toward, away from, and against; cognition, emotion, and action; mediators and moderators.

Some behaviors in specific motivation domains are explained, including evaluation in achievement contexts, reactions to the stigmatized, help giving, punishments for those who have transgressed because of various power sources, and aggressive retaliation.

An array of affects can be accounted for, particularly anger and sympathy, and perhaps to a lesser extent admiration, envy, gratitude, guilt, indignation, jealousy, regret, Schadenfreude, scorn, and shame.

Some insights or at least alternative views have been provided into a number of philosophical, theological, and/or legal issues, including the determinants of moral responsibility, the relation between free will and determinism, the distinction between cause and reason, the contrast between utilitarian and retributive punishment, the designation of moral and immoral emotions, and the functions of excuses, justifications, and confessions.

A number of personality inferences are amenable to explanation, including arrogance and modesty, as well as general positive (moral) and negative (immoral) characteristics.

The theory sheds light on, and is able to incorporate, *individual differences,* such as political ideology; *dyadic behaviors,* such as those between couples in a marriage; *family dynamics,* as occur between a mentally or physically ill person and others within the family; *organizational behavior,* as when companies account for transgressions; and *cultural disparities,* such as the differential reactions to the obese in Mexico and America.

Impression management techniques, or accounts, can be brought within the theoretical umbrella (as previously remarked when discussing philosophical/ theological contributions). Excuses, for example, typically attempt to alter causation from controllable to uncontrollable; justifications are mitigators that reduce responsibility rather than perceived volitional choice; and confessions alter inferences about the characteristics of the person and perceived stability of the cause of the transgression.

Innumerable demonstration experiments can be undertaken that are replicable in virtually any context. These include, for example, greater punishment given failure caused by lack of effort than lack of ability; more condemnation for AIDS than for Alzheimer's disease; more condemnation for AIDS due to promiscuous sexual behavior than because of a transfusion with contaminated blood; greater negative reactivity to one transgressing because of a promised reward than a feared punishment; more help given when a job is lost because the company went out of business as opposed to job loss due to repeated tardiness; greater likelihood of aggressive retaliation when the aggression of the other was intended rather than accidental; and on and on. These are merely instantiations; an infinite number of experimental variations capturing the same laws are possible. In a similar manner, documentation of the cognitive antecedents of emotions, including responsibility for anger and nonresponsibility for sympathy, are certain, just as are the emotional antecedents of inferred causal beliefs, as exemplified when anger indicates that the other is regarded as responsible. And the value and consequences of various impression management strategies are equally demonstrable, as are the goals of punishment evoked by contrasting causal ascriptions.

The theory has been, or is being, applied in various contexts, including school settings, marital counseling, counseling regarding mentally ill family members, interventions with aggressive parents and peers, and in organizations.

In my most positive moments, I believe this combination of breadth, both across disciplines and within the field of motivation; depth; certainty of prediction; and amenability to application is not descriptive of any other theory of human motivation.

THE NEGATIVES

In the light of this ringing endorsement, are there negatives? The answer is an unequivocal yes. In my mind, the most salient problem is that the theory is unable to account for why humans seek food, water, or sexual activity. Nor can it capture which particular restaurant is selected, unless there have been attributions for prior successes and failures (as opposed to being able to specify one determinant of the size of the waiter's tip). These shortcomings are because the theory lacks traditional motivation constructs including motive, need, instinct, incentive, value, habit, emotional anticipation, homeostasis, and even hedonism. The person does not seek to return to equilibrium nor to maximize pleasure and minimize pain. Behavior is not initiated by an absence of a commodity necessary for survival, a motive seeking an incentive, and so on. Rather, an observed outcome, event, or state activates a desire for understanding. The understanding, or causal ascription, is joined with other cognitions and has emotional significance; these cognitions and affects are the driving forces of behavior, with emotions pushing rather than pulling the person. The absence of longstanding friends of motivation, the core constructs such as viscerogenic needs and incentives proven so useful to generations of researchers, limits the focus and range of this theory.

Is this a fatal flaw? It is if one expects the theory to account for the behavior of a hungry person selecting a restaurant. In my view, there will not be a theory (in the near future) able to incorporate all the behaviors within a motivation domain, nor many behaviors across motivation domains. The theory explaining moral judgments is unlikely to account for eating behavior. For this reason, I suggested the use of metaphors as theory foundations because metaphors can stand side by side in the explanation of human behavior. The metaphors guiding this book, the person is a judge and life is a courtroom, do not provide a good fit, or foundation, to understand behaviors in service of survival needs, but they are pertinent to a wide swath of other human motivations.

It also would be foolhardy to believe that the issues raised and "solved" in the prior pages have in fact reached closure. For example, I am unsure what the motivation sequence will be in all domains and in all situations; it is unknown whether appraisals of responsibility must antedate anger, if anger must produce antisocial actions, or whether cognitions and/or emotions are sufficient (or even necessary) for action; I am uncertain about the linkage of attribution theory to folk or naïve psychology or even whether this is an important issue; and on and on. That is, the clearest evidence for the theory and its core presumptions often slip out of grasp in the complexities of the overdetermined and chaotic world of human motivated action.

THEORETICAL LONGEVITY

A pet psychological theory, like a cat or a dog, usually has a life of about 10 to 13 years, which is the equivalent of around 70 to 90 years of human existence.

Longevity in part depends on the size of the pet (the bigger the theory, the earlier the demise), breed, and so on. At around the age of 10, the pet often begins to weaken, does not see things too well, and is unable to adapt to new circumstances and the many obstacles in life. It can remember and account for the distant past better than recent events, and acts with rigidity.

As previously indicated, contemporary attribution theory was born with the publication of Heider's (1958) book, *The Psychology of Interpersonal Relations*. That was almost a half century ago; in pet years, the approach is about 350 years old. My neighbor's cat reached the age of 22 (or 154 years in human equivalency) and even this is rare among both animal pets and pet theories. The formulation of the attribution–affect–action theory proposed here is newer, perhaps first clearly formulated in my 1995 book, *Judgments of Responsibility*. Thus, even this specific variation of attribution theory is around 10 years old (70 in pet years).

Why has attribution theory endured so long and outlived its theoretical peers, including, for example, dissonance and other forms of balance, social comparison, and self-perception? We do still celebrate these old friends, and their memories do linger, but they must be regarded as no longer exhibiting élan vital. To what, then, do we attribute the vitality of attribution theory?

One reason for this longevity is that attribution theory focuses on the universal concern with explanation—why a particular event, state, or outcome has come about, and the consequences of phenomenal causality. Hence, it is not only of use and interest to social and motivation psychologists, but to those in other branches of psychology and in related disciplines as well. This cross-field fertilization has stimulated the theory and breathed new life in when it seemed in the autumn of existence. For cognitive psychologists, their general interest in epistemology and causal inference provided impetus for the examination and reformulation of attribution principles. For clinical psychologists, concern that the onset of depression might be brought about by dysfunctional causal beliefs and that recidivism is promoted by accusations from family members brought new attribution thinking. For personality psychologists, designating individuals as having "attributional styles," such as optimists and pessimists, based on their causal inferences, resulted in new research directions that extended to health psychology and coping with stress. In addition, important differences have been found in the causes individuals select for poverty, welfare, AIDS, and a number of other outcomes, states, and conditions. As Kelly (1955) noted, there are alternative construals of the world, and this surely includes causal beliefs. And for the educational psychologist, concern with explanations for success and failure by pupils and their teachers and parents provided avenues for attribution expansion. And these represent just some of the tenta-cles that grew from the attributional body.

A NAÏVE OR A SCIENTIFIC THEORY?

Attribution theory often is labeled a naïve theory or a theory of common sense (although even this has been questioned inasmuch as other folk theories have disagreed with or provided alternative folk explanations to that offered by at-tribution theory; see Haslam, 2003; Kelley, 1992; Malle, 2004). Sometimes at-tribution theory is pejoratively equated with *bubba* (granny) psychology. The reason for devaluation of bubba psychology is that predictions of the theory and/or observations supporting the theory are well-known or obvious to the av-erage person, thereby contributing little new knowledge. For example, it surely is no surprise to readers that one is held more responsible for intended than un-intended harm, so one who stepped on another's toes purposively is more faulted than the person pushed and unintentionally committing the same act. Furthermore, the average person understands that lack of effort as a cause of failure elicits more anger than an absence of ability. Thus, the talented baseball player not running fast to first base after hitting the ball is expected to be met with more negative affect than the teammate running her fastest. Forsterling and Rudolph (1988) have even shown that anger rather than resignation, given failure due to insufficient effort of others, is judged appropriate and indi-cates intelligence. And still further, it seems obvious a sympathetic other is more likely to help a person in need than a person who experiences anger or no affective reaction. These relations between controllability, responsibility, af-fect, and action are the focus of this theory. Thus, one may be prone to ask: "So, what's new? Didn't we know all this before? The reason findings from investiga-tions are so reliable is because they are obvious."

Indeed, empirical observations in the majority of studies reviewed in chap-ters 1 and 2 coincide with common sense, or with general knowledge. Attribu-tion theory, at times, studies the obvious, and as already stated when discussing responsibility beliefs as a determinant of anger, this theory best captures the or-dinary person doing ordinary things. It does not well represent religious people in their most religious moments. But I also documented that a number of phen-otypically diverse phenomena, including achievement evaluation, reactions to the stigmatized, help giving, compliance, and aggression, can be embraced within the same theoretical system. This search for generality is far from the goals and capabilities of the average person, who seeks to understand the par-ticular instance rather than attempting to develop fundamental laws of moti-vation. Furthermore, asking the average person to predict helping primarily is a matter of the heart whereas aggression is proximally related to the head as well as the heart is beyond their intuitions. This empirical contribution is certainly not characteristic of a naïve theory.

Somewhat paradoxically (to me) is that other theories in the psychology of motivation also make predictions that are part of naïve or everyday understanding, yet they do not attract the label of bubba psychology. For example, drive theory was regarded as the prototype of a scientific approach to motivation. A major prediction of the theory is animals high in drive, that is, animals hungry or thirsty, are more motivated by the anticipation of food or water than are sated (low drive) animals. I do not think this surprises anyone. In a similar manner, balance theory as formulated by Heider (1958) and others predicts that a situation where Jane likes Bill but Bill does not like Jane (or vice versa) results in greater desire to change than when they like one another. This is not surprising either. Yet balance theory is not considered a naïve psychology. Thus, the label of a common sense theory has not been applied consistently or systematically.

I consider the attribution conception in some sense a naïve theory in that many of its predictions are consistent with everyday understanding. In part, this is why the theory is so strongly confirmed. Yet I do not regard the study of common observations a shortcoming. In addition, key predictions of the theory, and the full pattern of sequential relations at its core, are not part of everyday understanding. Hence, what has been presented is both a naïve and a scientific theory, as I understand the meaning of these labels.

Finally, perhaps another reason this particular conception is considered naïve rather than scientific relates to the metaphors providing direction for the theory. The foundation for this book is not derived from biology and the metaphor of the person as a machine, which characterizes many prior theories of motivation, including those proposed by Freud and Hull. To the contrary, the background for the current work evolves from law and theology. The basic concepts and terms in the attribution approach to social motivation are causality, responsibility, anger, sympathy, and the like. These indeed are part of everyday understanding of the judge and the courtroom, my guiding metaphors, as opposed to being linked to mysterious workings of a machine, which are associated with laws of physics and are not part of naïve understanding.

WHAT NEXT?

A question likely to be raised by readers, as well as by this writer, is, "Now what?" What is the most fruitful direction for theoretical and empirical pursuits? The prior discussion suggests the road to continued theoretical life for attribution theory is to search for new theoretical directions, finding paths not previously explored. I am unsure where to find these roads or what they may look like. I recognize this could be a disappointment to the reader. Attribution theory has long amazed me with its richness and fertility—one puts a shovel somewhere in the ground and out come some nuggets.

On the other hand, it may be that increased breadth and new directions are not needed at this point in time. Rather, current loose ends should be secured, the knowledge made definitive. It could be argued that depth rather than (in addition to) breadth is called for. It is quite understandable that each re-searcher desires to blaze his or her own novel path. Replication-type studies are vastly undervalued and surely not as exciting as new directions. But they must be undertaken, along with "variation on a theme" research, for there to be em-pirical resolutions to already formulated questions.

Although I expressed uncertainty regarding the future direction of attribu-tion theory and research, I am convinced that any "ultimate" theory of motiva-tion will have to recognize the empirical and theoretical foundation, the definitive findings and conceptual tools, provided by attributional analyses. It is therefore very satisfying to be counted among the many contributors to attributional thinking. As indicated in the quote from the author Margaret Atwood at the front of this book, "We can't stand the idea of our own voices running silent finally, like a radio running down."

References

Abel, R. (1998). *Speaking respect, respecting speech.* Chicago, IL: University of Chicago Press.

Allred, K. G., Mallozzi, J. S., Matsui, F., & Raia, C. P. (1997). The influence of anger and compassion on negotiation performance. *Organizational Behavior an Human Decision Processes, 70,* 175–187.

Atkinson, J. W. (1957). Motivational determinants of risk-taking behavior. *Psychological Review, 64,* 359–372.

Atkinson, J. W. (1964). *An introduction to motivation.* Princeton, NJ: Van Nostrand.

Atwood, M. (2001). *The blind assassin.* Nelson, NZ: Anchor Press.

Averill, J. R. (1982). *Anger and aggression: An essay on emotion.* New York: Springer-Verlag.

Averill, J. R. (1983). Studies on anger and aggression. *American Psychologist, 38,* 1145–1160.

Azar, S. (1997). A cognitive behavioral approach to understanding and treating parents who physically abuse their children. In D. Wolfe, R. McMahon, & R. Peters (Eds.), *Child abuse: New directions in prevention and treatment across the lifespan* (pp. 79–101). Thousand Oaks, CA: Sage.

Azar, S., Robinson, D., Hekimian, E., & Twentyman, C. (1984). Unrealistic expectations and problem-solving ability in maltreated and comparison mothers. *Journal of Consulting and Clinical Psychology, 52,* 687–691.

Bailey, W. C., & Peterson, R. D. (1994). Murder, capital punishment, and deterrence: A review. In C. Aktaki & C. Brewin (Eds.), *Attributions and psychological change: Applications of attribution theories to clinical and educational practice* (pp. 177–194). London: Academic Press.

Bandura, A. (1986). *Social foundations of thought and action: A social cognitive theory.* Englewood Cliffs, NJ: Prentice-Hall.

Barnes, R. D., Ickes, W., & Kidd, R. F. (1979). Effects of the perceived intentionality and stability of another's dependency on helping behavior. *Personality and Social Psychology Bulletin, 5,* 367–372.

Baron, R. M., & Kenny, D. A. (1986). The moderator–mediator variable distinction in social psychological research: Conceptual, strategic, and statistical consideration. *Journal of Personality and Social Psychology, 51,* 1173–1182.

Barrowclough, C., & Hooley, J. M. (2003). Attributions and expressed emotion: A review. *Clinical Psychology Review, 23,* 849–880.

Barrowclough, C., Tarrier, N., & Johnston, M. (1994). Distress, expressed emotion and attributions in relatives of schizophrenic patients. *Schizophrenia Bulletin, 22,* 691–701.

Batson, C. D., Bowers, M. J., Leonard, E. A., & Smith, E. C. (2000). Does personal morality exacerbate or restrain retaliation after being harmed? *Personality and Social Psychology Bulletin, 26,* 35–45.

Bauerle, S. Y., Amirkhan, J., & Hupka, R. B. (2002). An attribution theory analysis of romantic jealousy. *Motivation and Emotion, 26,* 297–319.

Baumeister, R. F., & Ilko, S. A. (1995). Shallow gratitude: Public and private acknowledgment of external help in accounts of success. *Basic and Applied Social Psychology, 161,* 191–209.

Belgum, D. (1963). *Guilt: Where psychology and religion meet.* Englewood Cliffs, NJ: Prentice-Hall.

Bentham, J. (1962). Principles of penal law. In J. Browning (Ed.), *The works of Jeremy Bentham* (pp. 365–396). New York: Russell and Russell.

Ben-Ze'ev, A. (1992). Pleasure in another's misfortune. *Iyyan, The Jerusalem Philosophical Quarterly, 41,* 41–61.

Ben-Ze'ev, A. (1993). On the virtue of modesty. *American Philosophical Quarterly, 30,* 235–246.

Berkowitz, L. (1993). *Aggression.* New York: McGraw-Hill.

Berlyne, D. E. (1968). Behavior theory as personality theory. In E. F. Borgetta & W. Lambert (Eds.), *Handbook of personality theory and research* (pp. 629–690). Chicago: Rand McNally.

Berndsen, M., van der Pligt, J., Doosje, B., & Manstead, A. S. R. (2004). Guilt and regret: The determining role of interpersonal and intrapersonal harm. *Cognition and Emotion, 18,* 55–70.

Betancourt, H. (1990). An attribution–empathy model of helping behavior. *Personality and Social Psychology Bulletin, 16,* 573–591.

Betancourt, H., & Blair, I. (1992). A cognition (attribution)–emotion model of violence in conflict situations. *Personality and Social Psychology Bulletin, 18,* 343–350.

Betancourt, H., Hardin, C., & Manzi, J. (1995). Beliefs, value orientation, and culture in attribution processes and helping behavior. *Journal of Cross Cultural Psychology, 23,* 179–195

Bies, R. J., & Sitkin, S. B. (1992). Explanations as legitimization: Excuse-making in organizations. In M. L. McLaughlin, M. J. Cody, & S. Read (Eds.), *Explaining one's self to another: Reason giving in a social context* (pp. 183–198). Hillsdale, NJ: Lawrence Erlbaum Associates.

Blumstein, P. W., Carssow, K. G., Hall, J., Hawkins, B., Hoffman, R., Ishem, F., Maurer, C. P., Spens, D., Taylor, J., & Zimmerman, D. L. (1974). The honoring of accounts. *American Sociological Review, 39,* 551–566.

Bollen, K. A. (1989). *Structural equations with latent variables.* New York: Wiley.

Bradbury, T. N., Beach, S. R. H., Fincham, F. D., & Nelson, G. M. (1996). Attributions and behavior in functional and dysfunctional marriages. *Journal of Consulting and Clinical Psychology, 64,* 569–576.

Bradbury, T. N., & Fincham, F. D. (1990). Attributions in marriage: Review and critique. *Psychological Bulletin, 107,* 3–33.

Bradley, E., & Peters, R. (1991). Physically abusive and nonabusive mothers' perceptions of parenting and child behavior. *American Journal of Orthopsychiatry, 61,* 455–460.

Bugenthal, D. (1987). Attributions and moderator variables within social interaction systems. *Journal of Social and Clinical Psychology, 5,* 469–484.

Bugenthal, D., Blue, J., & Cruzcosa, M. (1989). Perceived control over caregiving outcomes: Implications for child abuse. *Developmental Psychology, 52,* 532–539.

Bush, G. W. (1999a, January 27). *State of the state address* [On-line]. Available on the Internet: http://www.georgebush.com/speeches/1-27-99sos.html

Bush, G. W. (1999b, July 22). *The duty of hope* [On-line]. Available on the Internet: http://www.georgebush.com/speeches/7-22-99_duty_of_hope.html

Buss, A. R. (1978). Causes and reasons in attribution theory: A conceptual critique. *Journal of Personality and Social Psychology, 36,* 1311–1321.

Butzlaff, R. L., & Hooley, J. M. (1998). Expressed emotion and psychiatric relapse: A meta-analysis. *Archives of General Psychiatry, 55,* 547–552.

Byrne, C. A., & Arias, I. (1997). Marital satisfaction and marital violence: Moderating effects of attributional processes. *Journal of Family Psychology, 11,* 188–185.

Caprara, G. V., Pastorelli, C., & Weiner, B. (1994). At-risk children's causal inferences given emotional feedback and their understanding of the excuse-giving process. *European Journal of Personality, 8,* 31–43.

Carlsmith, K. M., Darley, J. M., & Robinson, P. H. (2002). Why do we punish? Deterrence and just deserts as motives for punishment. *Journal of Personality and Social Psychology, 83,* 284–299.

Carlston, D. E., & Shovar, N. (1983). Effects of performance attributions on others' perceptions of the attributor. *Journal of Personality and Social Psychology, 44,* 515–525.

Carroll, J. S. (1979). Judgments by parole boards. In I. H. Frieze, D. Bar-Tal, & J. S. Carroll (Eds.), *New approaches to social problems: Applications of attribution theory* (pp. 285–308). San Francisco: Jossey-Bass.

Carroll, J. S., & Burke, P. A. (1990). Evaluation and prediction in expert parole decisions. *Criminal Justice and Behavior, 17,* 315–332.

Christensen, A., & Jacobson, N. S. (2000). *Reconcilable differences.* New York: Guilford.

Clinton, W. J. (1995). The President's radio address: January 1, 1994. In *Public papers of the Presidents of the United States: William J. Clinton, 1994, Book 1* (pp. 1–2). Washington, DC: U.S. Government Printing Office.

Clinton, W. J. (1996). Address before a joint session of the Congress on the state of the Union: January 24, 1995 (pp. 75–86). In *Public Papers of the Presidents of the United States: William J. Clinton, 1995, Book 1* (pp. 75–86). Washington, DC: U.S. Government Printing Office.

Cody, M., & McLaughlin, M. (1990). Interpersonal accounting. In H. Giles & W. Robinson (Eds), *Handbook of language and social psychology* (pp. 227–255). New York: Wiley.

Cook, T. D., Cooper, H. M., Cordray, T. S., Hartmann, H., Hedges, L. V., Light, R. J., Louis, T. A., & Mosteller, F. (Eds.). (1992). *Meta-analysis for explanation: A casebook.* New York: Russell Sage Foundation.

Cooper, E. T. (1984). A pilot study of the effects of the diagnosis of lung cancer on family relationships. *Cancer Nursing, 7,* 301–308.

Covington, M. (1992). *Making the grade: A self-worth perspective on motivation and school reform.* New York: Cambridge University Press.

Crandall, C. S. (1995). Do parents discriminate against their own heavyweight daughters? *Personality and Social Psychology Bulletin, 21,* 724–735.

Crandall, C. S., & Martinez, R. (1996). Culture, ideology, and anti-fat attitudes. *Personality and Social Psychology Bulletin, 22,* 1165–1176.

Crick, N., & Dodge, K. (1994). A review and reformulation of social information-processing mechanisms in children's social adjustment. *Psychological Bulletin, 115*, 74–101.

Crick, N., & Ladd, G. (1990). Children's perceptions of the outcomes of social strategies: Do the ends justify the means? *Developmental Psychology, 26*, 612–620.

Crocker, J., & Major, B. (1989). Social stigma and self-esteem: The self-protective properties of stigma. *Psychological Review, 96*, 608–630.

Dagnan, D., Trower, P., & Smith, R. (1998). Care staff responses to people with learning disabilities and challenging behavior: A cognitive-emotional analysis. *British Journal of Clinical Psychology, 37*, 59–68.

Darley, J. M., & Pittman, T. S. (2003). The psychology of compensatory and retributive justice. *Personality and Social Psychology Review, 7*, 324–336.

Deci, E. L. (1975). *Intrinsic motivation.* New York: Plenum.

Dijker, A. J., & Kooman, W. (2003). Extending Weiner's attribution-emotion model of stigmatization of ill persons. *Basic and Applied Social Psychology, 25*, 51–68.

Dillon, K. M. (1998). Reasons for missing class. *Psychological Reports, 83*, 435–441.

Dodge, K. A. (1980). Social cognition and children's aggressive behavior. *Child Development, 51*, 162–170.

Dodge, K. A., & Crick, N. (1990). Social information-processing biases of aggressive behavior in children. *Personality and Social Psychology Bulletin, 16*, 8–22.

Dwyer, S. (2003). Moral development and moral responsibility. *The Monist, 86*, 181–199.

Dyck, R. J., & Rule, B. G. (1978). Effect on retaliation of causal attributions concerning attack. *Journal of Personality and Social Psychology, 36*, 521–529.

Eagly, A. H., & Crowley, M. (1986). Gender and helping behavior: A meta-analytic review of the social psychological literature. *Psychological Bulletin, 100*, 283–308.

Eisenberg, N. (1986). *Altruistic emotion, cognition, and behavior.* Hillsdale, NJ: Lawrence Erlbaum Associates.

Ellsworth, P. C., & Gross, S. R. (1994). Hardening of the attitudes: Americans' views of the death penalty. *Journal of Social Issues, 50*, 19–52.

Emmons, R. A., & McCullough, M. E. (2003). Counting blessings versus burdens: An experimental investigation of gratitude and subjective well-being in daily life. *Journal of Personality and Social Psychology, 84*, 377–389.

Enzle, M. E., & Shopflocher, D. (1978). Instigation of attribution processes by attribution questions. *Personality and Social Psychology Bulletin, 4*, 595–599.

Epstein, S., & Taylor, S. P. (1967). Instigation to aggression as a function of degree of defeat and perceived aggressive intent of the opponent. *Journal of Personality, 35*, 265–289.

Eysenck, H. (1993). Creativity and personality: An attempt to bridge divergent traditions. *Psychological Inquiry, 4*, 238–246.

Farwell, L., & Weiner, B. (1996). Self-perception of fairness in individual and group contexts. *Personality and Social Psychology Bulletin, 22*, 867–881.

Farwell, L., & Weiner, B. (2000). Bleeding hearts and the heartless: Popular perceptions of liberal and conservative ideologies. *Personality and Social Psychology Bulletin, 26*, 845–852.

Feagin, J. (1972). Poverty: We still believe that God helps those who help themselves. *Psychology Today, 6*, 101–129.

Feather, N. T. (1974). Explanations of poverty in Australian and American samples: The person, society, or fate? *Australian Journal of Psychology, 26*, 199–216.

Feather, N. T. (1985). Attitudes, values, and attributions: Explanations of unemployment. *Journal of Personality and Social Psychology, 48,* 876–889.

Feather, N. T. (1989). Attitudes toward the high achiever: The fall of the tall poppy. *Australian Journal of Psychology, 41,* 239–267.

Feather, N. T. (1991). Attitudes toward the high achiever: Effects of perceiver's own level of competence. *Journal of Psychology, 43,* 121–124.

Feather, N. T. (1996). Reactions to penalties for an offense in relation to authoritarianism, values, perceived responsibility, perceived seriousness, and deservingness. *Journal of Personality and Social Psychology, 71,* 571–587.

Feather, N. T. (1999). *Values, achievement, and justice.* New York: Kluwer Academic.

Feather, N. T., Boeckmann, R. J., & McKee, I. R. (2001). Jail sentence, community service, or compensation? Predicting reactions to a serious corporate offence. *Australian Journal of Psychology, 53,* 92–102.

Festinger, L. (1980). Looking back. In L. Festinger (Ed.), *Retrospections on social psychology* (pp. 236–254). New York: Holt, Rinehart & Winston.

Fiendler, E., & Becker, J. (1994). Interventions in family violence involving children and adolescents. In L. Eron, J. Gentry, & P. Schlegel (Eds.), *Reasons to hope: A psychosocial perspective on violence and youth* (pp. 405–433). Washington, DC: American Psychological Association.

Fincham, D. F. (2000). The kiss of the porcupines: From attributing responsibility to forgiving. *Personal Relationships. 7,* 1–23.

Fincham, D. F. (2002). Forgiveness in marriage: The role of relationship quality, attributions, and empathy. *Personal Relationships, 9,* 27–37.

Fincham, F. D., & Jaspers, J. M. (1980). Attribution of responsibility: From man the scientist to man as lawyer. In L. Berkowitz (Ed.), *Advances in experimental social psychology* (Vol. 13, pp. 82–139). New York: Academic Press.

Folkes, V. S. (1984). Consumer reactions to product failure: An attributional approach. *Journal of Consumer Research, 10,* 398–409.

Forsterling, F., & Rudolph, U. (1988). Situations, attributions, and evaluation of reactions. *Journal of Personality and Social Psychology, 54,* 225–232.

Frankfurt, H. G. (1988). *The importance of what we care about: Philosophical essays.* Cambridge, England: Cambridge University Press.

French, J. R., Jr., & Raven, B. H. (1959). The bases of social power. In D. Cartwright (Ed.), *Studies in social psychology* (pp. 150–167). Ann Arbor, MI: Institute for Social Research.

Freud, S. (1948). Instincts and their vicissitudes. In *Collected papers* (Vol. 4). London: Hogard Press and the Institute of Psychoanalysis. (Original work published 1915)

Freud, S. (1959). The question of lay analysis: Conversations with an impartial person. In L. Strachey (Ed.), *The standard edition of the complete psychological works of Sigmund Freud* (Vol. 20, pp. 177–258). London: Hogarth. (Original work published 1926)

Frijda, N. H. (1986). *The emotions.* Cambridge, England: Cambridge University Press.

Frijda, N. H., Kuipers, P., & Ter Schure, E. (1989). Relations among emotion, appraisal, and emotional action readiness. *Journal of Personality and Social Psychology, 57,* 212–228.

Gawronski, B. (2003). Implicational schemata and the correspondence bias: On the diagnostic value of situationally constrained behavior. *Journal of Personality and Social Psychology, 84,* 1154–1171.

George, D. M. (1997). *An attribution–affect–efficacy model of helping behavior.* Unpublished manuscript, University of California, Los Angeles.

George, D. M., Carroll, P., Kersnick, R., & Calderon, K. (1998). Gender-related patterns of helping among friends. *Psychology of Women Quarterly, 22,* 685–704.

George, D. M., Harris, S., & Price, I. (1998). *Determinants of helping behavior: An attributional perspective.* Unpublished manuscript, University of California, Los Angeles.

Gerber, J., & Engelhardt-Greer, S. (1996). Just and painful: Attitudes toward sentencing criminals. In T. Flanagan & D. Longmire (Eds.), *Americans view crime and justice.* Thousand Oaks, CA: Sage.

Gert, B. (1988). *Morality: A new justification of moral rules.* New York: Oxford University Press.

Goffman, E. (1971). *Relations in public: Micro studies of the public order.* New York: Basic.

Gold, J. G., & Weiner, B. (2000). Remorse, confession, group identity, and expectancies about repeating a transgression. *Basic and Applied Social Psychology, 22,* 291–300.

Golub, J. (1984). *Abusive and nonabusive parents' perceptions of their children's behavior: An attributional analysis.* Unpublished doctoral dissertation, University of California, Los Angeles.

Graham, S. (1984). Communicated sympathy and anger to black and white children: The cognitive (attributional) consequences of affective cues. *Journal of Personality and Social Psychology, 47,* 40–54.

Graham, S. (1990). Communicating low ability in the classroom: Bad things good teachers sometimes do. In S. Graham & V. S. Folkes (Eds.), *Attribution theory: Applications to achievement, mental health, and interpersonal conflict* (pp. 17–36). Hillsdale, NJ: Lawrence Erlbaum Associates.

Graham, S., & Barker, G. (1990). The downside of help: An attributional–developmental analysis of helping behavior as a low ability cue. *Journal of Educational Psychology, 82,* 7–14.

Graham, S., & Hoehn, S. (1995). Children's understanding of aggression and withdrawal as social stigmas: An attributional analysis. *Child Development, 66,* 1143–1161.

Graham, S., & Hudley, C. (1991). An attributional approach to aggression in African-American children. In D. Schunk & J. Meece (Eds.), *Student perceptions in the classroom: Causes and consequences* (pp. 75–94). Hillsdale, NJ: Lawrence Erlbaum Associates.

Graham, S., & Hudley, C. (1994). Attributions of aggressive and nonaggressive African-American male early adolescents: A study of construct accessibility. *Developmental Psychology, 30,* 365–373.

Graham, S., Hudley, C., & Williams, E. (1992). Attributional and emotional determinants of aggression among African-American and Latino young adolescents. *Developmental Psychology, 28,* 731–740.

Graham, S., & Weiner, B. (1991). Testing judgments about attribution-emotion-act linkages: A lifespan approach. *Social Cognition, 9,* 254–276.

Graham, S., Weiner, B., & Benesh-Weiner, M. (1995). An attributional analysis of the development of excuse giving in aggressive and nonaggressive African-American boys. *Developmental Psychology, 31,* 274–284.

Graham, S., Weiner, B., Cobb, M., & Henderson, T. (2001). An attributional analysis of child abuse among low-income African American mothers. *Journal of Social and Clinical Psychology, 20,* 233–257.

Graham, S., Weiner, B., & Zucker, G. S. (1997). An attributional analysis of punishment goals and public reactions to O. J. Simpson. *Personality and Social Psychology Bulletin, 23,* 331–346.

Greitemeyer, T., & Rudolph, U. (2003). Help giving and aggression from an attributional perspective: Why and when we help or retaliate. *Journal of Applied Social Psychology, 3*, 1058–1068.

Greitemeyer, T., Rudolph, U., & Weiner, B. (2003). Whom would you rather help: An acquaintance not responsible for her plight or a responsible sibling? *Journal of Social Psychology, 14*, 331–340.

Greitemeyer, T., & Weiner, B. (2003). The asymmetrical consequences of reward and punishment on attributional judgments. *Personality and Social Psychology Bulletin, 29*, 1371–1382,

Guralnik, D. B. (1971). Webster's *New World Dictionary.* Nashville, TN: Southwestern Co.

Hareli, S., & Weiner, B. (2000). Accounts for success as determinants of perceived arrogance and modesty. *Motivation and Emotion, 24*, 215–236.

Hareli, S., & Weiner, B. (2002). Dislike and envy as antecedents of pleasure at another's misfortune. *Motivation and Emotion, 26*, 257–277.

Hareli, S., Weiner, B., & Yee, J. (2004). *Honesty doesn't always pay—The role of honesty accounts for success in inferences of modesty and arrogance.* Unpublished manuscript, University of California, Los Angeles.

Hart, H. L. A., & Honoré, A. M. (1959). *Causation in the law.* Oxford: Clarendon Press.

Hartup, W. W. (1983). Peer relations. In E. W. Hetherington (Ed.), *Handbook of child psychology* (Vol. 4, pp. 104–196). New York: Wiley.

Haslam, N. (2003). Folk psychiatry: Lay thinking about mental disorder. *Social Research, 7*, 621–644.

Heider, F. (1958). *The psychology of interpersonal relations.* New York: Wiley.

Henderson, M., & Hewstone, M. R. (1984). Prison inmate's explanations for interpersonal violence: Accounts and attributions. *Journal of Consulting and Clinical Psychology, 52*, 789–794.

Henry, P. J., Reyna, C., & Weiner, B. (2004). Hate welfare but help the poor: How the attributional content of stereotypes explains the paradox of reactions to the destitute in America. *Journal of Applied Social Psychology, 34*, 34–58.

Higgins, N. C., & Watson, C. E. (1995). *Negative life experiences predict attributional and emotional determinants of aggression.* Paper presented at the annual meeting of the American Association for the Advancement of Science, Pacific Division. University of British Columbia, Vancouver, Canada.

Ho, R., & Venus, M. (1995). Reactions to a battered woman who kills her abusive spouse: An attributional analysis. *Australian Journal of Psychology, 47*, 153–159.

Holtgraves, T. (1989). The function and form of remedial moves: Reported use, psychological reality and perceived effectiveness. *Journal of Language and Social Psychology, 14*, 363–378.

Hooley, J. M. (1985). Expressed emotion: A review of the critical literature. *Clinical Psychology Review, 5*, 119–139.

Hooley, J. M. (1987). The nature and origins of expressed emotion. In K. Hahlweg & M. J. Goldstein (Eds.), *Understanding major mental disorder: The contribution of family interaction research* (pp. 176–194). New York: Family Process Press.

Hudley, C. (1991). *An attribution retraining program to reduce peer-directed aggression among African-American male elementary students.* Unpublished doctoral dissertation, University of California, Los Angeles.

Hudley, C., & Graham, S. (1993). An attributional intervention to reduce peer-directed aggression among African American boys. *Child Development, 64*, 124–138.

Hull, C. L. (1943). *Principles of behavior.* New York: Appleton-Century-Crofts.

Ickes, W. (1996). On the deep structure of attribution-affect-behavior sequences. *Psychological Inquiry, 7,* 236–240.

Izard, C. E. (1977). *Human emotions.* New York: Plenum.

Johnson, T. E., & Rule, B. G. (1986). Mitigating circumstance information, censure, and aggression. *Journal of Personality and Social Psychology, 50,* 537–542.

Jones, E. E., & Davis, K. E. (1965). From acts to dispositions: The attribution process in person perception. In L. Berkowitz (Ed.), *Advances in experimental social psychology* (Vol. 2, pp. 219–266). New York: Academic.

Jones, E. E., Davis, K. E., & Gergen, K. J. (1961). Role playing variations and their informational value for person perception. *Journal of Abnormal and Social Psychology, 63,* 302–310.

Jones, E. E., Farina, A., Hastorf, A. H., Markus, H., Miller, D. T., & Scott, R. A. (1984). *Social stigma.* San Francisco: Freeman.

Jung, C. G. (1933). *Modern man in search of a soul.* New York: Harvest Books.

Juvonen, J. (1991). Deviance, perceived responsibility, and negative peer reactions. *Developmental Psychology, 27,* 672–681.

Juvonen, J. (2000). The social functions of attributional face-saving tactics among early adolescents. *Educational Psychology Review, 12,* 15–32.

Juvonen, J., & Murdock, T. B. (1993). How to promote social approval: The effects of audience and outcome on publicly communicated attributions. *Journal of Educational Psychology, 85,* 672–681.

Kahneman, D., & Tversky, A. (1979). Prospect theory: An analysis of decision under risk. *Econometrical, 47,* 263–291.

Karasawa, K. (1991). The effects of onset and offset responsibility on affects and helping judgments. *Journal of Applied Social Psychology, 21,* 482–499.

Karney, B. R., & Bradbury, T. N. (2000). Attributions in marriage: State or trait? A growth curve analysis. *Journal of Personality and Social Psychology, 78,* 295–309.

Katz, L. (1987). *Bad acts and guilty minds.* Chicago: University of Chicago Press.

Kelley, H. H. (1967). Attribution theory in social psychology. In D. Levine (Ed.), *Nebraska symposium on motivation* (Vol. 15, pp. 192–238). Lincoln: University of Nebraska Press.

Kelley, H. H. (1992). Common-sense psychology and scientific psychology. *Annual Review of Psychology, 43,* 1–23.

Kelly, G. A. (1955). *The psychology of personal constructs.* New York: Norton.

Kim, S., & Shanahan, J. (2003). Stigmatizing smokers: Public sentiment toward cigarette smoking and its relationship to smoking behaviors. *Journal of Health Communications, 8,* 343–367.

Klein, R. J., Newman, I., Weis, D. M., & Bobner, R. F. (1982). The Continuum of Criminal Offenses instrument: Further development and modification of Selling and Wolfgang's original criminal index. *Journal of Offender Counseling, Services and Rehabilitation, 7,* 33–53.

Kleinke, C. L., Wallis, R., & Stadler, K. (1992). Evaluation of a rapist as a function of expressed intent and remorse. *Journal of Social Psychology, 132,* 525–537.

Kluegel, J. R. (1990). Trends in Whites explanations of the Black–White gap in socioeconomic status, 1977–1989. *American Sociological Review, 55,* 512–525.

Kluegel, J. R., & Smith, E. R. (1986). *Beliefs about inequality.* New York: Aldine.

Kojima, M. (1992). An analysis of attributional processes in helping behavior. *Bulletin of the Tamagawa Guken Junior College for Women, 17,* 57–83.

Kun, A., & Weiner, B. (1973). Necessary versus sufficient causal schemata for success and failure. *Journal of Research in Personality, 7,* 197–207.

LaFave, F. W., & Scott, A. W., Jr. (1986). *Criminal law* (2nd ed.). St. Paul, MN: West.

Lakoff, G. (1996). *Moral politics: What conservatives know that liberals don't.* Chicago: University of Chicago Press.

Lane, R. (1962). *Political ideology: Why the American common man believes what he does.* New York: Macmillan.

Lee, F., & Robinson, R. (2000). An attributional analysis of social accounts: Implications of playing the blame game. *Journal of Applied Social Psychology, 30,* 1853–1879.

Lerner, J. S., Goldberg, J. H., & Tetlock, P. E. (1998). Sober second thoughts: The effects of accountability, anger, and authoritarianism on attributions of responsibility. *Personality and Social Psychology Bulletin, 24,* 563–574.

Lerner, M. J. (2003). The justice motive: Where social psychologists found it, how they lost it, and why they may not find it again. *Personality and Social Psychology Review, 7,* 388–399.

Lerner, M. J., & Miller, D. T. (1978). Just world research and the attribution process: Looking back and ahead. *Psychological Bulletin, 85,* 1030–1051.

Lewin, K. (1935). *A dynamic theory of personality.* New York: McGraw-Hill.

Lewin, K. (1938). *The conceptual representation and the measurement of psychological forces.* Durham, NC: Duke University Press.

Lopez, S. R., Nelson, K. A., Snyder, K. S., & Mintz, J. (1999). Attributions and affective reactions of family members and the course of schizophrenia. *Journal of Abnormal Psychology, 108,* 307–314.

MacGeorge, E. L. (2003). Gender differences in attributions and emotions. *Sex Roles, 48,* 175–182.

Major, B., Kaiser, C. R., & McCoy, S. K. (2003). It's not my fault: When and why attributions to prejudice protect self-esteem. *Personality and Social Psychology, 29,* 772–781.

Malle, B. F. (1999). How people explain behavior: A new theoretical framework. *Personality and Social Psychology Review, 3,* 23–48.

Malle, B. F. (2004). *How the mind explains behavior: Folk explanations, meaning, and social interaction.* Cambridge, MA: MIT Press.

Malle, B. F., & Knobe, J. (1997). The folk concept of intentionality. *Journal of Experimental Social Psychology, 33,* 101–121.

Malle, B. F., Knobe, J., O'Laughlin, M. J., Pearce, G. E., & Nelson, S. E. (2000). Conceptual structure and social functions of behavior explanations: Beyond person–situation attributions. *Journal of Personality and Social Psychology, 79,* 309–326.

Margolin, G., & Weiss, R. L. (1978). Comparative evaluation of therapeutic components associated with behavioral marital treatments. *Journal of Consulting and Clinical Psychology, 46,* 1476–1484.

Matsui, T., & Matsuda, Y. (1992). *Testing for the robustness of Weiner's attribution-affect model of helping judgments for exogenous impact.* Unpublished manuscript, Rikkyo University, Tokyo, Japan.

McCullough, M. E. (2000). Forgiveness as human strength: Theory, measurement, and links to well-being. *Journal of Social and Clinical Psychology, 1,* 43–55.

McLaughlin, M. L., Cody, M. J., & O'Hair, H. D. (1983). The management of failure events: Some contextual determinants of accounting behavior. *Human Communication Research, 9,* 208–224.

Menec, V. H., & Perry, R. P. (1995). Reactions to stigmas: The effects of target's age and controllability of stigmas. *Journal of Aging and Health, 7,* 365–383.

Menec, V. H., & Perry, R. P. (1998). Reactions to stigmas among Canadien students: testing an attribution-affect-help judgment model. *Journal of Social Psychology, 138,* 443–454.

Meyer, J. P., & Mulherin, A. (1980). From attribution to helping: An analysis of the mediating effects of affect and expectancy. *Journal of Personality and Social Psychology, 39,* 201–210.

Meyer, W., Bachmann, M., Biermann, U., Hempelmann, M., Ploeger, F., & Spiller, H. (1979). The informational value of evaluative behavior: Influence of praise and blame on perceptions of ability. *Journal of Educational Psychology, 71,* 259–268.

Mikulincer, M., Bizman, A., & Aizenberg, R. (1989). An attributional analysis of social-comparison jealousy. *Motivation and Emotion, 13,* 235–258.

Milner, J. S. (1993). Social information processing and physical child abuse. *Clinical Psychology Review, 13,* 275–294.

Milner, J. S., & Foody, R. (1994). The impact of mitigating information on attributions for positive and negative child behavior by adults at low and high risk for child-abusive behavior. *Journal of Social and Clinical Psychology, 13,* 335–351.

Moore, M. (1987). The moral worth of retribution. In F. Schoeman (Ed.), *Responsibility, character, and the emotions* (pp. 179–219). New York: Cambridge University Press.

Morse, S. J. (1978). Crazy behavior, morals, and science: An analysis of mental health law. *Southern California Law Review, 51,* 527–654.

Morse, S. J. (1985). Excusing the crazy: The insanity defense reconsidered. *Southern California Law Review, 58,* 777–837.

Murphy, J. G., & Coleman, L. J. (1990). *Philosophy of law: An introduction to jurisprudence.* Boulder, CO: Westview Press.

National Research Council. (1993). *Understanding child abuse and neglect.* Washington, DC: National Academy Press.

Neff, J. A., & Husaini, B. A. (1985). Lay images of mental health: Social knowledge and tolerance of the mentally ill. *Journal of Community Psychology, 13,* 3–12.

Neff, L. A., & Karney, B. R. (2004). How does context affect intimate relationships? Linking external stress and cognitive processes within marriage. *Personality and Social Psychology Bulletin, 30,* 134–148.

Nickel, T. W. (1974). The attribution of intention as a critical factor in the relation between frustration and aggression. *Journal of Personality, 42,* 484–492.

Nozick, R. (1981). *Philosophical explanations.* Cambridge, MA: Harvard University Press.

Ohbuchi, K., Agarie, N., & Kameda, M. (1989). Apology as aggression control: Its role in mediating appraisal of and response to harm. *Journal of Social Psychology, 134,* 5–17.

Orth, U. (2003). Punishment goals of crime victims. *Law and Human Behavior, 27,* 173–186.

Ortony, A., Clore, G. L., & Collins, A. (1988). *The cognitive structure of emotions.* Cambridge, England: Cambridge University Press.

Overholser, J. C., & Moll, S. H. (1990). Who's to blame: Attributions regarding causality in spouse abuse. *Behavioral Sciences and the Law, 8,* 107–120.

Pandey, J., Sinha, Y., Prakash, A., & Tripathi, R. C. (1982). Right–left political ideologies and attribution of the causes of poverty. *European Journal of Social Psychology, 12,* 327–331.

Peterson, C. (1991). The meaning and measurement of explanatory style. *Psychological Inquiry, 2,* 1–10.

Petrucci, J. C. (2002). Apology in the criminal justice setting: Evidence for including apology as an additional component in the legal system. *Behavioral Sciences and the Law, 20,* 337–362.

Pintrich, P. R., & Schunk, D. H. (2002). *Motivation in education.* Englewood Cliffs, NJ: Prentice Hall.

Pitschel-Waltz, G., Leucht, S., Bauml, J., Kissling, W., & Engel, R. R. (2001). The effect of family interventions on relapse and rehospitalization in schizophrenia—meta-analysis. *Schizophrenia Bulletin, 27,* 73–92.

Rabiner, D., & Gordon, L. (1993). The relation between children's social concerns and their social interaction strategies: Differences between rejected and accepted boys. *Social Development, 2,* 83–95.

Raven, B. H. (1965). Social influence and power. In I. D. Steiner & M. Fishbein (Eds.), *Current studies in social psychology* (pp. 371–381). New York: Holt.

Rawls, J. (1955). Concepts of rules. *Philosophical Review, 64,* 4–5.

Reeder, G. L., & Spores, J. M. (1983). The attribution of morality. *Journal of Personality and Social Psychology, 44,* 736–745.

Reisenzein, R. (1986). A structural equation analysis of Weiner's attribution–affect model of helping behavior. *Journal of Personality and Social Psychology, 50,* 1123–1133.

Reisenzein, R., & Hoffman, T. (1990). An investigation of the dimensions of cognitive appraisal in emotion using the repertory grid technique. *Motivation and Emotion, 14,* 1–26.

Reyna, C., & Weiner, B. (2001). Justice and utility in the classroom: An attributional analysis of the goals of teachers' punishment and intervention strategies. *Journal of Educational Psychology, 93,* 309–319.

Richardson, S. A., Hastorf, A. H., Goodman, N., & Dornbusch, S. M. (1961). Cultural uniformity in reaction to physical disabilities. *American Sociological Review, 26,* 241–247.

Roberts, J., & Stalans, L. (1997). *Public opinion, crime, and criminal justice.* Boulder, CO: Westview Press.

Robinson, P. H., & Darley, J. M. (1995). *Justice, liability, & blame: Community views of the criminal law.* Boulder, CO: Westview Press.

Rodrigues, A. (1995). Attribution and social influence. *Journal of Applied Social Psychology, 25,* 1567–1577.

Rodrigues, A., & Lloyd, K. L. (1998). Reexamining bases of power from an attributional perspective. *Journal of Applied Social Psychology, 28,* 973–997.

Roseman, I. (1991). Appraisal determinants of discrete emotions. *Cognition and Emotion, 5,* 161–200.

Rosenberg, M., & Reppucci, D. (1983). Abusive mothers: Perceptions of their own and their children's behavior. *Journal of Consulting and Clinical Psychology, 51,* 647–682.

Rosenfeld, P., Giacalone, R. A., & Riordan, C. A. (1995). *Impression management inorganizations: Theory, measurement, practice.* New York: Routledge.

Rotter, J. B. (1954). *Social learning and clinical psychology.* Englewood Cliffs, NJ: Prentice-Hall.

Rotter, J. B. (1966). Generalized expectancies for internal versus external control of reinforcement. *Psychological Monograph, 80*(1, Whole No. 609).

Rozin, P., Lowery, L., Imada, S., & Haidt, J. (1999). The CAD Triad Hypothesis: A mapping between three moral emotions (contempt, anger, disgust) and three moral codes (community, autonomy, divinity). *Journal of Personality and Social Psychology, 76,* 574–586.

Rudolph, U., & Greitemeyer, T. (2001). *Autobiographical recollections of pro- and anti-social behavior: Evidence for Weiner's theory of responsibility.* Unpublished manuscript, University of Chemnitz, Germany.

Rudolph, U., Roesch, S. C., Greitemeyer, T., & Weiner, B. (2004). A meta-analytic review of help giving and aggression from an attributional perspective. *Cognition and Emotion, 18,* 815–848.

Scher, S. J., & Darley, J. M (1997). How effective are the things people say to apologize? Effects of the realization of the apology speech act. *Journal of Psycholinguistic Research, 26,* 127–140.

Schlenker, B. R. (1975). Group members' attributions of responsibility for prior group performance. *Representative Research in Social Psychology, 6,* 96–108.

Schlenker, B. R. (1980). *Impression management.* Monterey, CA: Brooks/Cole.

Schlenker, B. R. (1982). Translating actions into attitudes: An identity-analytic approach to the explanation of social conduct. In L. Berkowitz (Ed.), *Advances in Experimental Social Psychology* (pp. 1930–1947). New York: Academic.

Schlenker, B. R. (1997). Personal responsibility: Applications of the triangle mode. In L. Cummings & B. Staw (Eds.), *Research in Organizational Behavior,* 241–301.

Schlenker, B. R., & Leary, M. R. (1982). Audiences' reactions to self-enhancing, self-denigrating, and accurate self presentations. *Journal of Experimental Social Psychology, 18,* 89–104.

Schlenker, B., Pontari, B., & Christopher, A. (2001). Excuses and character: Personal and social implications of excuses. *Personality and Social Psychology Review, 5,* 15–32.

Schmidt, G., & Weiner, B. (1988). An attribution–affect–action theory of behavior: Replications of judgments of help giving. *Personality and Social Psychology Bulletin, 14,* 610–621.

Scott, M. B., & Lyman, S. M. (1968). Accounts. *American Sociological Review, 5,* 46–62.

Scully, D., & Marolla, J. (1984). Convicted rapist' vocabulary of motive: Excuses and justifications. *Social Problems, 31,* 530–544

Shadish, W. R. (1996). Meta-analysis and the exploration of causal mediating processes: A primer of examples, methods, and issues. *Psychological Methods, 1,* 47–65.

Sharrock, R., Day, A., Qazi, F., & Brewin, C. (1990). Explanation by professional care staff, optimism and helping behavior: An application of attribution theory. *Psychological Medicine, 20,* 849–855.

Shaver, K. G. (1985). *The attribution of blame: Causality, responsibility, and blameworthiness.* New York: Springer-Verlag.

Sigelman, C. K., & Begley, N. L. (1987). The early development of reactions to peers with controllable and uncontrollable problems. *Journal of Pediatric Psychology, 12,* 99–115.

Skitka, L. J. (1999). Ideological and attributional boundaries on public compassion: Reactions to individuals and communities affected by a natural disaster. *Personality and Social Psychology Bulletin, 25,* 793–808.

Skitka, L. J., Mullen, E., Griffin, T., Hutchinson, S., & Chamberlin, B. (2002). Dispositions, scripts or motivated correction? Understanding ideological differences in explanations for social problems. *Journal of Personality and Social Psychology, 83,* 470–487.

Skitka, L. J., & Tetlock, P. E. (1993a). On ants and grasshoppers: The political psychology of allocating public assistance. In B. Mellers & J. Baron (Eds.), *Psychological perspectives on justice* (pp. 205–233). New York: Cambridge University Press.

Skitka, L. J., & Tetlock, P. E. (1993b). Providing public assistance: Cognitive and motivational processes underlying liberal and conservative policy preferences. *Journal of Personality and Social Psychology, 65,* 1205–1223.

Smith, R., Parrott, W., Diener, E., Hoyle, R., & Kim, S. H. (1999). Dispositional envy. *Personality and Social Psychology Bulletin, 25,* 1007–1020.

Sniderman, P. M., Piazza, T., Tetlock, P. E., & Kendrick, A. (1991). The new racism. *American Journal of Political Science, 35,* 423–447.

Sniderman, P. M., & Tetlock, P. E. (1986). Interrelationships of political ideology and public opinion. In M. Hermann (Ed.), *Handbook of political psychology* (2nd ed., pp. 62–96). San Francisco, CA: Jossey-Bass.

Snyder, C. R., Higgins, R. L., & Stucky, R. J. (1983). *Excuses: Masquerades in search of grace.* New York, NY: Wiley/Interscience.

Spence, K. W. (1956). *Behavior theory and conditioning.* New Haven, CT: Yale University Press.

Spinetta, J., & Rigler, D. (1972). The child-abusing parent: A psychological review. *Psychological Bulletin, 77,* 296–304.

Steins, G., & Weiner, B. (1999). The influence of perceived responsibility and personality characteristics on the emotional and behavioral reactions to persons with AIDS. *Journal of Applied Social Psychology, 139,* 487–495.

Stiensmeyer-Pelster, J., & Gerlach, H. (1997). Aggressive behavior among children and adolescents from an attribution theoretical point of view. [Aggressives Verhalten bei Kindern und Jugendlichen aus attributionstheoretischer Sicht]. *German Journal of Educational Psychology, 11,* 203–209.

Strickland, L. H. (1958). Surveillance and trust. *Journal of Personality, 26,* 200–215.

Sunmola, A. (1994). Perceived controllability, affective reactions of sympathy and anger as determinants of subjects' tendency to offer help to government. *IFE-Psychologia: An International Journal, 2,* 113–122.

Takaku, S. (2000). Culture and status as influences on account giving: A comparison between the United States and Japan. *Journal of Applied Social Psychology, 30,* 371–388.

Tangney, J. P., & Fischer, K. W. (1995). *Self-conscious emotions.* New York: Guilford.

Tedeschi, J. T., & Riess, M. (1981). Verbal tactics of impression management. In C. Antaki (Ed.), *Ordinary language explanations of social behavior* (pp. 3–22). London: Academic.

Tesser, A., & Beach, S. R. H. (1998). Life events, relationship quality, and depression: An investigation of judgment discontinuity in vivo. *Journal of Personality and Social Psychology, 74,* 36–52.

Tesser, A., Gatewood, R., & Driver, M. (1968). Some determinants of gratitude. *Journal of Personality and Social Psychology, 9,* 233–236.

Thompson, S. C., Medvene, L. J., & Freedman, D. (1995). Care-giving in the close relationships of cardiac patients: Exchange, power, and attributional perspectives on caregiver resentment. *Personal Relationships, 2,* 125–142.

Thorndike, E. L. (1911). *Animal intelligence.* New York: Macmillan.

Tollefson, N., Hsia, S., & Townsend, J. (1991). Teachers' perceptions of students' excuses for academic difficulties. *Psychology in the Schools, 28,* 146–155.

Tsang, J., & McCullough, M. E. (2004). Annotated bibliography of research on gratitude. In R. A. Emmons & M. E. McCullough (Eds.), *The psychology of gratitude* (pp. 291–341). New York: Oxford University Press.

Turillo, C. J., Folger, R., Lavelle, J. J., Umphress, E. E., & Gee, J. O. (2002). Is virtue its own reward? Self-sacrificial decisions for the sake of fairness. *Organizational Behavior and Human Decision Processes, 89,* 839–865.

Tversky, A., & Kahneman, D. (1992). Advances in prospect theory: Cumulative representation of uncertainty. *Journal of Risk and Uncertainty, 5,* 297–323.

Twentyman, C., & Plotkin, R. (1982). Unrealistic expectations of parents who maltreat their children: An educational deficit that pertains to child development. *Journal of Clinical Psychology, 38,* 497–503.

Vala, J., Monteiro, M., & Leyens, J. P. (1988). Perception of observer's ideology and actor's group membership. *British Journal of Social Psychology, 27,* 231–237.

Van Dijk, W. W., & Zeelenberg, M. (2002). Investigating the appraisal patterns of regret and disappointment. *Motivation and Emotion, 26,* 321–331.

Van Dijk, W. W., Zeelenberg, M., & van der Pligt, J. (1999). Not having what you want versus having what you don't want: The impact of negative outcome on the experience of disappointment and related emotions. *Cognition and Emotion, 13,* 129–148.

Van Overwalle, F., Mervielde, I., & DeSchuyter, J. (1995). Structural modeling of the relationships between attributional dimension, emotions, and performance of college freshman. *Cognition and Emotion, 9,* 59–85.

Vidmar, N. (2000). Retribution and revenge. In J. Sanders & V. L. Hamilton (Eds.), *Handbook of justice and research in the law* (pp. 31–63). New York: Kluwer.

Vidmar, N., & Miller, D. (1980). Social psychological processes underlying attitudes toward legal punishment. *Law & Psychology Review, 14,* 565–602.

Waldron, J. (2003). Who is my neighbor? Humanity and proximity. *The Monist, 86,* 333–354.

Watkins, P. C., Woodward, K., Stone, T., & Kolts, R. L. (2003). Gratitude and happiness: Development of a measure of gratitude, and relationships with subjective well-being. *Social Behavior and Personality, 31,* 431–452.

Watson, J. E., & Higgins, N. C. (1999). *A test of Weiner's (1995) responsibility judgment model: Does the judgment target matter?* Unpublished manuscript, University of British Columbia, Vancouver, Canada.

Wearden, A. J., Tarrier, A., Barrowclough, C., Zastowny, T. R., & Rahill, A. A. (2000). A review of expressed emotion research in health care. *Clinical Psychology Review, 20,* 633–666.

Weber, M. (1958). *The Protestant ethic and the spirit of capitalism.* Now York: Scribner's Sons. (Original work published in 1904)

Weiner, B. (1980a). A cognitive (attribution)–emotion–action model of motivated behavior: An analysis of judgments of help giving. *Journal of Personality and Social Psychology, 39,* 186–200.

Weiner, B. (1980b). May I borrow your class-notes? An attributional analysis of judgments of help giving. *Journal of Educational Psychology, 72,* 676–681.

Weiner, B. (1985a). An attributional theory of achievement-related emotion and motivation. *Psychological Review, 29,* 548–573.

Weiner, B. (1985b). "Spontaneous" causal thinking. *Psychological Bulletin, 97,* 74–84.

Weiner, B. (1986). *An attributional theory of motivation and emotion.* New York: Springer-Verlag.

Weiner, B. (1990). Searching for the roots of applied attribution theory. In S. Graham & V. S. Folkes (Eds.), *Attribution theory: Applications to achievement, mental health, and interpersonal conflict* (pp. 1–13). Hillsdale, NJ: Lawrence Erlbaum Associates.

Weiner, B. (1992a). Excuses in everyday interaction. In M. L. McLaughlin, M. J. Cody, & S. R. Reed (Eds.), *Explaining one's self to others* (pp. 131–146). Hillsdale, NJ: Lawrence Erlbaum Associates.

Weiner, B. (1992b). *Human motivation: Metaphors, theories, and research.* Newbury Park, CA: Sage.

Weiner, B. (1995). *Judgments of responsibility: A foundation for a theory of social conduct.* New York: Guilford.

Weiner, B. (2000a). Attribution thoughts about consumer behavior. *Journal of Consumer Research, 27,* 382–387.

Weiner, B. (2000b). Intrapersonal and interpersonal theories of motivation from an attributional perspective. *Educational Psychology Review, 12,* 1–14.

Weiner, B., Amirkhan, J., Folkes, V. S., & Verette, J. A. (1987). An attributional analysis of excuse giving: Studies of a naïve theory of emotion. *Journal of Personality and Social Psychology, 52,* 316–324.

Weiner, B., & Graham, S. (1989). Understanding the motivational role of affect: Life-span research from an attributional perspective. *Cognition and Emotion, 3,* 401–419.

Weiner, B., Graham, S., & Chandler, C. C. (1982). Pity, anger, and guilt: An attributional analysis. *Personality and Social Psychology Bulletin, 8,* 226–232.

Weiner, B., Graham, S., Peter, O., & Zmuidinas, M. (1991). Public confession and forgiveness. *Journal of Personality, 59,* 281–312.

Weiner, B., Graham, S., & Reyna, C. (1997). An attributional examination of retributive versus utilitarian philosophies of punishment. *Social Justice Research, 10,* 431–452.

Weiner, B., Graham, S., Stern, P., & Lawson, M. (1982). Using affective cues to infer causal thoughts. *Developmental Psychology, 18,* 278–286.

Weiner, B., & Kukla, A. (1970). An attribution analysis of achievement motivation. *Journal of Personality and Social Psychology, 15,* 1–20.

Weiner, B., Perry, R. P., & Magnusson, J. (1988). An attributional analysis of reactions to stigmas. *Journal of Personality and Social Psychology, 55,* 738–748.

Weiner, B., & Peter, N. (1973). A cognitive-developmental analysis of achievement and moral judgments. *Developmental Psychology, 9,* 290–309.

Weisman, A. G., & Lopez, S. R. (1996). Family values, religiosity, and emotional reactions to schizophrenia in Mexican and Anglo-American cultures. *Family Process, 35,* 227–237.

Weisman, A., G., Lopez, S. R., Karno, M., & Jenkins, J. (1993). An attributional analysis of expressed emotion in Mexican American families with schizophrenia. *Journal of Abnormal Psychology, 102,* 601–606.

Wells, G. (1980). Asymmetric attributions for compliance: Reward vs. punishment. *Journal of Experimental Social Psychology, 16,* 47–60.

Williams, S. (1984). Left–right ideological differences in blaming victims. *Political Psychology, 5,* 573–581.

Wingrove, J., & Bond, A. J. (1998). Angry reactions to failure on a cooperative computer game: The effect of hostility, behavioral inhibition, and behavioral activation. *Aggressive Behavior, 24,* 27–36.

Wispé, L. (1991). *The psychology of sympathy.* New York: Plenum Press.

Yamauchi, H., & Lee, K. (1999). An attribution–emotion model of helping behavior. *Psychological Reports, 84,* 1073–1074.

Yang, L. H., Phillips, M. R., Licht, D. M., & Hooley, J. M. (2003). *Causal attributions about schizophrenia in families in China: Expressed emotion and patient relapse.* Unpublished manuscript.

Zhang, A. Y., & Siminoff, L. A. (2003). Silence and cancer: Why do families and patients fail to communicate? *Health Communication, 15,* 415–429.

Zimbardo, P. G. (2004). Does psychology make a significant difference in our lives? *American Psychologist, 59,* 339–351.

Zucker, G. S. (1999). Attributional and symbolic predictors of abortion attitudes. *Journal of Applied Social Psychology, 29,* 1218–1256.

Zucker, G. S., & Weiner, B. (1993). Conservatism and perception of poverty: An attributional analysis. *Journal of Applied Social Psychology, 23,* 925–943.

Zumkley, H. (1981). The influence of different kinds of intentionality attributions on aggressive behavior and activation. [Der Einfluß unterschiedlicher Absichtsattributionen auf das Aggressionsverhalten und die Aktivierung.] *Psychologische Beiträge, 23,* 115–128.

Author Index

Subject Index